MW01195102

CREATING PRIVATE SECTOR ECONOMIES IN NATIVE AMERICA

Native nation economies have long been dominated by public sector activities – government programs and services and tribal government-owned businesses – which do not generate the same long-term benefits for local communities that the private sector does. In this work, editors Robert Miller, Miriam Jorgensen, Daniel Stewart, and a roster of expert authors address the underdevelopment of the private sector on American Indian reservations, with the goal of sustaining and growing Native nation communities, so that Indian Country can thrive on its own terms. Chapter authors provide the language and arguments to make the case to tribal politicians, Native communities, and allies about the importance of private sector development and entrepreneurship in Indigenous economies. This book identifies and addresses key barriers to expanding the sector, provides policy guidance, and describes several successful business models – thus offering students, practitioners, and policymakers the information they need to make change.

Robert J. Miller is Professor of Law at the Sandra Day O'Connor College of Law, Arizona State University and Faculty Director of the Rosette LLP American Indian Economic Development Program. He is a member of the Navajo Nation Council of Economic Advisors and the American Philosophical Society. He is also the Interim Chief Justice for the Pascua Yaqui Tribe Court of Appeals and a citizen of the Eastern Shawnee Tribe. He sits on the Grand Ronde Tribe and Northwest Inter-Tribal Courts of Appeals. He is the author of *Reservation 'Capitalism': Economic Development in Indian Country* (2012).

Miriam Jorgensen is Research Director of the Native Nations Institute at the University of Arizona. She is co-founder of the University of Arizona Indigenous Governance certificate program and editor of *Rebuilding Native Nations: Strategies for Governance and Development* (2007). Her work – in the USA, Canada, and Australia – focuses on Indigenous governance and development and has addressed issues as wide-ranging as welfare policy, policing and justice systems, natural resources, cultural stewardship, land ownership, enterprise management, financial education, and entrepreneurship.

Daniel Stewart is Professor of Entrepreneurship and Director of the Hogan Entrepreneurial Leadership Program at Gonzaga University. He is an enrolled member of the Spokane Tribe of Indians and the co-editor of *American Indian Business: Principles and Practices* (2017). In addition to his academic work, Daniel is president of Dardan Enterprises, a diversified commercial construction firm.

Creating Private Sector Economies in Native America

SUSTAINABLE DEVELOPMENT THROUGH ENTREPRENEURSHIP

Edited by

ROBERT J. MILLER

Sandra Day O'Connor College of Law, Arizona State University

MIRIAM JORGENSEN

Native Nations Institute, The University of Arizona

DANIEL STEWART

Gonzaga University, Washington

CAMBRIDGE
UNIVERSITY PRESS

CAMBRIDGE
UNIVERSITY PRESS

University Printing House, Cambridge CB2 8BS, United Kingdom

One Liberty Plaza, 20th Floor, New York, NY 10006, USA

477 Williamstown Road, Port Melbourne, VIC 3207, Australia

314-321, 3rd Floor, Plot 3, Splendor Forum, Jasola District Centre, New Delhi - 110025, India

79 Anson Road, #06-04/06, Singapore 079906

Cambridge University Press is part of the University of Cambridge.

It furthers the University's mission by disseminating knowledge in the pursuit of education, learning and research at the highest international levels of excellence.

www.cambridge.org
Information on this title: www.cambridge.org/9781108703758
DOI : 10.1017/9781108646208

© Cambridge University Press 2019

This publication is in copyright. Subject to statutory exception and to the provisions of relevant collective licensing agreements, no reproduction of any part may take place without the written permission of Cambridge University Press.

First published 2019
First paperback edition 2020

A catalogue record for this publication is available from the British Library

ISBN 978-1-108-48104-5 Hardback
ISBN 978-1-108-70375-8 Paperback

Cambridge University Press has no responsibility for the persistence or accuracy of URLs for external or third-party internet websites referred to in this publication, and does not guarantee that any content on such websites is, or will remain, accurate or appropriate.

Contents

Figures

Tables

Contributors

Randall Akee is an associate professor in the Department of Public Policy and American Indian Studies at UCLA. Dr. Akee is an applied microeconomist and has worked in the areas of labor economics, economic development, and migration. His most recent publication is "First People Lost: Determining the State of Status First Nations Mortality in Canada using Administrative Data" (with Donna Feir), in *Canadian Journal of Economics*, volume 52, issue 2 (May 2019).

Stephanie L. Black, PhD, is a member of the Santee Sioux Nation of Flandreau, South Dakota and Assistant Professor of Management at The University of Texas A&M San Antonio, Texas. She teaches entrepreneurship, strategy, organizational behavior, and leadership classes, and she conducts research in ethnic entrepreneurship, social entrepreneurship, networking, and equity crowdfunding. She has published research in *The Journal of Management*.

David Castillo serves as CEO of Native Capital Access, a certified Native Community Development Financial Institution (CDFI). In that role he is active in developing strategic partnerships with banks, public sector agencies, CDFIs, and foundations to raise equity and debt resources to support economic development and small business financing on tribal lands. He is a board member for Construction in Indian Country, New Mexico Community Capital, and the Housing Assistance Council. Mr. Castillo holds undergraduate and graduate degrees from Stanford University and an MBA from Arizona State University. Mr. Castillo is of Nahua Indian descent.

Raymond Foxworth, PhD, is Vice President of Grantmaking, Development and Communications at First Nations Development Institute (First Nations). First Nations is a national nonprofit organization that works with Native American communities to restore Native American control of Native American assets. Foxworth has a PhD in political science from the University of Colorado at Boulder and is a citizen of the Navajo Nation; his family is from Coal Mine Canyon, Arizona.

Carla F. Fredericks is Director of the American Indian Law Clinic at the University of Colorado Law School and Director of the First Peoples Investment Engagement Program. She graduated from the University of Colorado and Columbia Law School. Fredericks' areas of expertise include Indigenous peoples law, federal Indian law, development, business, and human rights. She was previously a partner at Milberg LLP, where she founded the firm's Native American practice. Carla maintains an active pro bono practice focused on complex and appellate litigation and Native American affairs. She is a proud, enrolled citizen of the Mandan, Hidatsa and Arikara Nation.

Benjamin D. Horowitz is a project manager at the Federal Reserve Bank of Minneapolis. His work centers on efforts to strengthen the community development sector throughout the Bank's 9th district. He researches and writes about emerging trends and best practices for the Bank's *Community Dividend* publication. Horowitz's previous work has included time spent serving as staff on a campaign to improve job conditions for residential construction workers in the Southwest; analyzing the distribution of affordable housing resources in the wake of Hurricane Sandy; and advocating for better childcare and tax policy in Minnesota. He received a master of public affairs from Princeton University.

Miriam Jorgensen is Research Director of the Native Nations Institute at the University of Arizona. Her work – in the United States, Canada, and Australia – focuses on Indigenous governance and development and has addressed issues as wide-ranging as welfare policy, policing and justice systems, natural resources, cultural stewardship, land ownership, enterprise management, financial education, and entrepreneurship. She is Co-Founder of the University of Arizona Indigenous Governance certificate program, editor of *Rebuilding Native Nations: Strategies for Governance and Development* (2007), and co-author of *Structuring Sovereignty: Constitutions of Native Nations* (2014).

Deanna M. Kennedy, PhD, is a member of the Cherokee Nation of Oklahoma and Associate Professor and Academic Area Coordinator of the Operations Management and Information Systems Area in the School of Business at the University of Washington Bothell. Her research focuses on project teams involved in business operations and supply chain management and has been published in *Production Planning and Control, European Journal of Operational Research*, and *Decision Sciences*.

Patrice H. Kunesh is the Director of the Center for Indian Country Development at the Federal Reserve Bank of Minneapolis. Kunesh, of Standing Rock Lakota descent, has extensive experience representing American Indian tribes throughout the country. Among her numerous publications is the recently published *Tribal Leaders Handbook on Homeownership*. Kunesh received a master of public administration from the Harvard Kennedy School of Government and a juris doctor from the University of Colorado School of Law.

Krystal Langholz is the Chief Operating Officer for First Nation Oweesta Corporation (Oweesta), overseeing all financial education and capacity building programs. Before joining Oweesta, Langholz was the founding Executive Director of Hunkpati Investments, a certified Community Development Financial Institution on the Crow Creek Indian Reservation. She has an MA in anthropology from Colorado State University. Her publications include "Snapshot 2018: The Growing Native CDFI Movement" and various other practitioner-focused resources.

Mark C. Maletz is a senior fellow at the Harvard Business School and an internationally recognized thought leader in the areas of strategy, leadership development, and organizational transformation. He is also Faculty Chair for the HR-Executive Suite Connection program at HBS (the school's flagship executive education program for senior HR leaders). His research activities focus on helping companies to rethink their business strategies, improve their leadership capabilities, and reshape their cultures with an orientation toward entrepreneurship, innovation, values, and performance.

Robert J. Miller is a professor at the Sandra Day O'Connor College of Law, Arizona State University; the Faculty Director of the Rosette LLP American Indian Economic Development Program; a member of the Navajo Nation Council of Economic Advisors; the Interim Chief Justice for the Pascua Yaqui Tribe Court of Appeals; a justice on the Grand Ronde Tribe and Northwest Inter-Tribal Courts of Appeals; an elected member of the American Philosophical Society; and a citizen of the Eastern Shawnee Tribe. He is the author of *Reservation "Capitalism": Economic Development in Indian Country* (2012).

Elton Mykerezi is an associate professor of applied economics and an extension economist at the University of Minnesota, Twin Cities. His research interests include the study of human capital, causes of poverty, food insecurity and poor nutrition, rural business, and labor market development. His extension and outreach program aims to improve economic opportunities for vulnerable populations by focusing on access to healthy foods, a quality education, and opportunities for entrepreneurship and employment. His publications include "The Impact of Immigration Enforcement on the US Farming Sector" with Genti Kostandini and Cesar Escalante.

Lori Lea Pourier grew up on the Pine Ridge Indian Reservation and is a member of the Oglala Lakota Nation. Dedicated to reconnecting Native communities to cultural assets and to bringing new philanthropic resources to artists and culture bearers, Pourier has been involved in the arts, social justice, and community development fields for thirty years and has led the First Peoples Fund since 1999. She is a 2018 Ford Foundation Art of Change Fellow, currently serves on the board of the Jerome Foundation, and over the years, has served in an advisory role to many philanthropies.

Vena A-dae Romero-Briones, JD, LLM (Cochiti/Kiowa), is the Director of the Native Food Systems and Agricultural Program at First Nations Development Institute. She was born and raised in Cochiti Pueblo, New Mexico. She has written numerous publications on Indigenous food systems, policy issues, and legal considerations for tribal communities. Romero-Briones has a BA from Princeton University's Woodrow Wilson School of Public and International Affairs, a JD from Arizona State College of Law, and an LLM from the University of Arkansas Food and Agricultural Law Program.

Ezra Rosser is a professor of law at American University Washington College of Law. He writes about poverty law, property law, and Navajo economic development. Rosser is a co-author of *Poverty Law, Policy, and Practice* (2014) with Juliet Brodie, Clare Pastore, and Jeff Selbin and a co-editor of *The Poverty Law Canon* (2014) with Marie Failinger and *Tribes, Land, and the Environment* (2012) with Sarah Krakoff.

Jessica A. Shoemaker is Associate Professor of Law at the University of Nebraska College of Law. She is the author of numerous articles on Indigenous land tenure, including "Complexity's Shadow: American Indian Property, Sovereignty, and the Future," 115 Mich. L. Rev. 487 (2018) and "Transforming Property: Reclaiming Modern Indigenous Land Tenures," 107 Calif. L. Rev. (2019).

Daniel Stewart (PhD, Stanford) is a professor of entrepreneurship and Director of the Hogan Entrepreneurial Leadership Program at Gonzaga University. An enrolled member of the Spokane Tribe of Indians, he is the co-editor of *American Indian Business: Principles and Practices* (2017).

Richard M. Todd recently retired as a vice president of the Federal Reserve Bank of Minneapolis and Advisor to the Bank's Community Development Department and Center for Indian Country Development. He holds a PhD in agricultural and applied economics from the University of Minnesota.

Introduction

Miriam Jorgensen

In broad strokes, Indian Country[1] has experienced three waves of growth in jobs and incomes since the late 1960s. The first arose when the U.S. government shifted the agenda for its Indian policy from termination and relocation (ceasing to recognize tribal governments and strongly encouraging/compelling American Indians to move away from reservations) toward support of the poor. This shift placed Indian policy under the umbrella set of policies that constituted the War on Poverty and made reservation-based tribal communities a target population for Great Society programs. In aiding the poor, many of these programs also embraced the idea of community empowerment, in which impoverished communities had the opportunity to participate in program planning, direction, and administration. Thus, many federal Indian programs developed from the mid-1960s to the mid-1970s directly or indirectly involved tribal governments in their administration or implementation,[2] and job creation followed. At Zuni Pueblo, for example, tribal government expanded from nine employees in the 1950s to fifty-four by the late 1960s, largely with the support of federal funds; the Community Action Program, a primary funnel for poverty alleviation funding, was the single largest component of tribal government, with thirty-three employees.[3]

The second wave of growth in jobs and income resulted from Native nations' response to the 1975 Indian Self-Determination and Educational Assistance Act (Public Law 93-638) and its amendments. Substantively, the Act ended the Bureau of Indian Affairs' and Indian Health Service's management monopoly over the many programs and resources they managed on behalf of tribes. For the activities specified

---

[1] While there is a formal legal definition for "Indian country" (in 18 U.S. Code § 1151), the term is used here to describe the many reservation-based Native communities that share a geography with the United States. Both the terms "Indian Country" and "Indian country" are used throughout this book according to chapter authors' preferences and intentions.

[2] *See, e.g.,* George Pierre Castile, *To Show Heart: Native American Self-Determination and Federal Indian Policy, 1960–1975* (Tucson: University of Arizona Press, 1998), chapters 1 and 2; and Sar A. Levitan and Barbara Hetrick, *Big Brother's Indian Programs—With Reservations* (New York: McGraw-Hill, 1971), chapter 6.

[3] T. J. Ferguson, E. Richard Hart, and Calbert Seciwa, "Twentieth Century Zuni Political and Economic Development in Relation to Federal Indian Policy," in C. Matthew Snipp (ed.), *Public Policy Impacts on American Indian Economic Development* (Albuquerque: Native American Studies, Institute for Native American Development, University of New Mexico, 1988).

in the legislation, tribes could contract or compact to take over a portion or all of a federal budget outlay and replace federal employees with tribal employees who performed similar functions.[4] Programs as diverse as law enforcement, general assistance, and road maintenance were available to tribes for contracting and compacting, as were opportunities to manage tribal mineral reserves, forests, and grazing lands, among other resources – which meant that if a tribe embraced the whole range of contracting and compacting opportunities, it could create a large number of tribal government jobs.[5] For example, as the Jicarilla Apache Tribe shifted toward management control over its forest resources, the share of forestry workers employed by the tribe as opposed to the federal government rose from 5 percent in 1984 to 90 percent in 1989, and the number of tribal forestry employees rose from five to thirty-nine.[6] Subsequent federal legislation made still other federal agencies' Indian program funding streams available for tribal management – including funding for housing development, environmental management, workforce development, and child protection – further bolstering jobs and income opportunities in tribal communities. In some cases, employees simply changed paymasters, but in many others, the shift to tribal control replaced non-Native "guest workers" with reservation-resident American Indians.

A third wave of jobs and income growth in Native communities resulted from tribes' significant efforts to leverage their comparative advantages in support of economic development and tribal government revenue. Natural resource development and gaming enterprise development have been particularly important parts of this trend. For example, many tribal governments rapidly developed casinos and related hospitality sector businesses (golf courses, hotels, restaurants) in response to the clarification in U.S. law that tribes, not states, had the right to regulate gaming on tribal lands. Economic development followed. In the 1990s, on average, tribes that entered into the gaming industry saw real median household income gains of $5,000–$6,000.[7]

Two things stand out about these drivers of growth. For one, each is linked directly to the political change that characterizes the modern period – Native nation self-determination. Tribes grew their economies, and job and income opportunities for their citizens, through active assertions of their right to control what happens in their

---

[4] The language here can be confusing. Tribes are contractors, but as such, do not manage someone else's resources. They contract to take back the right to manage their *own* resources.

[5] For a general discussion of how Public Law 93-638 increased the opportunities for tribal bureaucratic expansion, *see* David L. Vinje, "Native American Economic Development on Selected Reservations: A Comparative Analysis," *American Journal of Sociology and Economics*, Volume 55, number 4, October 1996, 427–42.

[6] From the data file for Matthew B. Krepps and Richard E. Caves, "Bureaucrats and Indians: Principal–Agent Relations and Efficient Management of Tribal Forest Resources," *Journal of Economic Behavior and Organization*, Volume 24, July 1994, 133–51.

[7] Jonathan B. Taylor and Joseph P. Kalt, *American Indians on Reservations: A Databook of Socioeconomic Change Between the 1990s and 2000 Censuses* (Cambridge, MA: The Harvard Project on American Indian Economic Development, Harvard University, 2005).

communities and on their lands. For another, all three primarily relied on the public sector as the economic engine for Indian Country. Put differently, for half a century economic development in Native America has been highly dependent on the Native public sector, through the growth of Native nation governments and tribal government-owned corporations.

Certainly, this growth led to greater well-being for many Native reservation residents. Yet as ongoing lags in income and employment levels attest, public sector growth alone cannot create truly flourishing Native community economies. Reservation economies also need strong and thriving private sectors, built up by Native entrepreneurs and tribal citizen-owned enterprises. Such private sector growth has the potential to catalyze another wave of transformative Native nation economic development, making these economies more resilient to shocks, more diverse, and more productive for tribal citizens.

And, properly regulated, private sector growth may reflect another aspect of self-determination – the ability of tribal members to create the kinds of community development they want. By strengthening local retail and service sectors, Native entrepreneurship can reproduce the opportunities, experiences, and choices that reservation residents once may have thought existed only outside their communities. Alternatively or additionally, the resultant reservation economies may have marked differences from the mainstream. Given Native nations' various preferences, traditions, geographies, and belief systems, reservation-based private sector development might result in a richer mix of social enterprises, culturally connected businesses, sustainable practices, and relationship-based trade arrangements than is present in the mainstream. Put somewhat differently, entrepreneurship and business development outside the tribal public sector have the potential to create distinctive quality of life benefits for Native communities.

The need for more private sector development, more entrepreneurship, and more sustainability and resilience in reservation economies is the motivation for this book. Our goal as editors and authors is to move beyond the observation, and to provide tools – in the form of data, arguments, ideas, and examples – that can help make such change happen. In our experience, very little has been written

- for tribal economic development practitioners that helps them make the case to tribal leadership about the importance of tribal citizen entrepreneurship and the on-reservation private sector;
- for tribal policymakers that helps them know what laws and policies need to be developed or revised in order to encourage private sector development;
- for students of business to help them learn about entrepreneurship and private sector development in Indian Country and that gives them models of such work;
- for Native entrepreneurs who wish to understand the unique contextual factors that affect the success of privately owned reservation-based businesses; and
- for tribes' and Native entrepreneurs' sectoral allies (lenders, insurers, etc.) that helps them be better partners in on-reservation private sector development.

This book responds.

The first section, Chapters 1 and 2, sets the scene. Robert Miller describes the economic conditions on many reservations, and against these, identifies the benefits to Native communities of private sector development. He puts to rest the argument that such development is somehow antithetical to Native cultures, pointing to the strong entrepreneurial traditions characteristic of many North American tribes. He also lays out nine critical factors necessary for private sector development in Indian Country to proceed, challenging tribes and tribal citizens to address them and to renew their traditions of trade and exchange.

The chapter by Randall Akee, Elton Mykerezi, and Richard Todd presents newly available data on the comparative organization of reservation and nearby economies. Previous literature was unable to identify businesses by location, making it impossible to quantify the differences in market structure on- and off-reservation. On the one hand, the news is good: their data show that, in general, reservations and surrounding comparison geographies have similar numbers of jobs. On the other hand, the data also show fewer workplaces on reservations and significant employment concentration in the government sector and hospitality industry, putting the arguments for greater diversification and entrepreneurship development in tribal economies on even firmer footing.

The next section, consisting of Chapters 3 to 6, looks in greater depth at several specific barriers to tribal citizen-owned business development and points to needed policy responses. Jessica Shoemaker reviews the specific land tenure-related obstacles for reservation entrepreneurship, including transfer restraints, tax and regulatory issues, group rights, and jurisdictional complexity. But rather than reverting to the simple solution that has attracted many pundits – privatizing reservations and essentially reviving the era of tribal land allotment – Shoemaker looks with both hope and evidence at the possibilities for locally engineered, Indigenous, creative solutions to the property-related barriers to entrepreneurship.

Ezra Rosser takes the Navajo Nation as a case study of how difficult – and how necessary – tribal land tenure reform can be. By reviewing the nation's recent attempt to reform its homesite lease process, Rosser shows how colonial history, regulatory overlays, cost barriers, and tensions between local communities and the Navajo Nation central government all conspired to make changes to land tenure rules nearly impossible to implement. The challenge is for the Navajo Nation, both the people and the government, to find a way forward. The costs of retaining the status quo are simply too high: without a better approach to land use, the inherent development potential of one of the largest Indigenous nations in North America cannot be unlocked.

Patrice Kunesh and Benjamin Horowitz turn attention to another access to capital issue for many entrepreneurs in Indian Country – the lack of a tribal secured transactions system. Secured transaction laws, a lien filing system, and a contract enforcement or dispute resolution mechanism constitute a secured transactions system. Kunesh and Horowitz provide details about each of these elements and suggest system adaptations that tribes might want to adopt in response to community practices (e.g., whether property that might be used in a potlatch or giveaway can be secured as collateral), while making the point that tribes that take the time to create secured transactions systems help close the credit gap for entrepreneurs.

By way of personal reflection on his career in the field, David Castillo introduces an important set of institutional players in Indian Country finance – Native Community Development Financial Institutions (CDFIs). Recounting his work as the founder of a regional Native CDFI in Arizona, the stressors that challenge the industry, and the still-extant needs that only nonbank lenders can meet, Castillo nonetheless views the future with confidence. He notes that Native CFDIs have been engaged in reflective learning for two decades, which makes them stronger while remaining attuned to their community-based missions. He also highlights the new availability of operating and loan capital from the philanthropic sector, which is helping to sustain and grow the industry. The more than seventy Native CDFIs now extant are poised to be a critical source of capital and credit for both start-up and expanding private sector businesses in Indian Country.

The book's third section, Chapters 7 to 10, provides advice from business and business law scholars whose job it is to ask, "What can we learn and share from examples working on the ground?" Mark Maletz introduces several factors that he has concluded are required to create a culture and practice of entrepreneurship. Using expository case studies, Maletz then describes what entrepreneurship "looks like," how entrepreneurs thrive in hostile environments, and what constitutes an entrepreneurial mindset, which he posits is part of what it takes to manage through the "entrepreneurial lifecycle." Ultimately, Maletz's chapter reminds readers that entrepreneurship is something that can be learned and that there are a number of unchanging principles involved in the practice of entrepreneurship – even in tribal communities.

Daniel Stewart focuses on the sequential process of entrepreneurship from idea to implementation. As Stewart explains, the primary point of this sequence is "value creation," or the fact that businesses must produce things that customers are willing to purchase. In tracing out the process, he instructs entrepreneurs to ideate (form a new idea), to prototype (create a physical or virtual model that aids in "kicking the tires" of the idea), to validate (find evidence that the idea works, investing leanly to minimize risk), to pivot or proceed (adapt based on learning or move to roll out), and finally, to repeat, since entrepreneurship requires constant refinement to keep the product or service fresh. Usefully, Stewart points to numerous tribal community examples and applications throughout this discussion.

Stephanie Black and Deanna Kennedy drill down on supply chain management. A supply chain is the series of providers and buyers that supply the components and products necessary to create a good or service. Black and Kennedy note that any business can thrive or fail based on effective or ineffective supply chain management, yet to date, no guidance has been available to Native business owners that addresses their specific supply chain management concerns, let alone to Native business owners operating within reservation economies. The authors then detail a variety of considerations that should help Native business owners avoid potential pitfalls and increase their odds of success.

To close out this section, Carla Fredericks introduces the UN Sustainable Development Goals (SDGs) as a set of ideas that are influencing socially responsible business development outside Indian Country and raises these provocative questions: If the SDGs are important for human progress, where do Indigenous nations in the United States fit in? To the extent that tribes and tribal citizens are participants in the realization of the SDGs, what development options might be open to entrepreneurial tribes and people? Fredericks details how several tribes' efforts to develop renewable energy projects provide examples of how to address the goals and advance economic opportunity on reservations. The challenge is for Native communities to find even more ways to do so, in not just the public but also the private sector.

The final section, Chapters 11 and 12, provides concrete examples of practices and programs that promote entrepreneurship and private sector development in Indian Country. Lori Pourier describes the work of the First Peoples Fund (FPF), which began with the provision of grants to outstanding community-based artists and culture bearers to help them grow as artist-entrepreneurs. Research and experience proved that a focus on artists was important: in the Northern Plains tribal communities that FPF studied, as many as one-third of home-based Indigenous entrepreneurs were artists. Seeking to have an even greater impact on the communities and economies it serves, FPF now focuses its programming on the community arts "ecology," providing grants and other assistance to artists *and* community organizations. Growing community partners' capacity to serve artists spurs more community investment in culture and even more income growth for artists and culture bearers.

Foxworth, Langholz, and Romero-Briones close the book with a look at the important topic of youth entrepreneurship. Their starting point, however, is the food sovereignty movement, in which Native nations increasingly are taking back control over food production, food policy, and food distribution. They note that in several, and perhaps many, Native communities, the food sovereignty and youth entrepreneurship movements have proceeded together – youth are learning about growing, making, and preserving food (often traditional food) and also are marketing it. They are gaining traditional knowledge, self-confidence, access to healthy foods, and entrepreneurial skills through these ventures and laying the groundwork for an entirely changed food system, from field to market, in coming generations.

The past fifty years of economic change in Indian Country have created a mandate for more tribal-citizen entrepreneurship and greater private sector development. Meeting this mandate will be difficult. Growing the number and size of Native American-owned businesses on reservations will require persuasion, policy development, institution building, risk-taking, professional development, market-mindedness, and generational thinking. As editors and authors, our desire for *Creating Private Sector Economies in Native America: Sustainable Development Through Entrepreneurship* is that it will aid in this important work.

PART I

The Setting

Private Sector Economic Development in Indian Country

Robert J. Miller

I INTRODUCTION

American Indian reservations and communities in the United States are poor. More American Indian families per capita live below the U.S. poverty line than any other group. Conditions are even worse on the more than 300 Indian reservations where unemployment reaches 80–90 percent, inadequate housing and a lack of housing is at the highest rate in the United States, and health conditions and life expectancy rates are the worst in America. Many commentators, including President Bill Clinton in 1999, compare reservations to "third world countries."[1]

In contrast, before contact with Europeans, most Indian nations and peoples were fairly prosperous, healthy, and had thriving societies that existed for hundreds and thousands of years with established governmental and economic systems. Most Indians supported themselves with agriculture and lived in permanent towns and settlements. For example, when the English arrived in modern-day Virginia, there were at least 200 permanent Indian villages in the Tidewater region of Virginia and Maryland. Life was easy for the Powhatan Confederacy. They "had a relatively sophisticated economy" and lived very comfortably due to intensive agriculture. It is true that some tribal peoples across the continent were somewhat nomadic, following buffalo herds or fish migrations, but these nations lived what are called "seasonal rounds" and traveled annually to the identical locations to live, harvest fish and animals, and take maturing roots, nuts, and berries. These peoples were not wandering aimlessly about. All Indians pursued economic activities in a systematic and intelligent manner to create the foods and assets they needed and wanted.[2]

---

[1] Brenda Norrell, *Clinton's New Market Focus on Indian Country*, INDIAN COUNTRY TODAY, May 3, 2000, at A1.

[2] ROBERT J. MILLER, RESERVATION "CAPITALISM": ECONOMIC DEVELOPMENT IN INDIAN COUNTRY 9–23 (2012); Richard H. Steckel & Joseph M. Prince, *Nutritional Success on the Great Plains: Nineteenth Century Equestrian Nomads*, 33 J. INTERDISCIP. HIST. 353, 354 (2003); BRUCE D. SMITH, C. WESLEY COWAN & MICHAEL P. HOFFMAN, RIVERS OF CHANGE: ESSAYS ON EARLY AGRICULTURE IN EASTERN NORTH AMERICA 201–03 (1992).

Indian nations and societies also developed governmental institutions that controlled their economic activities. Tribal peoples had well-established legal rules that recognized private rights in the ownership of homes, tools, art, crops, horses, captured animals and fish, and land, for example. Individual Indians also conducted extensive trade that crisscrossed the continent and traded at regularly scheduled fairs or markets that were held annually at various locations. This trade was carried on by individual Indians through private initiative, manufacturing, and economic efforts to earn "profits" to support themselves and their families by producing and selling necessary and luxury items.

In light of the current poverty and negative economic and social conditions on most reservations, tribal governments are heavily focused on economic development. But one tribal institution, one economic activity, that I fear has been overlooked by almost all Indian nations, the federal government, and reservation communities is the historic institution of the tribal private sector economy. It is time for Indian peoples and governments to revive their traditions that promoted and protected private economic activities, and to look to their historical roots and traditions of individual and family economic development activities.

Creating private sector economies on reservations will take the intelligent and coordinated efforts of tribal governments, Indian individuals, reservation communities, non-Indians, the United States, and nonprofit organizations. Indian nations and Indians will have to revive their private business skills, the legal regimes that promoted and protected private economic activities, and their historic support for reservation-based entrepreneurs and businesses. The upside to these efforts is limitless, and success in this field will create untold benefits for reservation communities, economies, individual Indians, families, and their nations. Creating functioning economies will go a long way toward diversifying reservation economic activities and will benefit everyone as the "multiplier effect" of keeping money circulating in Indian Country will create even more businesses, jobs, income, and better conditions for everyone. There can be no higher goal than to improve the living conditions on reservations and to help ensure the sustainability and livability of Indian homelands and the continued existence of Indian nations and peoples. These improvements will only occur if tribal governments and Indian peoples can revive their traditional institutions and skills to create private sector economic activities.

II ECONOMIC CONDITIONS IN INDIAN COUNTRY

The extreme economic conditions that exist in Indian Country highlight the crucial need for Indian nations and Indian peoples to build functioning reservation economies. According to a 2013 Department of the Interior labor report, only 49–50 percent of Indians sixteen or older, who live on or near reservations, have full or even part-time employment. In addition, many studies and reservations report unemployment rates as high as 90 percent. In contrast, the United States unemployment rate was below 4 percent as of January 2019.[3]

With these statistics in mind, it is no surprise that the percentage of American Indian families living below the poverty line is higher than for any other identifiable group in the United States. Indians also have the lowest educational attainment levels as a group in the United States. In addition, reservation-based Indian families suffer from the highest rates of substandard housing, the shortest life spans, highest infant mortality rates, and worst malnutrition rates in the United States.[4]

Furthermore, the basic infrastructure that most Americans take for granted is missing or limited on most reservations. Adequate roads, housing, clean water, sanitation, telephones, electricity, and high-speed internet are in short supply in Indian Country. In 2001, only 47 percent of reservation Indian households had telephones, compared to 94 percent for non-Native rural Americans. And only 9 percent of rural Indian houses had personal computers and only 8 percent had internet access. Moreover, only 14 percent of Indian communities contained financial institutions. More than one in six American Indians had to travel over one hundred miles to find a bank, and one-third had to travel at least thirty miles to access an ATM or bank. As of 2008, up to 35 percent of Indian homes lacked adequate water and 10–15 percent of Indian homes did not have plumbing. The Department of Energy reported in 2000 that 14.2 percent of Indian homes on reservations had no access to electricity, compared to just 1.4 percent for the average U.S. household.[5]

Consequently, it is understandable why there are very few functioning private sector economies in Indian Country. Almost none of the over 300 reservations in the lower forty-eight states, and the more than 200 Alaska Native villages, have

---

3   U.S. Department of the Interior, Office of the Assistant Secretary-Indian Affairs, 2013 *American Indian Population and Labor Force Report* 10, www.bia.gov/sites/bia.gov/files/assets/public/pdf/idc1-024782. pdf (last visited January 15, 2019); U.S. Census Bureau, U.S. Department of Commerce, *American Indian, Alaska Native Tables from the Statistical Abstract of the United States: 2004–2005* 441, 451 (124th ed., 2005); Bureau of Indian Affairs, *2003 Indian Labor Force Report* ii; Shelly Hagan, *Where U.S. Unemployment Is Still Sky-High: Indian Reservations*, Bloomberg (April 5, 2018).

4   Miriam Jorgensen, *Access to Capital and Credit in Native Communities* 4 (2016); U.S. Department of Commerce, U.S. Census Bureau, *Poverty Rates for Selected Detailed Race and Hispanic Groups by State and Place: 2007–2011*; Raymond Cross, *American Indian Education: The Terror of History and the Nation's Debt to the Indian Peoples*, 21 U. Ark. Little Rock L. Rev. 941, 943 (1999); Ward Churchill & Winona LaDuke, *Native North America: The Political Economy of Radioactive Colonialism*, in The State of Natives America: Genocide, Colonization, and Resistance 246 (M. Annette Jaimes ed., 1992); U.S. Dept. Housing & Urban Dev., *Assessment of Am. Indian Housing Needs and Program: Final Report* xii, 66–67, 76–78, 80 (May 1996).

5   Federal Communications Comm., *2018 Broadband Deployment Report* (1.2 million residents of tribal lands, well above 50 percent, lack access to high-speed internet), www.fcc.gov/reports-research/reports/ broadband-progress-reports/2018-broadband-deployment-report (last visited January 16, 2019); *California's Largest Tribe Deploys 1st White Space Broadband*, News from Indian Country, June 2011, at 23; Jodi Rave, *U.S. Senators Seek $2B for Tribes*, Missoulian.com December 11, 2008; U.S. Department of the Treasury, *The Report of the Native American Lending Study*, 11, 14, 39–40 (2001); U. S. Department of Energy, *Indian Energy Study* (March 28, 2000).

functioning economies. Few reservations have large grocery stores and retail outlets, and there is an almost complete absence of businesses where people can obtain the necessities and luxuries of life. Not surprisingly, Indians own their own businesses at the lowest rate per capita for any group in the United States and the businesses they own produce less income on average.[6]

III AMERICAN INDIAN CULTURES AND ECONOMIC DEVELOPMENT

We must address, even briefly, the historical facts regarding Indian nations' and communities' economic development activities because the first question that is always asked in addressing this topic is "won't economic development hurt Indian cultures." The very question ignores the reality that Indian peoples, cultures, and nations have to have at least some moderate level of economic activity and income to survive and thrive. Here, we will just mention some of the ample evidence that demonstrates that Indigenous peoples and cultures across what is now the United States intelligently engaged in a wide variety of economic activities. Hopefully, we can put to rest this question whether modern-day tribal and individual Indian private economic activities are possibly harmful to, or in violation of, cultural norms.

A American Indian Entrepreneurial Activities Regarding Land and Personal Property

Indian nations and communities developed and possessed cultural and governmental institutions that promoted and supported private economic activities over many centuries. Thus, this chapter and book are not arguing for some radical new idea to address economic issues in Indian Country. Instead, we are calling for Indian nations and peoples to revive their historical and traditional values, behaviors, structures, and mechanisms to engage in economic activities and to restore their institutions and legal regimes that promoted and supported individual and family economic activities.

History demonstrates clearly that the Indigenous nations and peoples in what is now the United States supported themselves for thousands of years with all sorts of private economic activities. Many Indian tribes engaged in hunter-gatherer activities but the majority of tribal communities worked as individuals, and in small family groups, through privately initiated efforts to fulfill their daily needs by agriculture, or by manufacturing projects that sustained their lives. In fact, one historian noted that in the 1600s the Indians of New England produced 65 percent of their diet from

---

[6] U.S. Census Bureau, *2012 American Community Survey 1-Year Estimates*, https://factfinder.census.gov/bkmk/table/1.0/en/ACS/12_1YR/DP05/0100000US|0400000US41 (last visited January 14, 2019; U.S. Census Bureau, *Statistics for All U.S. Firms by Industry, Gender, Ethnicity, and Race for the U.S., States, Metro Areas, Counties, and Places: 2012 Survey of Business Owners*, https://factfinder.census .gov/bkmk/table/1.0/en/SBO/2012/00CSA01/0100000US|0400000US41 (last visited January 15, 2019).

agriculture. When Europeans arrived, the lives and economies of Indian peoples and nations were primarily based on agriculture, including maize/corn, beans, squash, and grains, and on long-distance trade, specialized labor, and manufacturing. English colonists in the Chesapeake region of Virginia and Maryland encountered a well-populated and well-governed area that was controlled by sophisticated cultures and sovereign governments. Clearly, these peoples worked in an organized and intelligent fashion to create the foods and material goods necessary to maintain their lives and families.[7]

Native peoples understood and developed principles that today we call private property and entrepreneurship. Historians note that almost all Indian assets were privately owned: "truly communal property was scant."[8] Indians voluntarily participated in producing excess crops and manufactured goods and engaged in trade. Indian peoples across North America regularly traded goods for survival and comfort. The extensive trade that took place for several thousand years was conducted in free market situations where private individuals came together to buy and sell items they had manufactured or amassed and that they exchanged by barter and even sold for exchange mediums we today call money or currencies.[9]

As mentioned above, the majority of Indian societies lived permanently or semipermanently in towns and villages and supported themselves primarily through farming. Even tribal groups who might be considered nomadic followed "seasonal rounds" in which they moved to the nearly identical locations year after year to utilize wild and domesticated food resources and, for example, seasonal fish runs, animal migrations, and wild foods. Many of these peoples also planted crops and returned to harvest them as part of their seasonal rounds. These "nomadic" peoples recognized property rights in their cultivated and gathered foods, hunting and gathering territories, and the homesites they returned to year after year.[10]

---

[7]   Thomas R. Wessel, *Agriculture, Indians and American History*, 50 AGRICULTURAL HIST. 9–10, 14 (1976); Leonard A. Carlson, *Learning to Farm: Indian Land Tenure and Farming Before the Dawes Act*, in PROPERTY RIGHTS AND INDIAN ECONOMIES 70–71 (Terry L. Anderson ed., 1992); THE OTHER SIDE OF THE FRONTIER: ECONOMIC EXPLORATIONS INTO NATIVE AMERICAN HISTORY 70–71, 86 (Linda Barrington ed., 1999); Neal Salisbury, *The Indians' Old World: Native Americans and the Coming of Europeans*, in AMERICAN ENCOUNTERS: NATIVES AND NEWCOMERS FROM EUROPEAN CONTACT TO INDIAN REMOVAL 1500–1850 5–10 (Peter C. Mancall & James H. Merrell eds., 2000); PETER C. MANCALL, VALLEY OF OPPORTUNITY: ECONOMIC CULTURE ALONG THE UPPER SUSQUEHANNA, 1700–1800 39–40, 125 (1991); 15 SMITHSONIAN INST., HANDBOOK OF NORTH AMERICAN INDIANS (NORTHEAST) 58–69, 162, 240–52, 253–70, 271–81, 324 (William C. Sturtevant ed., 1978).

[8]   2 FREDRICK WEBB HODGE, HANDBOOK OF AMERICAN INDIANS NORTH OF MEXICO 308 (1910).

[9]   OTHER SIDE OF THE FRONTIER, *supra* note 7, at 5, 72, 74, 108; CLARK WISSLER, INDIANS OF THE UNITED STATES 37, 39–41 (Rev. ed. 1966); RICHARD WHITE, THE ROOTS OF DEPENDENCY: SUBSISTENCE, ENVIRONMENT, AND SOCIAL CHANGE AMONG THE CHOCTAWS, PAWNEES, AND NAVAJOS 184, 198 (1983); Wessel, *supra* note 7, at 9–10, 14.

[10]   E. RICHARD HART, AMERICAN INDIAN HISTORY ON TRIAL: HISTORICAL EXPERTISE IN TRIBAL LITIGATION 18, 63, 147, 185, 190–91, 193 (2018); 9 SMITHSONIAN INST., HANDBOOK OF NORTH AMERICAN INDIANS 332

All Indian tribes and societies recognized forms of permanent and semipermanent private rights in land. The fact that most American Indian societies considered land to be communal property of the tribal group and society did not prevent individual citizens and families from exercising rights to use specific pieces of land. A right to use land that belongs to another is called a usufructuary, or use, right. There are many examples across history and across tribal nations of the widespread recognition of private usufructuary rights in Indian cultures. Among the Choctaw people, for example, families had their own farming plots near their cabins and "most Choctaws had specific fields marked out within the communally prepared town lands ... A family ... could take any uncultivated lands they thought suitable and hold it as long as they used it."[11] Moreover, Pawnee women planted corn, beans, melons, and squash in multiacre plots that had been assigned them by chiefs. The women were entitled to the lands and crops they produced as long as they wished, although the land would revert to the tribe upon a woman's death. Consequently, Indians in these societies acquired and exercised ownership and private rights over specific pieces of land even though the lands were owned in common by the community. In other tribal cultures, individual Indians and families that commenced farming, hunting, or trapping on unused lands in effect made those communal lands their own private property when they began individually developing and working it.[12]

Indian private use of communally owned lands is also demonstrated by the Navajos who considered communal agricultural lands to be assets that individuals and families could claim by using them. In the Pueblos of the Southwest, farming rights were allotted to individuals by community leaders. Commentators have characterized these rights for Pueblo and Hopi families and individuals as rights for individuals to use the land as private property and to own any improvements they built; including the sophisticated irrigation systems that some Native peoples built communally to serve tribal lands. The Pima Tribe, for example, worked cooperatively to build irrigation systems and village headmen would then assign specific plots to individuals and the land became the permanent property of the assignee and its heirs. Furthermore, the Havasupai Tribe also considered that communal tribal

(William C. Sturtevant ed., 1979); WILBUR R. JACOBS, DISPOSSESSING THE AMERICAN INDIAN: INDIANS AND WHITES ON THE COLONIAL FRONTIER 1, 5–9 (1972); 7 SMITHSONIAN INST., HANDBOOK OF NORTH AMERICAN INDIANS: NORTHWEST COAST 547, 548 (Wayne Suttles ed., 1990); 12 SMITHSONIAN INST., HANDBOOK OF NORTH AMERICAN INDIANS 378, 380, 448–49 (William C. Sturtevant ed., 1979); LYNDA NORENE SHAFFER, NATIVE AMERICANS BEFORE 1492: THE MOUND BUILDING CENTERS OF THE EASTERN WOODLANDS 3, 19–20, 28, 33–34, 38, 84–85 (1992).

[11]   WHITE, *supra* note 9, at 20.

[12]   MILLER, RESERVATION "CAPITALISM," *supra* note 2, at 12–15; WHITE, *supra* note 9, at 159, 200; TERRY L. ANDERSON, SOVEREIGN NATIONS OR RESERVATIONS? AN ECONOMIC HISTORY OF AMERICAN INDIANS 8 (1995); Julian H. Steward, *Ethnography of the Owens Valley Paiute*, 33 AM. ARCHAEOLOGY & ETHNOLOGY 253 (1934); MELVILLE J. HERSKOVITS, THE ECONOMIC LIFE OF PRIMITIVE PEOPLES 362 (2d ed., 1952).

lands were privately owned by individuals as long as the land was put to a productive use.[13]

In addition, many Eastern and Southeastern tribes produced the majority of their subsistence by farming, and individuals and families held usufructuary rights to specific lands. The Creek and Cherokee peoples from the American Southeast farmed their own lands and put their crops into privately owned storehouses. Moreover, farming plots among Native peoples of New England and Virginia "were either owned outright by families or held in usufruct by them."[14] In fact, all tribal communities that practiced agriculture "definitely recognized exclusive land use."[15]

Indian nations' institutions, laws, and cultures recognized other private rights in addition to agriculture. Indian cultures that relied on fishing developed and protected individual and private rights in these resources. Columbia River salmon fishing sites consisting of wooden platforms and well-located rocks were individually and family-owned properties that were passed on by established inheritance principles. Other people could fish at these sites only with the permission of the owners. Other Native cultures also developed principles of private property that included the right to exclude others from communally owned lands. Owners could pass these properties on by inheritance, and fishing sites could be rented out or sold. One historian commented that "Indians had well developed legal systems that emphasized individual rights and individual ownership."[16]

The Inuits and other peoples in modern-day Alaska also enforced precise concepts of private ownership and industry in tribally owned hunting and fishing territories; "usufructuary rights to trap in specific territories became established."[17] The Nootka peoples of the Pacific Northwest "carried the concept of ownership to an incredible extreme."[18] Under the legal regimes of these cultures, individuals held as "privately owned property"[19] land, houses, beaches, salvage rights, clam beds, river and ocean fishing spots, and even sea lion rocks in the ocean. The Tlingit Tribe of Alaska also

---

[13] Carlson, *supra* note 7, at 70–71; HERSKOVITS, *supra* note 12, at 362; GRAHAM D. TAYLOR, THE NEW DEAL AND AMERICAN INDIAN TRIBALISM: THE ADMINISTRATION OF THE INDIAN REORGANIZATION ACT, 1934–1945 69–70 (1980); 9 SMITHSONIAN INST., *supra* note 10, at 554–57; ANGIE DEBO, A HISTORY OF THE INDIANS OF THE UNITED STATES 13–14 (1970); ANDERSON, *supra* note 12, at 32–34.

[14] 15 SMITHSONIAN INST., *supra* note 7, at 84.

[15] Carlson, *supra* note 7, at 70–71. *See also* DEBO, *supra* note 13, at 13–14; ANDERSON, *supra* note 12, at 32–34.

[16] Andrew P. Vayda, *Pomo Trade Feasts*, in TRIBAL AND PEASANT ECONOMIES 498 (George Dalton ed., 1967). *See also id.* at 495–96; OTHER SIDE OF THE FRONTIER, *supra* note 7, at 71; CHARLES F. WILKINSON, CROSSING THE NEXT MERIDIAN: LAND, WATER, AND THE FUTURE OF THE WEST 185 (1992); 7 SMITHSONIAN INST., *supra* note 10, at 536–37.

[17] Ronald L. Trosper, *That Other Discipline: Economics and American Indian History*, in NEW DIRECTIONS IN AMERICAN INDIAN HISTORY 210, 212 (Colin G. Calloway ed., 1988).

[18] Phillip Drucker, *The Northern and Central Nootkan Tribes*, 144 BUREAU AM. ETHNOLOGY BULL. 247 (1951).

[19] *Id.*

protected private rights in hunting grounds, salmon streams, sealing rocks, and the accumulation of individual wealth, and most of these rights were inheritable.[20]

In the vast majority of Indian nations, individuals and families owned their own housing and homesites. Many tribal cultures also recognized exclusive rights to valuable plants such as berry patches, and fruit and nut trees. The property rights recognized in most of these assets were inheritable and could be bought and sold.[21]

These Indigenous economic and property systems obviously encouraged entrepreneurial, individually directed, and privately owned food production and manufacturing activities on specific pieces of land. Individuals and their families owned the fruits of their labors and left their property to their descendants under well-established tribal laws and customs.

Furthermore, all American Indian cultures recognized and protected private property and entrepreneurship in items other than land. For example, in a form of intellectual property law, in some tribes, individuals and families owned exclusive rights to specific images, dances, marriage ceremonies, names, songs, stories, masks, medicines, and rituals. These rights were inheritable. And all Indian peoples owned as private personal property their clothing, cooking utensils, housing, animals, tools, weapons, canoes, handicraft and trade goods, and the foods they produced. From the Native peoples of Alaska to the Havasupai of Arizona, items of personal use were "clearly owned by the individual."[22]

The horse also demonstrates how Indian cultures viewed private property and individual economic activities. Horses were always items of private property. Among the Pawnee, for example, the horse "took its place as a peculiar form of property ... [and] began to denote wealth and created the beginnings of a social standing ... Horses were personal property ...."[23] Well-trained horses were very valuable private assets, and some Indians leased them out for payments of captured game or booty. In addition, principles of private property acquired by personal initiative were well demonstrated by the fact that in communal hunting, raiding, and warfare, most tribes recognized and protected individual rights in captured items.[24]

---

[20] *Id.*; John C. McManus, *An Economic Analysis of Indian Behavior in the North American Fur Trade*, 32 TASKS ECON. HIST. 36, 39 (1972); 15 SMITHSONIAN INST., *supra* note 7, at 84; Robert J. Miller, *Exercising Cultural Self-Determination: The Makah Indian Tribe Goes Whaling*, 25 AM. INDIAN L. REV. 165 (2001); KALERVO OBERG, THE SOCIAL ECONOMY OF THE TLINGIT INDIANS 35 (1973); ELIZABETH COLSON, THE MAKAH INDIANS: A STUDY OF AN INDIAN TRIBE IN MODERN AMERICAN SOCIETY 4 (1953).

[21] 7 SMITHSONIAN INST., *supra* note 10, at 418; COLSON, *supra* note 20, at 4; Carlson, *supra* note 7, at 71; OTHER SIDE OF THE FRONTIER, *supra* note 7, at 71, 108; 9 SMITHSONIAN INST., *supra* note 10, at 554–57; K. N. LLEWELLYN & E. ADAMSON HOEBEL, THE CHEYENNE WAY: CONFLICT AND CASE LAW IN PRIMITIVE JURISPRUDENCE 213–14, 216–20, 233 (1941).

[22] HERSKOVITS, *supra* note 12, at 376. *See also id.* at 372–73; 7 SMITHSONIAN INST., *supra* note 10, at 418; COLSON, *supra* note 20, at 4; OBERG, *supra* note 20, at 55, 62–63, 79–83, 91–94.

[23] WHITE, *supra* note 9, at 180.

[24] ANDERSON, *supra* note 12, at 43, 62; THE CHEYENNE WAY, *supra* note 21, at 223, 225, 229, 233; Alan M. Klein, *Political Economy of the Buffalo Hide Trade: Race and Class on the Plains*, in THE POLITICAL ECONOMY OF NORTH AMERICAN INDIANS 133, 141–42 (John H. Moore ed., 1993).

Indians from many nations also engaged in specific occupations other than farming or hunting and even hired out their personal services and expertise. For example, in the Makah Tribe there were specific occupations to which people aspired because there was a "degree of specialization into whale hunters, seal hunters, doctors, gamblers, warriors and fishermen."[25] In other tribal cultures, including the Powhatan Confederacy in Virginia, people specialized in professions such as healers, shamans, manufacturers, singers, and songwriters and were paid fees for their services. Ample agricultural surpluses allowed some individuals to pursue career paths other than farming, including as tribal administrators, artisans, and soldiers.[26]

This brief review of the private entrepreneurial activities that Indian individuals and families engaged in regarding lands and personal properties demonstrates that Native societies supported themselves via private economic endeavors to gain profits in assets in land, crops, and personal properties. Indian peoples and families worked diligently and intelligently to acquire the rights and profits they needed to support themselves and their families.

B American Indian Traditional Economic Activities and Skills

Indian peoples also engaged in other private economic activities that demonstrated their use of trade, barter, and the buying and selling of goods they had produced to earn profits to support their families. Indian communities across the continent regularly hosted annual and semiannual trade fairs and markets to trade and sell surplus foods and manufactured items to other peoples near and far. These markets were so important that Indian nations, and later the Spanish, would call truces so the markets could be held. In addition, trade networks crisscrossed North America and goods were traded hundreds and even a thousand miles from their sources. These trading activities were controlled and motivated by issues of private property, entrepreneurship, and individual initiative.[27]

Thousands of years before European settlers arrived, long-distance trade networks including Indigenous nations in modern-day Mexico and Canada were developed across North America to serve Indigenous peoples' interests in acquiring goods. Trade developed in all kinds of products including food, manufactured items,

---

[25] COLSON, *supra* note 20, at 249–50.

[26] 11 Smithsonian Inst., HANDBOOK OF NORTH AMERICAN INDIANS 315–16 (William C. Sturtevant ed., 1986); OBERG, *supra* note 20, at 94–95; 10 SMITHSONIAN INST., HANDBOOK OF NORTH AMERICAN INDIANS 714–15 (William C. Sturtevant ed., 1983); HERSKOVITS, *supra* note 12, at 123–24; EDMUND S. MORGAN, AMERICAN SLAVERY, AMERICAN FREEDOM: THE ORDEAL OF COLONIAL VIRGINIA 50, 56 (1975).

[27] 7 SMITHSONIAN INST., *supra* note 10, at 150, 208–09, 418, 560, 580; 9 SMITHSONIAN INST., *supra* note 10, at 25–26, 71–72, 79, 127–28, 149, 189, 201; OBERG, *supra* note 20, at 105, 111–12; 10 SMITHSONIAN INST., *supra* note 26, at 8, 712–13; 15 SMITHSONIAN INST., *supra* note 7, at 45, 83; JOHN C. EWERS, PLAINS INDIAN HISTORY AND CULTURE 24–25 (1997); SHAFFER, *supra* note 10, at 25; Salisbury, *supra* note 7, at 5, 13; MANCALL, *supra* note 7, at 24, 47–48; RICK RUBIN, NAKED AGAINST THE RAIN: THE PEOPLE OF THE LOWER COLUMBIA RIVER 1770–1830 69 (1999); HERSKOVITS, *supra* note 12, at 223–24.

stones, shells, and minerals. Jewelry and luxury items were manufactured and traded. In addition, these extensive and well-established trade networks spread new European goods to many Indians long before they actually encountered a Euro-American. Indian peoples and nations had no problems incorporating new goods and new trade partners – even for example the fur trade – into their trade networks.[28]

In light of all this prolonged economic activity, it is no surprise that Indian peoples exhibited advanced economic abilities and sophistication and were proficient at operating their business endeavors, trading, and manipulating markets to their advantage over many centuries. Native societies developed business and trading practices long before Euro-Americans arrived. Some Indian businesspeople and their regional trade fairs used standardized measurements and had established rules of trade. Some Indians gave guarantees on their goods, and some extended credit and lent out currencies and goods at interest. Moreover, individual Indians and tribal governments well understood the value of gaining monopolies, controlling trade routes, and being the middlemen in transactions.[29]

Surprising to many, no doubt, is that Indian peoples and tribal nations used currencies as a medium of trade exchange and a substitute for a barter system. Indians used seashells, manufactured shell belts, beads, Hudson Bay Company blankets, turquoise, dentalia, and deerskins as money to engage in business with other Indians and with Euro-Americans. Many Indians and non-Indians used these currencies exactly as we use money today.[30]

Another aspect of Indigenous economic activities that might be surprising is that many Indians and tribal cultures engaged in wealth accumulation, and honored and protected the related activities and assets. Amassing a surplus of food and goods led to ample leisure time, the manufacture of art and handicrafts, time to practice social and religious ceremonies, and even the use of these surpluses for the public display of wealth. Indians and their families worked hard at activities – which were sometimes dangerous – to acquire the goods they needed and wanted. Many Indian

[28]   MICHELE STRUTIN, CHACO: A CULTURAL LEGACY 50–51 (1994); OTHER SIDE OF THE FRONTIER, *supra* note 7, at 5, 86, 506; 7 SMITHSONIAN INST., *supra* note 10, at 120–21, 125, 208–09; 9 SMITHSONIAN INST., *supra* note 10, at 201–05, 305, 559–61; SHAFFER, *supra* note 10, at 21–23, 35–37, 44–45, 75–80; 10 SMITHSONIAN INST., *supra* note 26, at 691–707, 711–22; 15 SMITHSONIAN INST., *supra* note 7, at 83, 85, 202–06, 344–47, 763–64.

[29]   7 SMITHSONIAN INST., *supra* note 10, at 119–20, 123–25, 130–31, 153, 208, 282, 319–20, 369, 407–08, 471, 585; 15 SMITHSONIAN INST., *supra* note 7, at 84, 199, 204–06, 344–47, 430; Wessel, *supra* note 7, at 11–13; MANCALL, *supra* note 7, at 50–51, 83, 91–94; OBERG, *supra* note 20, at 35–36, 55–56, 60–61, 105–06, 110, 132; JACOBS, *supra* note 10, at 9–10, 32–33; THE CHEYENNE WAY, *supra* note 21, at 228–29; HERSKOVITS, *supra* note 12, at 86, 93–94; Trosper, *supra* note 17, at 205, 209; RUBIN, *supra* note 27, at 69–71; Klein, *supra* note 24, at 143.

[30]   9 SMITHSONIAN INST., *supra* note 10, at 149; 10 SMITHSONIAN INST., *supra* note 26, at 720–21; 15 SMITHSONIAN INST., *supra* note 7, at 166, 202–03, 384; 7 SMITHSONIAN INST., *supra* note 10, at 29, 122, 369, 417, 493, 505, 536–37, 540, 548, 551, 565, 573, 580, 585, 591; RUBIN, *supra* note 27, at 27, 69, 71; OBERG, *supra* note 20, at 50–51, 96, 112, 132, 152; JACOBS, *supra* note 10, at 41, 48, 490, 609 n.61; HERSKOVITS, *supra* note 12, at 209, 251–53.

communities were so successful in their work and ingenuity in gathering and preserving their necessities that their "economic year," the time it took them to produce their annual subsistence needs, was only four to five months. These short economic years left time for individuals and communities to engage in leisure, culture, and ceremonies.[31]

In conclusion, this overview demonstrates that historically Indian nations, cultures, and individuals had well-established economies, private property regimes, and economic rights. Indians and tribal governments understood and protected the ownership of rights in land, river and ocean fishing sites, hunting sites, and wild plants; personal property such as horses and manufactured items; and professional services. Indian peoples worked hard to create and acquire these individual benefits by investing their human capital of labor, expertise, and time, and their physical capital of tools and assets, to manufacture foods and other items for their own use and profit. Almost all Indian nations and peoples were well acquainted throughout their histories with private entrepreneurial economic activities. Consequently, developing private entrepreneurial activities and private sector economies in Indian Country today are not new ideas to Indian peoples and cultures and cannot on their own be harmful to Native cultures.

IV CRUCIAL FACTORS FOR PRIVATE SECTOR DEVELOPMENT IN INDIAN COUNTRY

Creating private sector economies from scratch seems a daunting task. Of course, every reservation has informal or underground private sectors composed of part-time workers and entrepreneurs that residents can employ. But what strategies can Indian nations, reservation communities, and individual Indians pursue to purposely build functioning and formalized private sector economies?

This section analyzes nine factors or elements that Indian nations and individuals could pursue to help develop reservation private sector economies. Such an effort entails reviving the institutions and entrepreneurial activities that Indian peoples successfully used for centuries.

A Improving Financial Literacy

American Indians and reservation communities have long suffered from extreme poverty and an absence of privately operated businesses. Not surprisingly, the levels of financial literacy and skills needed to start and successfully operate private businesses might be lacking. Consequently, one of the necessary factors for Indians and Indian nations is to increase their overall financial literacy. Indian

---

[31] 7 SMITHSONIAN INST., *supra* note 10, at 346, 493, 505, 540, 548, 551, 564, 580, 591; MORGAN, *supra* note 26, at 50, 56; OBERG, *supra* note 20, at 35, 56, 60–61, 132–33; 9 SMITHSONIAN INST., *supra* note 10, at 82, 979; RUBIN, *supra* note 27, at 27, 69, 71.

nations could mandate teaching financial, business, and accounting topics from kindergarten through college in tribal schools. Tribes could also advocate for these topics to be taught in schools operated by the Bureau of Indian Affairs and the Bureau of Indian Education, and in state schools on or near reservations. Tribal governments could also offer adult financial literacy classes through their economic development or education departments or by using other organizations. Materials are available for these kinds of efforts.[32]

B Developing Human Capital

The conditions on most reservations have left many residents with poor credit scores and limited job experience and business skills. Indians and tribal governments need to improve these aspects of "human capital," that is, the assets and physical and mental abilities needed to operate a business, and to develop their reservation-based workforces. One of the first questions for businesses or entrepreneurs considering locating on a reservation is what is the available workforce, and is it experienced and motivated.

Tribal governments can play an enormous role in developing reservation human capital. Hiring tribal citizens to work in and manage tribal departments and programs will increase the experience and abilities of Indians. Consequently, the preference already held by most Indian nations for hiring their citizens, and Indians in general, is a valuable tool to develop Indigenous human capital. As more Indian nations undertake an increasing number of social welfare and economic activities, they are improving their human capital if they hire Indians and reservation inhabitants. We can expect the future pool of successful Indian Country entrepreneurs to come from people who have gained experience and skills working for tribal nations.

In addition to improving the financial literacy of reservation communities as mentioned above, there are now thirty-seven tribal colleges on various reservations and Indian peoples are graduating with college degrees in ever increasing numbers from on- and off-reservation institutions. This is another important aspect of improving human capital and expanding the pool of possible reservation-based entrepreneurs. When Indian nations provide higher education and create business and employment opportunities on their reservations, they both help to improve their

---

[32]   *See, e.g.*, John L. Murphy, Alicia Gourd & Faith Begay, *Financial Literacy Among American Indians and Alaska Natives* (2014), www.ssa.gov/policy/docs/rsnotes/rsn2014-04.html (last visited January 13, 2019); William Anderson, Noorie Brantmeier, Miriam Jorgensen & Amber Lounsberg, *Financial Education in South Dakota's High Native-Enrollment Schools: Barriers and Possibilities* (2010), https://firstnations.org/knowledge_center/download/financial_education_south_dakota's_high_native_enrollment_schools_barrier (last visited January 13, 2019); First Nations Development Inst., *Building Native Communities: Financial Skills for Families*, www.firstnations.org/knowledge-center/publications/achieving-native-financial-empowerment/?pub-sub-categories=building-native-communities-financial-education-curriculum (last visited January 13, 2019).

human capital and also alleviate the "brain drain," the loss of young, motivated, and talented people from their reservations.

C Creating Entrepreneurs

Indian governments, political leaders, and reservation communities should concentrate on developing and attracting more Native and non-Native entrepreneurs to Indian Country. Again, with the decades of poverty and the absence of privately owned businesses on reservations, there are few role models, mentors, and examples to inspire Native peoples and youth to dream of owning their own businesses. Tribal governments can start overcoming the lack of private business owners by establishing economic development departments and programs that help develop the private sector, teaching business and entrepreneurial classes, sponsoring business plan development competitions, publicizing private business owners, and giving community awards to entrepreneurs. Successful tribal models already exist for these kinds of endeavors.[33]

There are at least three nationally known Indian-related organizations that are well recognized for offering training programs, counseling services, and assistance to Native entrepreneurs. First, the Lakota Funds has operated on the Pine Ridge Indian Reservation in South Dakota since 1986. It was the first Native Community Development Financial Institution ("CDFI") in the nation. In 1986, there were only two Indian-owned businesses on the reservation, 85 percent of the Oglala Lakota people had never had bank accounts, 75 percent had never had loans, and 95 percent had no business experience. Lakota Funds started as a micro-lender of $500 loans. To date, it has helped create more than 1,600 permanent jobs on the reservation, made over 1,000 loans totaling more than $10 million, helped establish 600 businesses, and assisted thousands of artists and entrepreneurs. Its loan portfolio now exceeds $2 million and it awards loans up to $300,000.[34]

Second, the Oregon Native American Business and Entrepreneurial Network ("Onaben") was created in 1991 by four Oregon tribes as a nonprofit organization to develop and train Indian entrepreneurs who would hopefully open businesses on reservations. For more than twenty-five years, Onaben has helped hundreds of Indians in the Pacific Northwest start their own businesses though training classes that assist people to draft fundable business plans and to start and operate businesses. Onaben serves Native entrepreneurs and community-based economic development

---

[33] *See* Stephen Cornell, Miriam Jorgensen, Ian Wilson Record, and Joan Timeche, *Citizen Entrepreneurship: An Underutilized Development Resource*, in REBUILDING NATIVE NATIONS: STRATEGIES FOR GOVERNANCE AND DEVELOPMENT (Miriam Jorgensen ed., 2007); Navajo Nation Dept. Economic Dev., 3rd Annual Navajo Nation Economic Summit 2018, Business Plan Competition, April 23, 2018, www.nneconomicsummit.com (last visited January 15, 2019).

[34] https://lakotafunds.org (last visited January 15, 2019).

organizations with its culturally relevant business curriculum and programs, and with help accessing financing and business-to-business relationships.[35]

Onaben has hosted its annual conference, "Trading at the River," for more than a decade to help Native entrepreneurs share information, make business contacts, and find marketing opportunities. It also puts on Native youth entrepreneurship camps and focuses on financial literacy for youth. But Onaben is best known for creating the widely used culturally relevant training materials entitled Indianpreneurship ®. Onaben and others have used these materials to train thousands of Native peoples to consider their suitability for business, to draft business plans, and to launch their enterprises.[36]

Third, the Cheyenne River Sioux Tribe created the Four Bands Community Fund in 2000 to provide entrepreneurial training services. At that time, less than 1 percent of the businesses on the reservation were Indian owned, although the population was 75 percent Indian. Four Bands has had a major impact in transforming the economic landscape at Cheyenne River and now assists Native peoples throughout South Dakota to improve their financial literacy, human capital, and funding options, and to enter the business world. At its creation, it made loans of only $500. In the first fifteen years of its existence, Four Bands provided technical assistance to over 6,600 customers, made over 1,000 loans totaling nearly $10 million, approved 671 "credit builder loans" to help people improve their credit scores, created or retained on the reservation nearly 600 jobs, graduated 445 people from its business training courses, increased the financial literacy of 810 people, placed nearly 200 Native youth in internship positions, invested nearly half a million dollars in a savings program that raises money for education, business, or home ownership, and assisted people in filing tax returns who then received more than $5 million in refunds. Those are spectacular results.[37]

These entities teach educational classes and provide services to create and assist new entrepreneurs. These organizations and programs are excellent models for any Indian nation attempting to build a private sector. In fact, every Indian nation should consider creating similar entities and programs or using these existing programs to assist in creating and training entrepreneurs.

D Funding Privately Owned Businesses

The poverty in Indian Country has left most Indians unable to finance start-up businesses. In fact, individual Indians almost universally lack access to the three

---

[35] http://onaben.org/about-us/our-history/ (last visited January 15, 2019); Robert J. Miller, *Economic Development in Indian Country: Will Capitalism or Socialism Succeed?*, 80 ORE. L. REV. 757, 839–40 (2001).

[36] Onaben Annual Report 2015, www.onaben.org/userfiles/Documents/2015%20ONABEN%20Annual%20Report.pdf (last visited January 15, 2019); www.onaben.org/indianpreneurship (last visited January 15, 2019).

[37] http://fourbands.org/about/ (last visited January 15, 2019).

primary sources that the average American uses to start private businesses. Indian entrepreneurs have to overcome generational poverty, spotty credit and job histories, and a lack of financial resources that many reservation-based people suffer. Hence, Indian nations and private organizations must assist individual Indians to obtain the seed funding necessary to start businesses.

A few Indian nations have the resources to provide fairly significant amounts of money to tribal citizens to open businesses. It seems to be a very appropriate use of tribal funds to assist tribal citizens to create private businesses on reservations. Furthermore, tribal governments could pressure the banks they do business with to open bank branches on reservations, and to grant tribal citizens business loans. My own tribe, the Eastern Shawnee Tribe of Oklahoma, for a time used our bank, Peoples Bank of Seneca, to issue loans to tribal citizens, which the tribe guaranteed.

Successful models of the value of micro-lending exist internationally and, as demonstrated by the Lakota Funds and the Four Bands Community Fund, for Indian peoples as well. As both those entities prove, loan funds and entrepreneurial assistance can make dramatic improvements in reservation economic conditions and are worth the attention of tribal governments.

E Enacting and Improving Tribal and Federal Buy Indian Acts

Federal and tribal governments need to be the clients of reservation-based businesses to help in the creation and success of such businesses, and to help reservation communities benefit from what economists call the "multiplier effect." The multiplier effect is the idea that the economic health and wealth of a region is increased dramatically if dollars can be retained within a town, county, or reservation by circulating between local consumers, businesses, and employees, and between businesses.

The United States was pursuing this very idea when it enacted the federal Buy Indian Act in 1908. This Act encourages the Secretary of Interior to employ "Indian labor" and "products ... of Indian industry" in carrying out federal duties in Indian affairs.[38] The problem with this good idea is that the federal provision is totally discretionary and has not had much effect in Indian Country. Indian nations should lobby Congress to strengthen this Act by requiring the federal government to spend some set percentage of the total federal budget, or the total General Services Administration budget, or at least the Bureau of Indian Affairs and Indian Health Services budgets on the purchase of Indian labor and products. Since Congress appropriates the BIA and IHS budgets for the direct benefit of Indian nations and peoples, it should be straightforward to convince Congress to earmark a certain percentage of these funds for direct spending that benefits Indians and tribal nations by purchasing Indian labor and products.

---

[38]   25 U.S.C. § 47 (2012).

In addition, tribal governments must themselves take more direct actions to become the customers of reservation-based privately owned businesses. Many Indian nations have very large annual budgets and they possess the legal right to give preferences to tribal citizens and other Indians. Tribes should enact tribal "Buy Indian" Acts and order tribal departments to spend as much money as possible, or at least a set percentage of their budgets, buying goods and services from tribal citizens and Indian-owned private businesses.

This kind of policy would have at least two major and immediate impacts. First, there is a "chicken and egg" problem in Indian Country. Tribal leaders and departments often say, correctly, that there are few or no Indian-owned businesses they can do business with. But this just highlights the fact that tribal governments must actively work to increase the number of Native-owned businesses so that tribal governments can then engage them in business. Think of the major incentive to create new Indian-owned businesses on reservations that would result if Indian nations made public and binding commitments through ordinances that they would spend say 3 percent or 5 percent of their annual budgets on Indian-owned businesses. Tribal departments would have to actively seek out Indian-owned businesses to do business with the nation and every person with an ounce of entrepreneurial spirit would notice this new opportunity with their own tribal government. This should go a long way to solving the "chicken and egg" issue because new businesses would be formed and/or Indians would locate their existing businesses or branches on reservations to benefit from tribal Buy Indian Acts.

Second, reservations would benefit significantly from other economic principles if tribal governments made directed purchases such as I am suggesting. Even if goods and services cost a bit more from newly created and Indian-owned businesses than from major chain stores and producers, reservations would receive a guaranteed benefit by slowing the "leakage" of their money from reservation economies to border towns and beyond. Reservations would instead benefit from the proven results of the multiplier effect by keeping money in the local economy to circulate and multiply a couple of times. Economists unanimously agree that towns, cities, counties, and states are injured when money "leaks" away from the local economy. Indian Country well understands this principle because most reservations are surrounded by "border towns" where reservation inhabitants spend their money on goods and services that are unavailable on their reservation. But if tribes could work to increase the number of businesses on reservations and begin to build functioning private sector economies, they would begin to benefit from the multiplier effect and see increased economic activities, businesses, and jobs created on the reservation.

I know of only two Indian nations that have enacted tribal Buy Indian Acts; the Navajo Nation and the Salt River Pima-Maricopa Indian Community. (There are no doubt others.) But both of these tribal ordinances suffer from the same lack as the federal Buy Indian Act; they are not mandatory and they do not allocate a set percentage of tribal expenditures to be spent on Indian privately owned businesses.

The Navajo Nation enacted its Business Opportunity Act because its studies showed that while 90 percent of the reservation population was Navajo, "76% of the contracts by the Navajo Nation between the years 1994 and 2003 were awarded to non-Navajos …"[39] The Nation recognized that Indian preferences would help develop privately owned businesses on its reservation and that would "promote economic development and the growth of Navajo-owned businesses within the Navajo Nation."[40] But the Act is discretionary in the sense that it only allows a "'first opportunity' and/or preference in contracting to Navajo and/or Indian owned and operated businesses."[41]

The Salt River Pima-Maricopa Indian Community enacted its Administrative Policies Procurement Policy in 2014 (or maybe earlier). One of the purposes is to "[p]romote the success and growth of Community-owned and Community Member-owned businesses and individual Community Members through the application of preference as set forth in this policy … "[42] This policy comes close to requiring tribal departments to contract with qualified tribal citizens or tribal citizen-owned businesses but it does not provide a guarantee that tribal citizens will receive a particular tribal contract.[43]

In sum, the federal government and Indian nations need to impose requirements upon themselves that will help increase the number of Indian-owned businesses in Indian Country and assist in developing private sector economies.

F Improving Legal Institutions

Commentators have long recommended that Indian nations must improve their legal infrastructures to attract investors and develop economies. There is no question that sophisticated investors and businesses carefully analyze the courts, laws, bureaucracies, and governing bodies of the states, counties, and reservations where they are considering investing or locating.[44]

Many Indian nations, however, lack the basic commercial laws that business needs to function smoothly. Tribal governments have particularly been encouraged for decades to enact the Uniform Commercial Code, for example, and there are several tribal models available. Tribes should also consider adopting

---

[39]   5 Nav.Nat. § 201(B)(6) (2005).
[40]   *Id.* at (F).
[41]   *Id.* at (C)(1) & (E).
[42]   SRPMIC 3–5, § I(A)(3) (Procurement Policy) (2014).
[43]   *Id.* at § IV(D)(2)(d).
[44]   Jorgensen, *supra* note 4, at 73–87; Miller, *Economic, supra* note 35, at 842–48; ABA Business Law Section, *Lending in Indian Country*, www.americanbar.org/content/dam/aba/publications/blt/2005/11/lending-indian-country-200511.authcheckdam.pdf (last visited January 14, 2019).

other commercial and consumer protection codes. Some tribes have enacted very extensive codes. The value of publicly available codes is that businesses need certainty and need to know the laws of a region before they will invest or open a business in an area. By adopting and publicizing such laws, Indian nations demonstrate they are taking steps to encourage economic activities in their jurisdictions.

Two examples demonstrate the kinds of laws that Indian nations could consider enacting to make their reservations more business friendly. First, very few tribal nations (only two apparently) have enacted constitutional provisions that prevent the tribal government from impairing the obligation of contracts. Enacting such provisions in tribal constitutions or statutes, such as in the U.S. Constitution, could prevent a new tribal council from trying to defeat projects and contractual rights that were approved by a prior council. Some infamous examples of this have occurred and have no doubt stopped or stalled many investors' interest in Indian Country. If tribes were to enact provisions such as a no impairment of contracts law, this could help assure investors that their contractual rights will be protected and can be enforced in tribal courts.[45]

Second, many tribal governments have not enacted separation of powers provisions to make their court systems fully independent from the legislative branch, the tribal council. Such provisions would also help to reassure financial investors and entrepreneurs considering investments in Indian Country.

According to many commentators, tribal court systems need to be analyzed and perhaps modified to help attract investment and to build economies. Tribes could consider creating specialized business courts, and should at least ensure that their court systems are independent and nonpoliticized. Tribal judges need to be legally trained and to have some form of guaranteed tenure and independence from the other political branches. The importance of these safeguards to economic development is proven by multidecade studies conducted by the Harvard Project on American Indian Economic Development. Harvard's studies demonstrate that tribal governments with truly independent court systems have a 5 percent better employment rate on their reservations than Indian nations without such courts, and that tribes that create truly independent court systems and effective separation of powers provisions enjoy 15 percent better employment rates than tribal nations that have not instituted such systems and provisions. The higher employment rate for Indian nations with independent courts and separation of powers provisions demonstrates that businesses and investors

---

[45] CONSTITUTION OF THE SNOQUALMIE TRIBE OF INDIANS, art. XI, § 1(9), www.snoqualmietribe.us/sites/default/files/linkedfiles/constitution.pdf (last visited January 14, 2019); Elmer R. Rusco, *Civil Liberties Guarantees Under Tribal Law: A Survey of Civil Rights Provisions in Tribal Constitutions*, 14 AM. IND. L. REV. 269, 289 (1990) (Salt River Pima-Maricopa Indian Community); MILLER, RESERVATION "CAPITALISM," *supra* note 2, at 101–05.

recognize well-governed areas and gravitate to localities where contractual and property interests are protected and courts are free from political control.[46]

Tribal courts are a particular concern for investors and businesses who enter contracts with tribal governments, tribal entities, and reservation-based Indians, and/or work on tribally and Indian-owned lands on reservations. Disputes regarding such investments will no doubt be litigated in tribal courts. While the available evidence proves that in the vast majority of cases non-Indian litigants are treated as fairly as Indian litigants, non-Indians probably feel at a disadvantage in tribal courts.

Investors considering Indian Country are well aware of the tribal court issue. Sometimes Indian nations have had to waive their sovereign immunity and allow suits in federal or state courts, or accept arbitration agreements, when potential business partners have demanded them. Tribal governments that want to attract entrepreneurs, businesses, and investors need to critically examine their courts to see if they are established and operated so as to create legitimate and fair legal systems where the rule of law applies.

Indian nations also need to develop efficient bureaucracies and reasonable regulations to govern business operations. It is a truism that business hates red tape. The Harvard Project has proven that efficient tribal bureaucracies and administrative agencies play important roles in helping tribal governments attract economic development. An efficient, knowledgeable, and fair bureaucracy that assists investors, entrepreneurs, and businesses is a major attraction to investment.[47]

In conclusion, tribal governments and reservation communities need to evaluate and decide whether and how to make the legal, institutional, and systemic changes they think will help develop their economies. Indian nations need to be aware of these factors and the concerns of investors that might prevent them from considering Indian Country. Ultimately, however, the economic and legal policies that an Indian nation and its citizens choose might not satisfy all commentators or all investors. But the decision on how business friendly a tribal community wants to become is up to that government and its citizens. Indian Country does need to be aware that there is no question that building economies requires creating legal institutions that respect the rule of law, ensure the performance of contracts and the repayment of debts, and assist as much as possible in the success of business ventures.

---

[46] Stephen Cornell & Joseph P. Kalt, *Culture and Institutions as Public Goods: American Indian Economic Development as a Problem of Collective Action*, in PROPERTY RIGHTS, *supra* note 7, at 215, 227, 235, 237; Stephen Cornell & Joseph P. Kalt, *Reloading the Dice: Improving the Chances for Economic Development on American Indian Reservations*, in WHAT CAN TRIBES DO? STRATEGIES AND INSTITUTIONS IN AMERICAN INDIAN ECONOMIC DEVELOPMENT 25–26 (1992).

[47] Stephen Cornell, *Sovereignty, Prosperity and Policy in Indian Country Today*, 5 CMTY. REINVESTMENT 5, 5–7, 9–13 (1997).

G Developing Reservation Physical Infrastructure

Indian Country lacks the physical infrastructure that the vast majority of the United States enjoys and that private businesses need to operate. Paved roads, highways, railroads, potable water, electricity, high-speed internet, cell phone connectivity, and banking institutions are missing or in poor condition on most reservations. Some of these items are so costly that to remedy these issues tribal governments are probably forced to rely on federal or state governments to finance such projects. Some tribes, however, have used tax-free bond financing to construct items such as hospitals, roads, and sewer projects themselves.

Indian Country also suffers from an absence of another form of physical infrastructure: banks. There are very few banking institutions and credit unions on reservations. A 2017 report stated that there are only eighteen Native-owned banks in the United States although there are 573 federally recognized tribes. It is a truism that money burns a hole in one's pocket and people will spend their money where they cash their checks. Without banks on reservations, where can Indians open accounts and learn the fundamentals of financial management, and where can they cash checks and then spend money? Tribal governments must explore whatever options they have to open financial institutions on their reservations. Indian nations should use their financial muscle and coerce the banks they deal with to open branches on reservations. Tribes could also buy or create banks under federal or state banking laws, open federal credit unions, or at least create Community Development Financial Institutions on their lands. Reservation communities absolutely have to find solutions for this particular lack of physical infrastructure.[48]

By contrast, Indian Country seems to have a surplus of one infrastructure need – land. Yet even here, Indian entrepreneurs often encounter serious problems in acquiring site leases on reservations to operate businesses. Many reservations have lots of apparently open space, but preexisting rights and other issues can limit where businesses and storefront establishments can be established. In addition to land issues, a lack of utilities, internet connectivity, and telephone service limits where businesses can locate. There are also reports of the extraordinary lengths of time and numerous steps faced by someone who wants to obtain a business land lease on some reservations.

Indian nations could address the scarcity of land issue by designating in advance, and clearing preexisting claims to, locations where land leases would be immediately available and where efficient tribal bureaucracies are ready to facilitate leasing. Federal and tribal governments could even install utilities at these designated locations and/or build incubator spaces, a currently popular idea where new business start-ups share space and perhaps even get space for free. Furthermore, tribes

---

[48] Miriam Jorgensen & Randall K. Q. Akee, *Access to Capital and Credit in Native Communities: A Data Review* iii–iv, 4–10 (2017); MILLER, RESERVATION "CAPITALISM," *supra* note 2, at 2, 148–49.

could build business parks and strip malls with small spaces for lease where businesses could open very quickly and cheaply.

Creating incubators, buildings, and strip malls where multiple businesses can locate offers another benefit to new businesses. Research shows that clusters of entrepreneurs succeed more often and are more profitable than solo entrepreneurs because clusters of entrepreneurs innovate new ideas, services, and products off of each other, and they support each other by being both suppliers and customers of each other. So the more entrepreneurs and businesses attracted to a reservation, the more businesses, business, and new entities that will result. Establishing incubators and strip malls can encourage the formation of entrepreneurial clusters.[49]

It is clear that Indian Country must create solutions for infrastructure issues if significant progress is to be made in developing private sector economies. Addressing these ideas could even produce a multiplier effect of its own because many tribal governments already operate utility departments and construction companies or departments and these entities could be the developers and builders of much of the infrastructure discussed above. This would create a win-win situation because these projects would employ tribally and Indian-owned companies who employ many Indian people and this would help keep that money circulating in tribal communities to further benefit reservations from the multiplier effect.

H Attracting Human and Financial Capital Investments

Indian nations can greatly increase their chances of creating private sector economies by undertaking targeted strategies that attract human capital and financial investments to their reservations. We have already discussed similar strategies above: developing human capital, creating and funding entrepreneurs, patronizing on-reservation businesses, and improving the legal and physical infrastructure in Indian Country. This section raises the issue that Indian nations could use tribal partnerships and tax and regulatory incentives to attract private businesses and investments.

Many tribal governments have already entered joint venture arrangements with private industry to develop major economic projects. Indian nations could also consider partnerships or joint ventures on a smaller scale with private sector businesses and non-Indian companies to operate economic concerns or franchises on reservations.

The Navajo Nation provided an excellent example of this strategy when it worked with the Bashas' food company to build thirteen privately owned medium-sized grocery stores on the Navajo reservation. The economic and human benefits have been enormous. As of 2014, thirteen Bashas' stores were operating on the reservation,

---

[49] Vincent J. Pascal & Daniel Stewart, *The Effects of Location and Economic Cluster Development on Native American Entrepreneurship*, INT'L J. ENTREPRENEURSHIP & INNOVATION (May 1, 2008).

employing 365 people, and Navajo women were the managers of all the stores. The stores provide quality fruits and vegetables that are mostly absent on remote reservations. This appears to be a valuable partnership and points the way to further partnerships between tribal governments and private businesses that can also create economic, employment, and social benefits.[50]

Tribes should also consider using tax and regulatory enticements to attract businesses and investments. It is, of course, a political decision for each tribal government and community to make whether to aggressively wield taxation and regulatory powers or to consider modifying or reducing them and to use them instead as incentives to entice investors. In 2001, the Navajo Nation provided an example of these tactics when it approved a 25 percent business activity tax break for reservation-based coal companies. Similarly, tribal governments could tempt investments of financial and human capital via tax incentives. Contractual and statutory promises of reduced tax rates for a number of years, or even offers of financial assistance to induce businesses to locate in a particular jurisdiction, are well-known strategies used by non-Indian governments to attract business and industry. States and counties have aggressively used these tactics to attract businesses. Indian nations are obviously in competition with non-Indian cities, counties, and states to attract business development. Tribal governments need to consider using similar strategies to attract investments.

Tribal governments also need to consider making their reservations places that are "open for business" to entice entrepreneurs to invest their financial capital and their time, efforts, and expertise operating businesses. These tribal efforts obviously include working to attract tribal citizens, other Indians, and non-Indians to invest their human capital and create businesses in Indian Country.

It is even more crucial for Indian nations to make reservations business friendly when attempting to attract capital investments. Investors invest wherever they wish and they do so in locations and in financial instruments that promise the highest and safest returns. By necessity, Indian nations must make Indian Country a secure and profitable place to invest. Utilizing the points discussed in this section will contribute to more profitable and stable economic environments in Indian Country.

I Developing Nonprofit and Nongovernmental Social Welfare Organizations

Nonprofit organizations, nongovernmental organizations, and social welfare organizations create enormous ancillary economic benefits that assist the regions where they work. They are important parts of the non-Indian American economy. Such organizations and activities can help attract financial and human capital, employment, and more economic activities to reservations. Indian Country could benefit

---

[50]   Susan F. Calder, *Bashas' Diné Markets and the Navajo Nation: A Study of Cross-Cultural Trade*, 39 AM. IND. CULTURE & RESEARCH J. 47 (2015).

greatly from emphasizing and assisting the creation of such entities and adopting policies to attract these kinds of programs.

One example demonstrates graphically the economic benefits that social policies can create. In 2003, the Tohono O'otham Nation completed a sixty-bed skilled nursing facility on its reservation. The facility was built to serve the social and cultural goals of the Nation to help elders live on the reservation and to be closer to their families. Apparently, no one was thinking of economic issues, but this project ended up creating one hundred permanent jobs on the reservation, the majority of which are held by Tohono O'otham citizens. The facility later added employee housing and a ten-bed assisted living annex. This project ended up serving both communal social interests and economic interests on the reservation.[51]

There are many nonprofit entities working on American Indian issues but I am aware of only a very few that are actually located on reservations and thus are contributing to Indian Country economies. Tribal governments and Indian Country economic development advocates should work to attract such organizations to locate and operate in Indian Country. Certainly, being located on reservations should assist these organizations to better carry out their missions, as related to Indian peoples, and would assist Indian Country economic development.

In sum, Indian nations must make reservations attractive to businesses and investors by enforcing the rule of law, adopting and enforcing sound business codes and regulations, creating effective bureaucracies, and establishing courts that are independent from politics. In essence, tribes must develop conditions that attract new and existing entrepreneurs, businesses, and investments. The ideas discussed in this section set out some important factors for Indian nations and reservation communities to consider if they choose to develop private sector economies.

V CONCLUSION

American Indians and tribal nations need to revive their traditional private sector economic activities. This endeavor is crucial for the continued existence of reservations as the homelands of tribal governments, Indian peoples, and their cultures. A failure to address these issues will continue to allow the leakage of money from reservations to border towns and beyond, and the "brain drain" problem that reservations and rural America face of young people and young families moving away. This situation is a death knell for the sustainability of

---

[51] Email from Judith Dworkin, Sacks Tierney, to Robert J. Miller (June 8, 2018, 3:07 p.m.). *Accord* Mississippi Band of Choctaw Indians, *Economic Development History* (2016), www.choctaw.org/government/development/economicDevHistory.html (last visited January 14, 2019) (Tribe was purposefully trying to diversify its economy when it opened a 120-bed nursing home that employs 125 people.).

reservation communities. If young Indian people and families cannot find living wage jobs, adequate housing, good schools, and the necessities of life on reservations, they will be forced to work and live elsewhere. This loss of human capital and economic activity is a potential disaster for the future of tribal nations and homelands.

The goal of this chapter and book is to stimulate analysis and action on improving economic conditions in Indian Country. The goal is not to make some individual Indians rich, but to help make Indian Country and reservations sustainable homelands where Indian nations, governments, cultures, communities, and peoples can survive and thrive. American Indian nations, peoples, and cultures have existed on their homelands for thousands of years. Will they be able to preserve their existence? Many tribal citizens and families are ready to move to reservations if they can only find decent housing and employment. Surely, diversifying reservation economies and improving economic conditions will go a long way toward strengthening reservation communities, making reservations viable places to live, and sustaining American Indian cultures and identities.

Some of the best ways to diversify and strengthen reservation economies are to revive the Native institutions that supported private sector business activities. The private sector is crucial because it allows a community to benefit from the "multiplier effect" where the same dollar circulates within an area creating new economic activities, new businesses, and new jobs. The longer a dollar stays in a local area the greater the benefit. The only way to create the multiplier effect is to have multiple locations in a community where money can be spent on goods and services. This requires the creation of private sector economies on reservations.

The importance of developing privately owned businesses in Indian Country is emphasized by the fact that small businesses are the primary ingredient of the United States economy. As of 2001, small businesses created 93 percent of the new jobs in the United States. In Oregon, for example, as of 2008 small and family-owned businesses made up 90 percent of the state's economy, created 78 percent of new jobs, and paid more than 65 percent of all wages.[52] When we compare these facts to the absence of small businesses and private sector economies in Indian Country it is no surprise that poverty exists on reservations.

In reviving traditional and historic attitudes toward private, entrepreneurial economic activities, Indian nations and peoples will not be injuring their own cultures. As Section III demonstrates, it is a myth that being involved in economic activities is somehow anti-Indian or anti-Native culture. In fact, over many centuries, Indians supported themselves through economic activities operated by individuals and families, and through hard work. Those economic activities are part of Indian

---

[52]   Amy Hsuan, *Success, Caring Infuse the Sacks Family Tradition*, THE OREGONIAN, May 15, 2008, at D1.

cultures, histories, and institutions. One Navajo Nation chairman affirmed this point: "Traditional Navajo values do not include poverty."[53] And frankly, it is clear that allowing Indian Country and Indian families to suffer from poverty injures cultures and imperils the continued existence of reservations as our homelands. Creating reservation private sector economies is a tool to ensure our continued existence.

Moreover, this point bears reemphasizing: improving economic conditions in Indian Country greatly helps tribal cultures, reservation health and welfare, and the existence of Indian nations. Improved conditions encourage families to move home, increase salaries, and produce private profits and public tax dollars that can be used to support the study and practice of Native cultures, create and support language programs, sustain and improve governmental services, and improve social issues on reservations. Better economic conditions make families healthier.

Not surprisingly, there are concrete examples of this point. An ongoing twenty plus-year study by Duke University School of Medicine demonstrates that these statements are true. Since 1996, Duke has studied the mental health of children from the Eastern Band of Cherokee Indians in North Carolina. As the Band began operating a successful casino and distributing some profits annually to Cherokee families, the mental health of the children improved dramatically. These improvements are still evident today as these Cherokee children enter their thirties.

In addition, the Mississippi Choctaw Tribe has demonstrated the fantastic beneficial health and cultural results that have arisen from improving economic conditions among its citizens. In the 1950s and 1960s, the tribe suffered from the lowest life expectancy rate and the highest infant mortality rate in the United States, and almost every family lived in poverty and on less than $2,000 annual income. Up to 90 percent of their houses had no plumbing, only 7 percent of the Choctaw people had high school degrees, and educated Choctaws were leaving the reservation seeking better opportunities. After several decades of the tribal government and community working to create sustained and diverse economic activities, Choctaw families were moving home to the reservation for employment and improved incomes. Chief Phillip Martin stated in 1998: "It used to be that everyone moved away. Now they're all coming back."[54] The tribe also significantly improved its housing and increased educational attainment levels, and is now one of the top ten employers in the state. Choctaws are now enjoying increasing life spans and as of 1998, had the lowest infant

---

53 RICHARD H. WHITE, TRIBAL ASSETS: THE REBIRTH OF NATIVE AMERICA 277 (1990).

54 UNIVERSITIES AND INDIAN COUNTRY: CASE STUDIES IN TRIBAL-DRIVEN RESEARCH 15 (Dennis K. Norman & Joseph P. Kalt eds., 2015) (quoting Chief Phillip Martin speech, Harvard University, September 29, 1998). *Accord* Kevin Abourezk, *Winnebago Tribe Continues to See More Return to Homelands*, Indianz.com (January 16, 2019), www.indianz.com/News/2019/01/16/winnebago-tribe-continues-to-see-more-re.asp (last visited January 16, 2019) (discussing the Winnebago Tribe in Kansas building middle-class housing and attracting young Winnebago families to live on reservation).

mortality rate in the United States! It is impossible to imagine more beneficial results for an Indian nation, its families, and its culture.[55]

In conclusion, Indian nations and Indian peoples need improved economic conditions. Indian Country needs living wage jobs and adequate housing, schools, and health care. These kinds of conditions and services require public and private economic activities and money. Indian nations and reservation communities need to revive their traditional governmental and cultural institutions that supported and promoted private sector economies and use them today as additional tools to address the economic issues they face.

[55] E. Jane Costello, William Copeland & Adrian Angold, *The Great Smoky Mountains Study: Developmental Epidemiology in the Southeastern United States* (March 24, 2016), www.ncbi.nlm .nih.gov/pmc/articles/PMC4846561/ (last visited January 14, 2019); PETER J. FERRARA, THE CHOCTAW REVOLUTION 13–14, 46–47, 82–85 (1998); Rhonda G. Phillips, *The Choctaw Tribe of Mississippi: Managing Skills for Workforce Transformation*, Organisation for Economic Cooperation and Development 155, 156, 158–63, 169–72 (November 16, 2009), http://dx.doi.org/ 10.1787/9 789264066649-6-en (last visited January 14, 2019).

2

Opportunities to Diversify: Reservation Workplaces and Job Numbers Compared to Nearby County Areas

Randall Akee, Elton Mykerezi, and Richard M. Todd

I INTRODUCTION

In his book *Reservation Capitalism*, legal and tribal economies scholar Robert Miller laments (p. 113) the "few employers and jobs available in Indian Country" and specifically points to (p. 136) a dearth of grocery stores, retail outlets, movie theaters, motels, clothing stores, restaurants, and bank branches. In the same book, he also strikes a more positive tone, noting that "tribal governments and Indian communities are currently engaged in a wide array of business and economic activities," pointing to sectors such as timber, minerals, manufacturing, agriculture, tourism, fishing, housing, and public administration. At first glance, these statements may appear to conflict, but they are not logically inconsistent. Comprehensive data are needed to assess and possibly reconcile them.

However, comprehensive data on reservation workplaces and jobs are scarce (Jorgensen 2016a, p. 53). Miller and others tend to rely on general impressions, anecdotes, and infrequent or county-based data collections covering a few reservations. This chapter presents and discusses some of the most comprehensive data on workplaces and jobs in Indian Country. These data partly support both of Miller's statements. Workplaces, also referred to as establishments, are the physical places, whether privately owned or in the public sector, where people engage in income-generating labor. They are distinct from firms, in that a firm is a legal entity that may have multiple workplaces.[1] Workplaces are in fact relatively scarce on federally recognized American Indian reservations as a group, compared to a group of off-reservation comparison areas selected from counties near reservations. And yet these workplaces do indeed encompass a wide array of activities, in the sense that the distribution of workplaces across industries is similar for reservations and nearby county areas. In contrast to the relatively low number of workplaces, the overall number of jobs located within

---

[1] For example, a single firm might have a management headquarters establishment in one place, a manufacturing factory in a second place, a warehouse or distribution establishment in a third place, a retail establishment in a fourth place, etc.

reservations is roughly on par with or even somewhat higher than in the county comparison areas, largely due to high job counts in sectors such as Arts/ Entertainment/Recreation, Accommodation and Food Services, and Public Administration. These statements apply to reservations as a group, so that high job numbers on some reservations – such as those with large casino-related enterprises – can compensate for other reservations with very low job numbers. Outcomes can vary significantly from one reservation to another within the overall group of reservations. Nonetheless, these patterns suggest an opportunity to expand tribal economies by diversifying their private sectors beyond the recreational and government workplaces that dominate reservation job numbers today.

II DATA SET CREATION AND DESCRIPTION

The information used here is from Akee, Mykerezi, and Todd (2017) and Akee, Mykerezi, and Todd (2018), hereafter jointly noted as AMT. AMT compile the first comprehensive data set on reservation businesses and reservation employers.[2] Their underlying sources are primarily the U.S. Census Bureau's Center for Economic Studies' Longitudinal Business Database (LBD) and Integrated Longitudinal Business Database (ILBD). The LBD contains annual employment and industry classification data for all workplace establishments that file Social Security taxes or withhold federal payroll taxes for employees. The ILBD provides annual information on the industry classification and revenue of nonemployer establishments.

Akee, Mykerezi, and Todd (2017) link the 2010 LBD records to establishment data in the U.S. Census Bureau's 2010 Standard Statistical Establishment List (SSEL) in order to obtain the SSEL's establishment location information – the mailing and/or physical address of almost all 2010 employer establishments, as well as the census-provided longitude, latitude, and census block codes corresponding to many but not all of these addresses. They also (2018a) use the similar location information for nonemployer establishments available in the ILBD.[3]

AMT then geocode (i.e., assign longitude and latitude coordinates to) the address of each establishment and use the location coordinates to create new

---

[2]   Their data are limited to federally recognized American Indian reservations in the contiguous forty-eight states, which we may at times refer to simply as "reservations." The data on establishments with employees contain all workplaces where management files Social Security taxes or withholds federal payroll taxes for employees. This includes most private business employers and most nonprofit and government-held establishments with employees. The data for nonemployer establishments derive primarily from income tax filings by the owners of those establishments.

[3]   The ILBD typically provides mailing addresses taken from tax returns (Davis et al., 2007; Table 2.1), and Akee, Mykerezi, and Todd assume that nonemployers' place of work (physical address) is identical to their mailing address, which may contribute to geographic measurement error.

variables that identify whether an establishment is located in a federally recognized American Indian reservation (and if so, which one). They geocode the physical addresses, where available, and the mailing address otherwise (on the assumption that the mailing address is also the physical address for those records). Then they assign establishments to reservations based on their geographic coordinates and TIGER/Line Shapefiles® for reservation boundaries. Finally, they override a small percentage of these reservation codes in cases where the establishment's five-digit zip code is inconsistent with their geocoding results.[4]

These methods do not precisely geocode the location of all establishments. In some cases, the primary source of spatial measurement error is a spatially uninformative address, such as a post office box number instead of a street number. For example, Akee, Mykerezi, and Todd (2017) report that longitude and latitude were assigned based on a relatively precise street address for only about 71 percent of the employer establishments in the construction industry that their methods assigned to a reservation. For almost 29 percent, longitudes and latitudes were based on the centroid of the establishment's zip code area, so that AMT could not eliminate nontrivial spatial measurement error in their assignment of establishments to reservations. Overall, their results are likely to broadly reflect general reservation business patterns while falling short of precise measures of the number of workplaces and jobs on each reservation.

AMT analyzed only federally recognized reservations in the contiguous forty-eight states and their nearby nonreservation areas. To operationalize their "comparison group" of nonreservation areas, they used geographic information systems software to partition counties that intersect with reservations into reservation and nonreservation components. They generated new areas, called "county complements," that were identical to the county itself for all counties that do not intersect with any reservations and the nonreservation portion of counties that do intersect with at least one reservation. They then restricted the set of county complements to those of counties included in at least one reservation's list of ten nearest county neighbors, based on centroid-to-centroid distance.

AMT also limited their sample to reservations and county complements with a 2010 population of less than 50,000. Among reservations, this excludes only Navajo, whose exceptionally large area and population would make it an extreme outlier in their statistical analysis. Overall, they analyzed statistics on 277 American Indian reservations and 514 county complements. These statistics summarize information on about 966,000 employer and nonemployer establishments across the eighteen industries shown in Table 2.1, including, as shown in Table 2.2, almost 54,000 establishments on reservations.

---

[4] For details see AMT.

TABLE 2.1: *North American Industrial Classification System (NAICS) codes for major industries*

Industry	NAICS Codes
Agriculture, Forestry, Fishing and Hunting	11
Mining	21
Utilities	22
Construction	23
Manufacturing	31, 32, 33
Wholesale Trade	42
Retail Trade	44, 45
Transportation and Warehousing	48, 49
Information	51
Finance and Insurance; Real Estate and Rental and Leasing	52, 53
Professional, Scientific, and Tech. Services	54
Mgmt. of Companies and Enterprises; Administrative and Support; and Waste Mgmt. and Remediation	55, 56
Educational Services	61
Health Care and Social Assistance	62
Arts, Entertainment, and Recreation	71
Accommodation; Food Services	72
Other Services	81
Public Admin.	92

III CONCEPTUAL FRAMEWORK

AMT compare reservations and nearby county complement areas with respect to both the number of workplaces per capita and number of jobs per capita, across eighteen industries. Multiple factors might cause the per-capita number of establishments or jobs to differ between reservations and county complements.

Social scientists have identified political, legal, and historical or institutional factors on American Indian reservations that may impede business development. For example, the underlying title to most of the land on federally recognized American Indian reservations is held by the U.S. federal government as trustee for the tribal governments and the individual American Indians who in turn hold the beneficial use rights. Trust land differs from fee simple land in that it cannot be used as easily as collateral for a commercial mortgage. This is due to the fact that commercial banks must make nonstandard

TABLE 2.2: *Count of employer and nonemployer establishments by industry in 2010 Note: Figures are approximate, in keeping with Census Bureau disclosure rules. See Table 2.1 for a listing of the industries associated with each sector's code number.*

| NAICS Codes | Implied Number of Reservation Estb. | | | Percent of Total Estb. on Reservations | Parity Index* for Total Estb. |
	Nonemployer	Employer	Total		
11	1768	1363	3131	4.54%	0.55
21	532	264	796	11.37%	1.39
22	47	101	149	4.79%	0.58
23	4370	1581	5951	4.84%	0.59
31, 32, 33	864	552	1416	5.06%	0.62
42	838	590	1428	6.80%	0.83
44, 45	3899	2040	5939	5.12%	0.62
48, 49	1597	638	2235	5.08%	0.62
51	392	224	615	5.81%	0.71
52, 53	3796	1104	4900	5.05%	0.62
54	4316	867	5183	6.25%	0.76
55, 56	3167	560	3727	6.11%	0.75
61	1445	299	1744	9.48%	1.16
62	3969	1296	5265	6.75%	0.82
71	2235	292	2527	6.94%	0.85
72	927	1250	2177	5.58%	0.68
81	5160	1222	6382	5.07%	0.62
92		358	358	6.40%	0.78
Total	39322	14601	53923	5.58%	0.68

* Index = Percent on Reservations/8.2, where 8.2 is the percentage of the population (reservations plus county complements) on reservations.

arrangements and use often unfamiliar procedures to secure their interest in or foreclose upon lands, or leases on lands, held in trust by the U.S. federal government for tribes or tribal members. Possibly as a result, Dimitrova-Grajzl et al. (2015) find a low usage of consumer mortgage credit on reservations as compared to adjacent areas. Despite some mitigating factors,[5] it is quite plausible that reservation businesses' access to mortgages is similarly low.

[5] Akee (2009) and Akee and Jorgensen (2014) have shown that extension of leasing options can facilitate housing and business infrastructure investment that mirrors that of off-reservation land parcels in Southern California. Additionally, Native-owned Community Development Finance Institutions (CDFIs) have proliferated throughout Indian Country and, for a variety of purposes, provide increased access to credit and financial services to Native communities. And for American Indian home buyers,

In addition, only some tribes have adopted business laws for non-real-estate collateral that closely parallel the relevant title (IX) of the Uniform Commercial Code (UCC) that state collateralized-lending laws are based on (Woodrow 2011). There is a positive association between adoption of uniform commercial codes and the prevalence of self-employment reported on American Indian reservations included in the small sample of reservations studied by Akee (2012), suggesting that the failure of some tribal business codes to parallel the UCC may be a barrier to reservation business development.[6]

Additional factors potentially impeding business development on reservations include underfunded, underdeveloped infrastructure; a lack of financial institutions on or near reservations; many Native Americans' relatively limited experience with the financial world; lenders' and investors' general failure to understand tribal government or legal systems; the historical absence of trust between tribes and banks; and discrimination against and stereotyping of tribal community members (NNI 2016).

Demographic and socioeconomic differences between reservations and nearby areas may also lead to different business patterns. To the extent, for example, that reservations have small populations or relatively low household incomes, the effective demand for goods and services may not be sufficient to support the number of consumer-oriented establishments found in more populated or affluent off-reservation locations (Berry and Garrison 1958). Alternatively, workforce issues, such as small populations or limited educational attainment, may inhibit placement of production facilities on reservations. This can feed back into other sectors as well, given the finding of Shonkwiler and Harris (1996) that retail firms in rural areas are dependent upon the presence of retail demand from other industries and the finding of Blair et al. (2004) that the presence of a large manufacturing sector in rural areas has a positive association with a strong retail sector. The effects of population size and density, household income, and education are allowed for in the results discussed below.

One area that has been little studied is whether tribal governments fill the void when the number of commercial business enterprises on American Indian reservations is low. Legislation and court decisions since the 1970s have clarified the authority of tribal governments to establish and operate business enterprises on reservation trust land. The Indian Gaming Regulatory Act (IGRA) gives many tribes the option of owning casinos, and Title 17 of the Code of Federal Regulations provides additional authority for the establishment of tribal corporations that may

---

the U.S. Department of Housing and Urban Development (HUD) offers the Indian Home Loan Guarantee program that guarantees mortgages on American Indian lands and helps to encourage home mortgage lending by commercial lenders. In recent years, however, the vast majority of loans made under this HUD program have been on fee simple land, not trust land (Jorgensen 2016b).

[6]   However, Akee's findings are based on a small sample of American Indian reservations, and additional data and analysis would be required to identify true causal effects.

own and operate commercial enterprises for the purpose of raising revenue for tribal governments.[7] Tribally owned and operated businesses may have certain tax and jurisdictional advantages (as well as disadvantages) over that of businesses located in nearby county areas. Existing research provides little information about whether tribally owned enterprises offset some of the disadvantages that reservations face in attracting businesses and jobs, but Title 17 employer establishments are included in the results below.

IV OVERALL PATTERNS FOR ESTABLISHMENTS

This chapter focuses on how reservations and nearby county areas differ, on average, in their type and number of establishments and jobs. We summarize the count of employer and nonemployer establishments within reservations by industry category for 2010 in Table 2.2. The first column provides the industry's two-digit NAICS code. Columns 2 and 3 show the estimates of, respectively, the number of employer and nonemployer establishments within reservations. Column 4 sums columns 2 and 3 to estimate the total number of establishments within reservations. Column 5 shows, by sector, reservations' percentage share of all establishments (i.e., the employer plus nonemployer establishments in both reservations and nearby county complements). The final column divides the reservation establishment share from column 5 by 8.2 percent, the percentage of the relevant population that lives in a reservation.[8] We call the resulting ratio the establishment parity index. It is below or above 1 to the extent that the share of establishments in reservations is below or above the share of the adult population in reservations.

Figure 2.1 is based on column 4 of Table 2.2 and similar establishment counts for county complements. It shows that the distribution of establishments across industries is similar in reservations and county complements. The black bars show each industry's percentage share in the total number of reservation establishments, with the percentages adding to 100 percent across the eighteen industries shown. The gray bars provide the corresponding shares for the county complements. For example, about 11 percent of all workplaces on reservations are retail businesses, whereas retailers make up about 12 percent of the workplaces in nearby county areas. Overall, the differences in the distribution of establishments across industries for these two geography types appear small. The largest differences, proportionally, are in Mining, Quarrying, and Oil and Gas Extraction (hereafter "Mining"), and Educational Services, but these two sectors account for just a small share of the total number of

---

[7] Most tribally owned enterprises will be included in our LBD data set, since most will have employees and be required to withhold federal payroll taxes for them.

[8] Specifically, 8.2 percent represents the number of people who live in one of the reservations we study, expressed as a percentage of the total number of people living in either one of these reservations or one of our county complement areas.

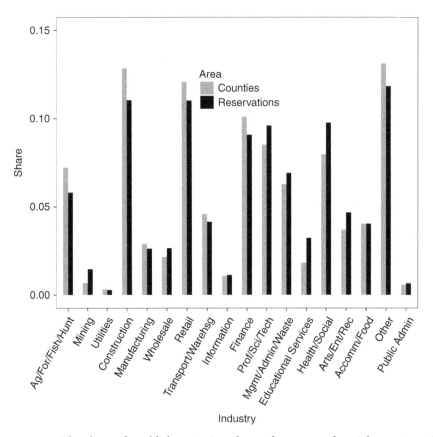

FIGURE 2.1: The share of establishments (employer plus nonemployer) by sector and place, 2010

all establishments. These results show that, at least across these eighteen broad categories, reservation workplaces engage in the same array of industrial activities as workplaces in nearby county areas, with only minor differences in the share of each industry within the local reservation or county complement economy.

Although the distribution of establishments across sectors is similar in reservations and nearby county areas, the number of establishments per person is typically lower on reservations than in county complements, overall and in most sectors. Figure 2.2 shows this by plotting Table 2.2's reservation establishment parity ratios by industry. The "Total" row of Table 2.2 shows an overall parity ratio of 0.68 (or 5.58/8.2), indicating almost a third fewer establishments per person on reservations than in nearby county complement areas overall. The industry-specific parity ratios in Figure 2.2 show that reservations have a large deficit of establishments per person in most industries. The biggest exceptions are again the Mining sector (parity ratio of 1.39) and the Education sector (parity ratio of 1.16).

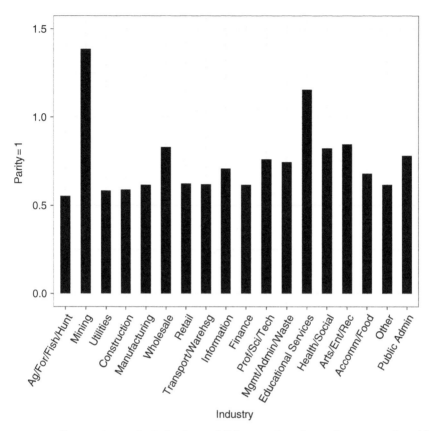

FIGURE 2.2: Reservation parity index for establishments (employer plus nonemployer) by sector, 2010

V OVERALL PATTERNS FOR JOBS

To analyze jobs, AMT assume that each nonemployer establishment employs one worker. This simple assumption is clearly not true in all cases. For example, some family-owned businesses may provide work for multiple family members even though none of them may technically need to be reported as employees, while other nonemployer establishments may provide only very part-time work for one person. Better information about the number of "jobs" that should be attributed to nonemployer establishments could be used to enhance AMT's analysis; they view the assumption of one job per nonemployer establishment as a practical and informative alternative until better data are available.

Table 2.3 provides a snapshot of the number of employer and nonemployer jobs by industry in 2010 for reservations. The columns are provided in a similar manner to that of Table 2.2. We use these figures to create Figure 2.3, which

TABLE 2.3: *Count of employer and nonemployer jobs by industry in 2010*
Note: Figures are approximate, in keeping with Census Bureau disclosure rules. See
Table 2.1 for a listing of the industries associated with each sector's code number.

| | Implied Number of Reservation Jobs | | | Percent of Total Jobs on | Parity Index* for |
NAICS Codes	Nonemployer	Employer	Total	Reservations	Total Jobs
11	1768	6734	8502	4.78%	0.58
21	532	2840	3372	5.75%	0.70
22	47	1296	1343	4.21%	0.51
23	4370	10296	14666	6.21%	0.76
31, 32, 33	864	14426	15290	3.75%	0.46
42	838	6940	7778	7.01%	0.85
44, 45	3899	27082	30980	6.30%	0.77
48, 49	1597	5971	7568	6.05%	0.74
51	392	3662	4054	8.39%	1.02
52, 53	3796	9446	13243	6.56%	0.80
54	4316	5652	9968	6.39%	0.78
55, 56	3167	12132	15299	9.56%	1.17
61	1445	27519	28963	8.14%	0.99
62	3969	29245	33214	6.44%	0.78
71	2235	33978	36213	31.49%	3.84
72	927	45394	46321	13.20%	1.61
81	5160	16625	21785	9.35%	1.14
92		42395	42395	21.63%	2.64
Total	39322	301632	340954	8.58%	1.05

* Index = Percent on Reservations/8.2, where 8.2 is the percentage of the population (reservations plus county complements) on reservations.

shows the distribution of jobs by industry for reservations and county complements in 2010. There are more differences across the two geographic types for job shares than for the establishment shares shown in Figure 2.1. Counties tend to have higher shares of their jobs in industries such as Agriculture/Forestry/ Fishing/Hunting (sector 11), Construction (sector 23), Manufacturing (sectors 31, 32, 33), Retail (sectors 44, 45), and Health/Social Services (sector 62). On the other hand, reservations have higher shares of their jobs in Accommodation/ Food Services (sector 72) and, especially, Arts/Entertainment/Recreation (sector 71) and Public Administration (sector 92).

Although job provision per capita is lower on reservations in most sectors, reservations' large advantage in a few sectors causes overall jobs per capita on reservations to be somewhat higher than in nearby county complements. The bottom row of Table 3.3 shows that the jobs parity index for total reservation jobs is 1.06, which means that the share of jobs on reservations is 6 percent higher than the reservation share of total population (reservation plus county complement) in

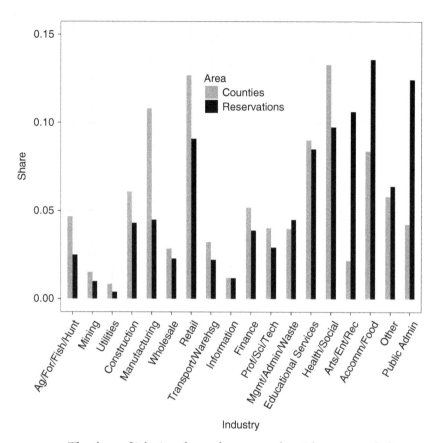

FIGURE 2.3: The share of jobs (employer plus nonemployer) by sector and place, 2010

our sample. Figure 2.4 shows the jobs parity index by industry. We compute these job parity index numbers in a similar fashion to those in Figure 2.2; the numerator is the percentage of all jobs in the sample that are located on reservations and the denominator is the total population residing on reservations (8.2 percent). Comparing jobs per capita for reservations and county complements shows that reservations have:

- very distinct advantages in Arts/Entertainment/Recreation and Public Administration, with the former strongly related to the gaming industry (based on work not shown here);
- a moderate advantage in Accommodation/Food Services;
- narrow advantages in Management of Companies and Enterprises/ Administrative and Support/Waste Management and Remediation Services (hereafter "Management") and Other Services (except Public Administration); and rough parity in the Educational Services and Information sectors.

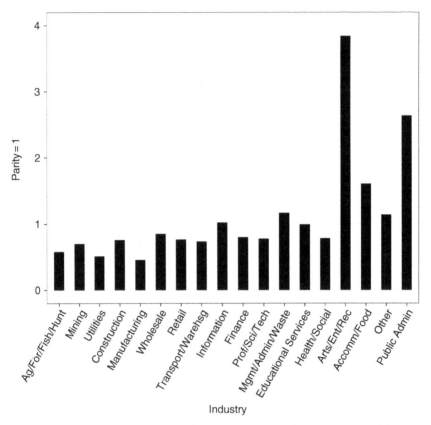

FIGURE 2.4: Reservation parity index for jobs (employer plus nonemployer) by sector, 2010

However, in several economically important sectors, such as Manufacturing, Retail Trade, and Health Care/Social Assistance, reservations display large deficits (relative to county complements) in jobs per capita, just as they showed for establishments per capita in Figure 2.2. Overall, the position of reservations relative to county complements is more varied by sector for jobs per capita than for the number of establishments per capita, and reservations hold a moderate advantage in total jobs per capita due to their very high job numbers in Public Administration and Arts/ Entertainment/Recreation, which mainly reflects the gaming industry.

It is important to note, however, that these results are averages across all the reservations and county complements in AMT's sample and do not hold uniformly for each reservation. The job situation on a remote reservation with at most a small casino could be very different from the overall average shown in Figure 2.4 or the situation on a near-urban reservation with a large casino.

VI ESTABLISHMENTS AND JOBS PER CAPITA BY POPULATION SIZE

The results above show a sizable deficit of establishments on reservations and mixed results for jobs per capita but leave many questions unanswered, such as whether the raw differences are statistically significant and how they vary across reservations. One factor that can lead to variation among reservations is population size, given the possibility of population threshold effects documented by Berry and Garrison (1958) and subsequent papers. Figure 2.5 shows the population distributions for the reservation and county complement areas examined by AMT. Threshold effects may be especially relevant to American Indian reservations, which cluster at the low end of the population distribution in Figure 2.5, below 15,000. The nearby county complement areas are much more evenly distributed across the population categories, up to AMT's sample cutoff point of 50,000. It is thus important to consider population size as an important characteristic in the comparison of establishment and job counts within and near reservations. Specifically, over half of the reservation population lives in communities of less than 15,000 people, and this alone may be an important predictive characteristic for the presence of employer establishments and the number of jobs.

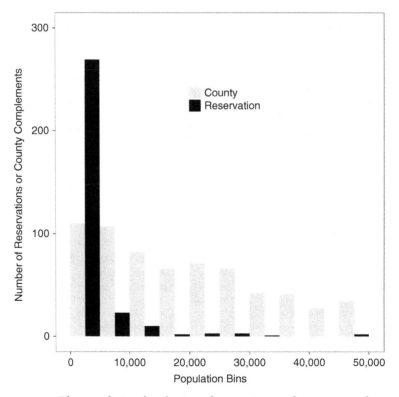

FIGURE 2.5: The population distribution of reservations and county complements

The statistical technique of regression analysis can shed some light on the threshold effects by estimating the typical relationship between population size and either establishments per capita or jobs per capita. The results show how the relative position of reservations and county areas tends to vary with population size.[9] This can be done both with and without additional variables that control for factors such as rural location, population density, income, poverty, and educational attainment in each geographic unit.

A complete set of results for eighteen industries on how establishment and job numbers vary with population on reservations as compared to nearby county complement areas is discussed in AMT. Results for the Agriculture/Forestry/Fishing/ Hunting industry are shown in Figures 2.6 and 2.7 to illustrate some typical patterns. The solid lines at the center of the shaded areas in Figures 2.6 and 2.7 show the overall best estimate of the relationship between population and the respective outcome measures, with the thinner solid line representing county complements and the thicker solid line representing reservations. Although the solid lines represent the best estimate of how population and outcomes are related, these relationships cannot be precisely determined. AMT use simulation methods to account for the uncertainty surrounding each relationship. The results appear in the shaded areas surrounding each line in Figures 2.6 and 2.7 (light gray for county complements and dark gray for reservations). These shaded areas depict a region, or confidence interval, containing 90 percent of the simulated outcomes around the lines that show the best estimate of the relationship.[10]

One important pattern is the tendency for the number of both establishments and jobs per capita to be lower on reservations than in county complements when the local population is below about 15,000. This occurs in most industries and is clearly shown for Agriculture/Forestry/Fishing/Hunting in Figures 2.6 and 2.7. Beyond

---

[9]   For further details, see AMT. We estimate the following equation and plot the estimated coefficients for the reservation and county complement estimated coefficients:

$$\left(\frac{E}{P}\right)_i = \alpha + \beta_1 Population_i + \beta_2 Population_i^2 + \beta_3 Reservation_i + \beta_4 (Reservation_i \times Population_i)$$
$$+ \beta_5 (Reservation_i \times Population_i^2) + X'\beta + \epsilon_i$$

In this equation *Population* is the size of the population for each reservation or county complement area. *Reservation* is a variable equal to one if the observation comes from a reservation geography and o otherwise. The vector X is excluded in the results shown in Figures 2.6 and 2.7. When included, X is a set of control variables: rural location and population density, per capita personal income, the poverty rate, and the percentage of adults (twenty-five years old and older) with a bachelor's degree.

[10]   In Figure 2.6, the 90 percent confidence interval for reservations noticeably widens as population increases, in part because the number of reservations in AMT's sample becomes very small at the high end of the population range. Specifically, only the eleven reservations shown in Table 2.4 have populations over 15,000 but below AMT's cutoff of 50,000. Because the county complements in their sample were more numerous and their population sizes are more evenly distributed, the 95 percent confidence intervals for those estimates were more precisely estimated and widen less as population increases, for most industries.

TABLE 2.4: *Reservations with 2010 population between 15,000 and 50,000 (American Community Survey, 2008–2012)*

Reservation	Population 2010
Nez Perce Reservation	18,437
Pine Ridge Reservation	18,834
Oneida (WI) Reservation	22,775
Uintah and Ouray Reservation	24,369
Agua Caliente Indian Reservation	24,545
Isabella Reservation	26,274
Wind River Reservation	26,481
Flathead Reservation	28,359
Yakama Nation Reservation	31,219
Puyallup Reservation	46,813
Osage Reservation	47,472

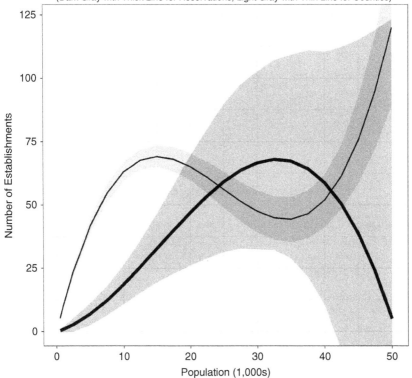

FIGURE 2.6: Employer establishments in the agriculture, forestry, fishing, and hunting industry

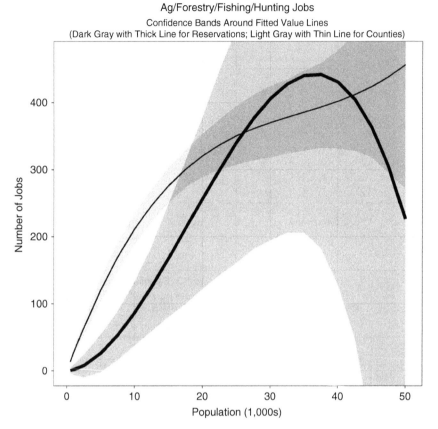

Ag/Forestry/Fishing/Hunting Jobs

Confidence Bands Around Fitted Value Lines
(Dark Gray with Thick Line for Reservations; Light Gray with Thin Line for Counties)

FIGURE 2.7: Estimated number of jobs at employer establishments in the agriculture, forestry, fishing, and hunting industry, by place

15,000, the confidence intervals are often wide (especially for reservations) and often overlap.

This pattern – significantly lower numbers of both establishments per capita and jobs per capita on reservations over a range of lower population values – prevails in a majority of broadly defined industries for both employer and nonemployer establishments. Akee, Mykerezi, and Todd (2017, 2018) documented this across eighteen industries with graphs similar to Figures 2.6 and 2.7. An alternative summary of these findings for employer establishment numbers appears in Table 2.5, which covers all eighteen sectors. Industry categories are presented along the Y-axis. Population size is given along the X-axis (in thousands). Each sector-population cell in the table reports its respective establishment count gap – the best estimate of the typical number of county complement establishments minus the best estimate of the typical number of reservation establishments. For each industry, darkest shaded cells show

TABLE 2.5: *Differences in the number of employer establishments between counties and reservations by population size and industry in 2010. See Table 2.1 for a listing of the industries associated with each sector's code number.*

SECTOR	0.5	1.0	2.5	5.0	7.5	10.0	12.5	15.0	17.5	20.0	22.5	25.0	27.5	30.0	32.5	35.0	37.5	40.0	42.5	45.0	47.5	50.0
11	5	9	21	35	42	44	42	36	28	18	7	-3	-12	-19	-23	-23	-18	-7	11	37	71	115
21	0	1	2	2	2	1	0	-2	-4	-7	-9	-12	-15	-17	-19	-21	-22	-22	-22	-21	-19	-16
22	0	0	1	2	2	2	3	2	2	1	1	1	0	0	0	1	1	1	2	3	5	7
23	2	3	7	11	14	16	16	15	13	11	8	6	4	2	1	1	3	6	11	18	27	39
31, 32, 33	0	1	2	4	5	6	7	8	8	8	8	8	8	7	7	6	5	5	4	3	2	1
42	-1	1	3	6	7	8	8	7	5	3	1	-2	-5	-9	-12	-16	-20	-23	-27	-30	-33	-36
44, 45	2	4	9	15	19	21	22	22	20	19	17	16	15	15	16	19	24	31	41	54	70	90
48, 49	-1	2	4	7	8	9	8	7	5	3	0	-2	-5	-8	-11	-13	-14	-15	-16	-15	-13	-11
51	0	1	3	3	3	3	3	2	2	1	1	0	0	-1	0	-1	-1	0	1	2	4	6
52, 53	1	3	6	10	13	14	14	12	11	9	6	4	2	1	0	2	2	5	10	16	26	37
54	-1	2	4	6	8	8	7	6	4	2	0	-2	-4	-5	-6	-6	-5	-3	1	6	13	22
55, 56	0	0	1	3	3	4	4	5	5	4	4	3	-3	0	-3	-3	-5	-7	-9	-11	-14	-16
61	0	0	1	1	1	-1	1	0	0	-1	-1	-2	-2	-3	-3	-3	-3	-2	-1	0	1	3
62	1	2	4	7	8	8	7	5	2	0	-2	-4	-6	-6	-5	3	3	9	18	30	45	63
71	0	0	1	2	3	4	4	5	5	6	6	6	6	6	6	7	7	7	7	7	8	8
72	1	3	7	11	14	15	15	13	12	10	8	6	5	5	6	9	13	20	29	40	55	73
81	1	3	6	11	15	17	18	18	18	17	15	14	12	11	10	9	9	10	12	16	20	27
92	1	1	3	4	5	6	6	6	5	5	4	3	3	3	3	3	4	6	8	11	16	21
Pop. (1000s)	0.5	1.0	2.5	5.0	7.5	10.0	12.5	15.0	17.5	20.0	22.5	25.0	27.5	30.0	32.5	35.0	37.5	40.0	42.5	45.0	47.5	50.0

Legend:

- Reservation significantly lower
- Reservation lower, not significant
- County lower, not significant
- County significantly lower

population-industry combinations for which the number of employer establishments on reservations is significantly lower, based on AMT's 90 percent confidence regions. The next darkest shading indicates a reservation deficit that is not significant. The lightest shading marks cells where reservations have an advantage that is not significant, and the unshaded cells show where reservations have significantly higher amounts of employer establishments as compared to county complements.

Table 2.5 clearly shows that statistically significant deficits in employer establishment counts on reservations are common across the eighteen industries when the local population is below 15,000. Such gaps appear in all industries for populations of 7,500 or less and in all but three industries in areas of up to 15,000 people. Beyond 15,000, there is often an overlap of the confidence intervals of the number of establishments for the two geography types. In a few cases – Mining (sector 21), Wholesale Trade (sector 42), and Transportation and Warehousing (sectors 48, 49) – there's evidence that at higher population sizes, reservations have a higher establishment count than the county complements.

The prevalence of light to intermediate shading at high population levels, signifying insignificant differences, may be due to the fact that there are relatively few American Indian reservations with large populations and, thus, standard errors are quite large, making it difficult to estimate differences efficiently. In addition, at higher population levels in a few industries – Mining (sector 21), Education (sector 61), Wholesale Trade (sector 42), and Transportation and Warehousing (sectors 48, 49) – AMT find significantly more predicted employer establishments on reservations. Again, however, these limited results pertain primarily and only on average to the eleven large but quite diverse reservations listed in Table 2.4 (and, in particular, should not be assumed to hold for all of the eleven individually or for the much larger Navajo reservation, which AMT did not analyze).

Table 2.6 provides a similar summary for the difference in the number of jobs at employer establishments between counties and reservations by industry in 2010. It shows significant job number deficits for reservations in many but not all industries when population is low. However, it also shows the reverse over some low population ranges in four industries: Management (sectors 55, 56), Arts/Entertainment/Recreation (sector 71), Other Services (sector 81), and Public Administration (sector 92). Table 2.6 also shows a greater number of reverse deficits (county complements significantly less than reservations) at higher population levels than for employer establishment numbers. Overall, the pattern for jobs at employer establishments is more mixed across sectors than the pattern for employer establishment numbers, although for reservations with populations below 12,500, a significant deficit remains the most common pattern, especially outside of the sectors related to tribal casinos and tribal government .

Table 2.7 summarizes AMT's results for nonemployer establishments. Only seventeen sectors are shown because no nonemployers are classified as in the Public Administration (government) industry. Also, one table covers both

TABLE 2.0: *Differences in the number of jobs at employer establishments between counties and reservations by population size and industry in 2010. See Table 2.1 for a listing of the industries associated with each sector's code number.*

SECTOR	0.5	1.0	2.5	5.0	7.5	10.0	12.5	15.0	17.5	20.0	22.5	25.0	27.5	30.0	32.5	35.0	37.5	40.0	42.5	45.0	47.5	50.0
11	13	25	57	95	117	125	121	109	89	64	37	10	−15	−36	−50	−55	−49	−29	7	60	134	231
21	9	16	36	55	59	51	34	10	−19	−50	−81	−109	−132	−147	−152	−144	−121	−81	−20	62	170	306
22	3	5	12	20	25	28	28	26	24	21	18	15	13	13	14	19	26	36	51	71	95	125
23	3	7	16	31	42	50	53	52	44	31	10	−19	−57	−104	−161	−229	−309	−401	−506	−624	−758	−906
31, 32, 33	3	6	21	61	114	179	250	324	399	469	532	584	621	640	637	609	551	460	333	166	−44	−302
42	7	13	31	56	75	87	91	88	75	52	20	−23	−77	−143	−222	−314	−419	−539	−674	−824	−991	−1174
44, 45	9	17	38	60	69	68	57	41	20	−1	−21	−38	−49	−52	−44	−22	14	69	144	242	365	515
48, 49	3	7	16	32	44	54	59	60	54	42	22	−7	−46	−95	−155	−228	−314	−414	−530	−661	−809	−975
51	2	4	8	12	12	9	3	−5	−16	−29	−44	−60	−77	−95	−114	−133	−152	−170	−188	−204	−219	−233
52, 53	6	12	24	33	29	15	−9	−39	−73	−109	−145	−178	−206	−228	−240	−241	−228	−199	−151	−84	7	122
54	5	9	21	35	42	43	37	27	11	−10	−34	−63	−94	−128	−165	−203	−243	−284	−325	−366	−407	−447
55, 56	−4	−7	−11	−2	21	51	82	108	124	122	96	41	−50	−183	−365	−601	−897	−1261	−1697	−2213	−2814	−3507
61	10	19	37	41	18	−27	−87	−157	−230	−301	−364	−412	−441	−444	−416	−349	−239	−80	134	410	753	1169
62	18	34	72	109	117	101	66	19	−35	−91	−143	−184	−210	−215	−193	−139	−47	89	274	515	815	1182
71	−45	−86	−191	−309	−363	−365	−325	−254	−161	−59	44	136	206	245	241	185	64	−130	−409	−783	−1262	−1858
72	−44	−85	−185	−285	−311	−276	−190	−65	87	255	427	593	739	856	931	952	909	790	583	277	−140	−679
81	−6	−12	−29	−56	−82	−104	−124	−140	−152	−159	−162	−159	−150	−134	−112	−82	−44	3	58	122	197	281
92	−17	−34	−85	−172	−259	−344	−424	−498	−562	−616	−656	−681	−689	−676	−642	−583	−499	−385	−241	−65	147	396
Pop. (1000s)	0.5	1.0	2.5	5.0	7.5	10.0	12.5	15.0	17.5	20.0	22.5	25.0	27.5	30.0	32.5	35.0	37.5	40.0	42.5	45.0	47.5	50.0

Legend:

- Reservation significantly lower
- Reservation lower, not significant
- County lower, not significant
- County significantly lower

TABLE 2.7: *Differences in the number of nonemployer establishments between counties and reservations by population size and industry in 2010. See Table 2.1 for a listing of the industries associated with each sector's code number.*

SECTOR	0.5	1.0	2.5	5.0	7.5	10.0	12.5	15.0	17.5	20.0	22.5	25.0	27.5	30.0	32.5	35.0	37.5	40.0	42.5	45.0	47.5	50.0
11	3	6	13	23	30	34	37	38	38	37	36	36	35	35	37	37	46	54	65	79	97	119
21	0	1	2	3	4	4	3	1	-1	-4	-8	-13	-18	-24	-31	-39	-48	-57	-68	-79	-91	-104
22	0	0	0	0	1	1	1	1	0	1	1	1	1	0	0	0	0	0	0	1	2	2
23	3	7	16	29	40	49	56	62	66	69	71	73	74	75	75	76	78	80	83	87	92	100
31, 32, 33	0	1	2	3	4	5	6	6	6	7	7	8	8	9	10	12	14	17	20	24	29	34
42	0	0	1	1	1	0	-1	-3	-4	-6	-7	-7	-8	-7	-6	-4	0	4	10	18	27	38
44, 45	4	7	16	27	35	39	40	39	37	34	30	27	25	25	27	32	40	53	70	93	122	158
48, 49	2	4	10	17	21	24	25	25	23	21	18	14	11	8	6	4	3	4	7	11	18	27
51	0	0	1	1	1	1	1	0	0	-1	-1	-2	-2	-2	-2	-2	0	1	3	6	9	13
52, 53	4	8	17	28	33	34	30	24	16	7	-4	-13	-22	-29	-33	-33	-29	-20	-5	17	47	85
54	2	4	8	13	14	13	10	6	0	-6	-12	-18	-22	-26	-27	-27	-23	-16	-6	9	29	54
55, 56	1	2	5	10	13	16	17	18	19	19	18	18	17	15	14	13	12	11	10	10	10	11
61	0	0	0	-1	-2	-5	-7	-10	-12	-15	-17	-19	-20	-20	-19	-17	-13	-8	-1	7	18	31
62	1	2	4	5	6	5	3	0	-3	-5	-8	-9	-9	-8	-6	-1	7	17	30	46	67	91
71	0	1	1	2	2	1	0	-1	-2	-3	-3	-4	-3	-1	1	5	10	17	25	35	48	62
72	1	1	3	5	7	7	7	6	5	4	3	2	1	0	1	1	3	5	9	14	20	28
81	5	9	21	37	48	54	57	57	55	51	46	41	37	33	31	31	34	41	51	67	88	116
Pop. (1000s)	0.5	1.0	2.5	5.0	7.5	10.0	12.5	15.0	17.5	20.0	22.5	25.0	27.5	30.0	32.5	35.0	37.5	40.0	42.5	45.0	47.5	50.0

Legend:

Reservation significantly lower

Reservation lower, not significant

County lower, not significant

County significantly lower

establishment numbers and jobs, given AMT's assumption that each nonemployer establishment creates the equivalent of one job. For populations of 7,500 or less, reservations have significantly fewer nonemployer establishments in fourteen of seventeen sectors. The exceptions are Wholesale Trade (sector 42) and Arts/ Entertainment/Recreation (sector 71), with few significant reservation–county differences at any population level, and Educational Services (sector 61), where reservations are estimated to have a significantly higher number of nonemployer establishments when the population is in the range of 7,500 to 35,000. Up to population levels of 15,000, reservations have significantly fewer nonemployer establishments in ten of seventeen sectors, and only in Educational Services is there a significant reservation advantage. Overall, the pattern for reservation nonemployer establishment numbers (and hence jobs) is less pervasively negative than the pattern for reservation employer establishment numbers but more negative than for reservation employer establishment jobs.

VII TAKING ACCOUNT OF ADDITIONAL FACTORS

Although AMT do not attempt a causal analysis of the reservation–county gaps, they examine the extent to which additional variables commonly used to analyze the spatial density of businesses affect the basic descriptive patterns discussed above. They first add two economic geography variables – rural location and population density[11] – that tend to change gradually with distance and are thus likely to affect reservations and their neighboring county areas somewhat evenly. In a second step, they add three measures of personal outcomes[12] – per capita personal income, the poverty rate, and the percentage of adults (twenty-five years old and older) with a bachelor's degree –whose values can vary significantly over short distances, depending on residential choices and the nature of the local economy. The causality links between this second group of variables and either establishment numbers or jobs can flow in either or both directions. By contrast, establishment and job numbers are somewhat less likely to strongly influence the two economic geography variables (rural location and population density), although such effects are clearly possible, especially for locally dominant industries.

AMT show that adding rural location and population density changes their employer establishment results very little.[13] That is, accounting for two important economic geography variables does not materially change the general pattern of establishment and job gaps between reservations and nearby county complements

---

[11] For county complements, rural location is an indicator variable equal to 1 if the U.S. Department of Agriculture's 2013 Rural–Urban Continuum Code is greater than 3 and 0 otherwise. Reservations are assigned the same value as their nearest county. Population density is measured as square miles per person. See AMT for details.

[12] The data are from the 2008–12 American Community Survey (ACS). See AMT for details.

[13] See AMT for the methodology and more detailed results.

discussed above. This may be partly due to their use of a geographically adjacent comparison group of nonreservation areas, limiting the sample variation in "rurality."

Much larger changes in the employer establishment results appear when AMT add the three measures of local area personal outcomes. A majority of industries still show a significant shortfall in the number of establishments on reservations when the local population is at or below 10,000, but several industries (Mining, Construction, Manufacturing, Management, Educational Services, Arts/Entertainment/Recreation) fail to show a significant shortfall of establishments even at low population levels. For jobs, only a few industries consistently show a significant reservation deficit for populations at or below 10,000 (Agriculture/Forestry/Fishing/Hunting, Utilities, Wholesale Trade, and Educational Services). Instances of the reverse, where reservations exhibit a significant job advantage even for relatively low values of population, also diminish somewhat. Overall for employer establishment numbers and jobs, an increase in the share of insignificant differences prevails in the lower population ranges, as compared to the results in Tables 2.5 and 2.6. In this sense, the additional personal outcome variables statistically account for many, but not all, of the reservation–county differences that were significant in Tables 2.5 and 2.6 at population levels of 15,000 or less.

Adding the same set of additional variables somewhat weakens the extent of statistically significant gaps that AMT find in the number of nonemployer establishments within reservations and nearby county complements. Compared to the relatively clear nonemployer establishment results in Table 2.7 here, AMT find that a majority of industries still exhibit a significant shortfall on reservations, at least when the local population is at or below 7,500. However, the opposite holds for the Arts/Entertainment/Recreation sector. Above 7,500 residents, reservation deficits predominate, but most differences are not statistically significant.

AMT stress that their multivariate regressions do not reveal the causal relationships between the additional control variables and the reservation–county differences in establishment or job numbers. For example, for relatively low levels of population, Tables 2.5 and 2.6 show that the Construction sector has significantly fewer establishments and jobs on reservations than in county complements, but the corresponding results become insignificant when AMT control for personal income, poverty, and college graduation. This change could arise because certain reservations and counties have resource endowments that promote the presence of a strong Construction sector, which in turn provides jobs, raises local incomes, and lowers local poverty. Alternatively, high (low) personal income could serve as a marker for underlying business environmental factors that promote (inhibit) the success of the Construction sector, and there are other possible linkages. AMT conclude the fact that the additional variables diminish the number of sectors with significant differences suggests that further work on the causal linkages would be useful.

VIII JOBS PER EMPLOYER ESTABLISHMENT

The fact that, for employer establishments, significant reservation establishment number gaps are more common across sectors than significant reservation job gaps, especially for reservations with fewer than 15,000 people, suggests that the average number of employees per employer establishment may be higher on small reservations in some sectors. Akee, Mykerezi, and Todd (2017) present figures that verify that this is indeed the case in many sectors, at least over some low population range. Higher reservation jobs per establishment for populations below 15,000 is very distinct in sectors such as Arts/Entertainment/Recreation, Accommodation/Food Services, Other Services, and Public Administration but prevails to a lesser degree and often over a more limited population range in some other sectors. In addition, for the eleven reservations with populations above 15,000, Tables 2.5 and 2.6 here imply that, on average, reservations have higher jobs per establishment than county complements in the following industries: Construction, Wholesale Trade, Transportation/Warehousing, Finance/Insurance/Real Estate/Rental/Leasing, Information, Management, and Educational Services.

IX ADDITIONAL EVIDENCE ON VARIATION AMONG RESERVATIONS

The patterns summarized above are based on averaging outcomes over a group of reservations and a group of counties. These averages may not reflect the experience of many individual reservations and counties. Disclosure restrictions inherent in working with confidential census microdata make it difficult to provide more detailed census-based information on how outcomes vary around these averages.

Alternative sources of data on business establishments can be used to shed light on the range of workplace and job densities in reservations and counties. One source is the National Establishment Time-Series (NETS) Database, which the firm Walls & Associates creates from annual Dun and Bradstreet (D&B) establishment data. Barnatchez, Crane, and Decker (2017) compare NETS data to official government business data. Although they express concerns about using NETS data over time, they conclude that the "NETS microdata can be useful and convenient for studying static business activity in high detail." That is, with some adjustments and for a given year, the NETS data can provide useful but more detailed information about the types of outcomes measured above with census data – spatial densities by sector. On that basis, the NETS data for 2014 were used to reexamine the average results presented above and then to provide new information about the range of reservation and county experiences for jobs per resident.

On average, the NETS data produce the same pattern of results as the census data. That is, establishments per resident are lower on reservations than in nearby counties, but jobs per resident are higher. The reservation disadvantage in establishments per resident computed with NETS data is similar in magnitude to the census result, or about 30 percent fewer overall. The reservation advantage in jobs per resident is greater in the NETS data. This may reflect the finding of Barnatchez, Crane, and Decker (2017) that "independent contractors and temporary workers . . . might be double counted in NETS (i.e., they may be counted both in the establishment in which they work and in the establishment that pays them)." Nonetheless, the average patterns are qualitatively similar between the NETS and census data, and the potential double count of workers will, to some extent, affect both reservations and counties.

NETS-based statistics on jobs per resident can go beyond these average patterns to explore the range of reservation and county outcomes. The results show that reservations are more likely than counties to experience extreme outcomes (very low or very high) but also that the majority of American Indian and Alaska Native people living on reservations experience very low levels of jobs per resident. Specifically, about 53 percent of the American Indians and Alaska Natives living on federally recognized reservations in the contiguous forty-eight states live on reservations whose jobs per resident would rank among the lowest 25 percent of the nearby counties. This also implies that the advantage that reservations have, on average, in jobs per capita is driven by very high jobs per resident figures in a relatively small group of reservations that are home to a minority of the American Indians and Alaska Natives residing on reservations. Living on a reservation with average or above-average jobs per resident (by county standards) is not the typical experience for reservation American Indians or Alaska Natives.

X CONCLUDING REMARKS

The research summarized here finds that, overall, reservations and county areas have a similar sectoral distribution of establishments, but in nearly all sectors reservations tend to have significantly fewer establishments per resident. This shortfall is clearest in reservations with fewer than 15,000 residents, which make up the majority of reservations. By contrast, the number of jobs provided by reservation establishments is, on average, at par with or somewhat higher than in nearby county areas but is concentrated in the Arts/Entertainment/Recreation, Accommodation/ Food Services, and Public Administration sectors. Jobs in other industries are typically sparser, per capita, within reservations. Geographic and demographic factors, such as population density and income, statistically account for some but not all of these differences. However, the result that reservations average more jobs per resident than the nearby counties reflects very high jobs per resident in a minority of reservations, and most American Indians and Alaska Natives residing on reservations do not experience those conditions.

These patterns suggest both the opportunity and the capacity for reservation economies to grow through greater employment diversification into sectors beyond those related to gaming and government. Figure 2.1 shows that reservations have the capacity to support the same diversity of workplaces as nearby county areas. At the same time, the establishment and job parity indices in Tables 2.2 and 2.3 and Figures 2.2 and 2.4 show that reservations have fewer establishments per capita in most industries and that jobs per capita are 20 to over 50 percent below nearby county norms in economically important sectors such as Health Care/Social Assistance, Professional/Scientific/Technical, Finance/Insurance/Real Estate/Rental/Leasing, Transportation and Warehousing, Retail Trade, Manufacturing, Construction, and Agriculture/Forestry/Fishing/Hunting. Assuming that job numbers in reservations' gaming-related and government sectors can be sustained near current levels, tribal leaders could foster significant additional growth through policies that bring other sectors' per capita numbers of workplaces and job numbers more in line with the levels that prevail in the nearby, mostly rural counties.

Implementing a diversification strategy along these lines will require a bundle of policies broadly grouped under the banner of good governance. As discussed in other chapters here and elsewhere (e.g., Cornell et al. 2007, Miller 2001, and Miller 2012), policies supporting this approach include:

- *Embracing a strong role for privately owned businesses*, without forgoing the option to use tribally owned entities to fill critical gaps. Fostering a local presence of business organizations such as Indian Chambers of Commerce, Indian Business Alliances, and industry-specific advocacy groups (e.g., the Native American Contractors Association) may help by providing a channel for business owners' issues to reach tribal community leaders.
- Maintaining a fair, efficient, and trusted system for *resolving business disputes*, including disputes between tribal members and outsiders. Components might include clear and accessible commercial law codes (e.g., Woodrow 2011) plus access to trusted courts (Flies Away, Garrow, and Jorgensen 2007) and other mechanisms (e.g., lien filing systems) needed to make effective use of the codes (Kunesh and Benjamin 2019).
- *Minimizing direct political or tribal government intervention* in the affairs of both privately owned businesses and tribal enterprises (Grant and Taylor 2007).
- *Ensuring that reservation land can be readily acquired or leased* for business purposes. This includes efficient processing of land titles and maintaining land use plans and regulations that provide appropriate sites for business use.
- Arranging the funding and administrative capacity to provide the *physical and digital infrastructure* businesses need to compete (National Congress of American Indians 2017).
- *Building a skilled workforce* through policies that support high-quality education from early childhood through post-secondary and vocational training, promote good-quality childcare options, and address other factors impeding employment (NCAI 2016, Kunesh and Todd 2018).

The evidence summarized here suggests that, for many reservations, implementing a "good governance" approach to diversifying beyond gaming-related and government jobs in order to bring work and workplaces in other sectors on par with nearby counties may be a practical economic development alternative to seeking narrowly based boom industries.

REFERENCES

Akee, Randall, 2009. "Checkerboards and Coase: The Effect of Property Institutions on Efficiency in Housing Markets." *The Journal of Law and Economics*, Volume 52, Number 2, pp. 395–410.

Akee, Randall. 2012. "Secured Transactions Laws and Economic Outcomes on American Indian Reservations: A Preliminary Analysis." Unpublished manuscript.

Akee, Randall, and Miriam Jorgensen. 2014. "Property Institutions and Business Investments on American Indian Reservations." *Regional Science and Urban Economics*, Volume 46, pp. 116–125.

Akee, Randall, Elton Mykerezi, and Richard M. Todd. 2017. "Reservation Employer Establishments: Data from the U.S. Census Longitudinal Business Database." Federal Reserve Bank of Minneapolis, Center for Indian Country Development Working Paper Number 2017–02.

Akee, Randall, Elton Mykerezi, and Richard M. Todd. 2018. "Reservation Nonemployer and Employer Establishments: Data from U.S. Census Longitudinal Business Databases." Federal Reserve Bank of Minneapolis, Center for Indian Country Development Working Paper Number 2018–01.

Barnatchez, Keith, Leland D. Crane, and Ryan A. Decker. 2017. "An Assessment of the National Establishment Time Series (NETS) Database." Board of Governors of the Federal Reserve System Finance and Economics Discussion Series 2017–110.

Berry, Brian J. L. and William L. Garrison. 1958. "A Note on Central Place Theory and the Range of a Good." *Economic Geography*, Volume 34, pp. 304–11.

Blair, John P., Thomas Traynor, and Manjiang Duan. 2004. "Retail Development in Rural Counties: Evidence from the Upper Midwest." *Journal of Regional Analysis and Policy*, Volume 34, Number 1, pp. 69–84.

Cornell, Stephen, Miriam Jorgensen, Ian Wilson Record, and Joan Timeche. 2007. "Citizen Entrepreneurship: An Underutilized Development Resource." In Miriam Jorgensen (ed.). 2007. *Rebuilding Native Nations*. Tucson, University of Arizona Press.

Dimitrova-Grajzl, Valentina P., Peter Grajzl, A. Joseph Guse, and Richard M. Todd. 2015. "Consumer Credit on American Indian Reservations." *Economic Systems*, Volume 39, Number 3, pp. 518–40.

Flies Away, Joseph Thomas, Carrie Garrow, and Miriam Jorgensen. 2007. "Native Nation Courts: Key Players in Nation Rebuilding." In Miriam Jorgensen (ed.). 2007. *Rebuilding Native Nations*. Tucson, University of Arizona Press.

Grant, Kenneth and Jonathan Taylor. 2007. "Managing the Boundary Between Business and Politics: Strategies for Improving the Chances for Success of Tribally Owned Enterprises." In Miriam Jorgensen (ed.). 2007. *Rebuilding Native Nations*. Tucson, University of Arizona Press.

Jorgensen, Miriam. 2016a. *Access to Capital and Credit in Native Communities*, digital version. Tucson, Native Nations Institute, The University of Arizona.

Jorgensen, Miriam. 2016b. "Mortgage Markets Outlooks Post-Recession and Impacts in Indian Country: A Response." Presentation at the conference "Mortgage Lending in Indian Country: Foundational Investments & Future Pathways to Homeownership," Scottsdale, Arizona (September). Available at www.minneapolisfed.org/~/media/files/com munity/indiancountry/events/2016-08/jorgensen-presentationat-mortgage-lending-in-indian-country.pdf?la=en.

Kunesh, Patrice H. and Benjamin D. Horowitz. 2019. "Access to Credit in Indian Country: The Promise of Secured Transaction Systems in Creating Strong Economies." In Robert J. Miller, Miriam Jorgensen, and Daniel Stewart (eds.) 2019. *Creating Private Sector Economies in Native America*. Cambridge: Cambridge University Press.

Kunesh, Patrice H. and Richard M. Todd. 2018. "Narrowing Gaps Through Educational Investments for American Indians and Alaska Natives." In Stuart Andreason, Todd Greene, Heath Prince, and Carl Van Horn (eds.) 2018. *Investing in America's Workforce: Improving Outcomes for Workers and Employers*. Kalamazoo, MI: W.E. Upjohn Institute for Employment Research.

Miller, Robert J. 2001. "Economic Development in Indian Country: Will Capitalism or Socialism Succeed?" 80 OR. L. REV. 757.

Miller, R. J. 2012. *Reservation "Capitalism": Economic Development in Indian Country*. Santa Barbara, CA: Praeger.

National Congress of American Indians (NCAI). 2017. *Tribal Infrastructure: Investing in Indian Country for a Stronger America*. An initial report by NCAI to the Administration and Congress, downloaded (08/28/2018) from www.ncai.org/attachments/PolicyPaper_RslnCGsUDiatRYTpP XKwThNYoACnjDoBOrdDlBSRcheKxwJZDCx_NCAI-InfrastructureReport-FINAL.pdf.

NCAI Partnership for Tribal Governance. 2016. Empowering Tribal Workforce Development: Indian Country's Policy Recommendations for the Federal Government (Version 1.0). Washington, D.C.: National Congress of American Indians, and related materials downloaded (08/28/2018) from www.ncai.org/ptg/work-force-development/fpb.

Shonkwiler, J. S. and Thomas R. Harris. 1996. "Rural Retail Business Thresholds and Interdependencies." *Journal of Regional Science*, Volume 36, Number 4, pp. 617–630.

Woodrow, Susan M. 2011. "Opportunities and Challenges for Economic Development in Indian Country." Testimony to the U.S. Senate Committee on Banking, Housing, and Urban Affairs. Available at www.minneapolisfed.org/indiancountry/research-and-articles/articles-and-reports/woodrow-testimony-2011.

Any opinions and conclusions expressed herein are those of the authors and do not necessarily represent the views of the U.S. Census Bureau, the Federal Reserve Bank of Minneapolis, the Federal Reserve System, or the U.S. Department of Agriculture. All results have been reviewed to ensure that no confidential information is disclosed. This material is based upon work that is supported by the National Institute of Food and Agriculture, U.S. Department of Agriculture, under award number MIN-14-G19. Contact Information: Center for Indian Country Development, Federal Reserve Bank of Minneapolis, 90 Hennepin Avenue, Minneapolis, MN 55401 (CICD@mpls.frb.org).

PART II

Policy Barriers and Policy Needs

3

The Challenges of American Indian Land Tenure and the Vastness of Entrepreneurial Potential

Jessica A. Shoemaker

Land tenure and economic development are closely connected. All economic activity has to physically occur somewhere, and so the legal rules that shape who gets to do what where – especially with valuable resources – can either facilitate individual enterprise or get in its way. In Indian Country, property rules for land tend to be particularly important, in part because the greatest areas of economic potential for many reservation communities are land based and land connected, including food and agriculture, energy development, forestry, tourism, and related industries.[1] In addition, many Indigenous communities are deeply connected to specific physical spaces in ways that are fundamental to Indigenous identities and cultures.[2] This is true not only socially and culturally but also legally. Under modern rules, self-governance rights in Indian Country are frequently dependent on persistent real property ownership; tribal governments can often only regulate or govern the physical spaces that remain in Indian ownership.[3]

Land tenure also impacts economic development in more foundational ways. Property systems fundamentally structure how markets and economies operate. Many economists and law and development scholars go so far as to argue that well-defined private property rights are *the* single most important precondition to successful economic development.[4] In this view, property law's most important function is to facilitate desirable market transactions. By communicating quickly and

---

[1] E.g., S. REP. NO. 103–186, at 2 (1993), *reprinted in* 1993 U.S.C.C.A.N. 2459, 2460 (finding that "[t]he farming and ranching sector provides the main source of entrepreneurial opportunity to the Indian people within Indian reservations and communities"); Judith V. Royster, *Practical Sovereignty, Political Sovereignty, and the Indian Tribal Energy Development and Self-Determination Act*, 12 LEWIS & CLARK L. REV. 1065, 1066–67 (2008) (collecting data on potential energy development within Indian Country).

[2] E.g., Rebecca Tsosie, *Land, Culture, and Community: Reflections on Native Sovereignty and Property in America*, 34 IND. L. REV. 1291, 1300–03, 1306–08 (2001).

[3] E.g., Plains Commerce Bank v. Long Family Land & Cattle Co., 554 U.S. 316, 327–28, 340 (2008) (categorically limiting some tribal jurisdiction after reservation lands are transferred to non-Indian ownership); City of Sherrill v. Oneida Indian Nation, 544 U.S. 197, 219–20 (2005) (limiting tribal authority over repurchased lands that had been previously owned, albeit illegally, by non-Indians in fee).

[4] *See* Amir N. Licht, *The Entrepreneurial Spirit and What the Law Can Do About It*, 28 COMP. LAB. L. & POL'Y. J. 817, 852 (2007) (collecting sources). Importantly, this is not limited to land rights necessarily

transparently about who owns what, clear property rules can simplify bargaining and make transferring assets easier.[5] In an economist's ideal world, these transactions ensure that resources move efficiently to their highest and best users and, by securing investments over time, encourage wise resource management.[6]

In Indian Country, however, property rights are notoriously complex and cumbersome. Reservation lands are commonly owned in complicated and heavily regulated tenure forms, often with competing claims by numerous owners, and many of these land assets cannot be sold or freely transferred on any kind of open market whatsoever.[7] Many scholars and policymakers, therefore, draw a straight line of blame from these complicated reservation property systems to persistent poverty in many reservation communities.[8] If only reservation property were more straightforward, more private, and more easily transferred, then the capital needed for development would flow more freely into reservation economies and more prosperity would spread broadly across the land, lifting up entire reservation communities. Or at least that is the hope.

This chapter challenges this simple analysis and explores in a more nuanced way the specific relationship between these specialized reservation property regimes and observed economic outcomes. The challenges of modern reservation property systems are complex and have emerged as a result of difficult policy trade-offs and after a long history of forced, top-down property law reforms used against Indigenous peoples for colonial ends.[9] Certainly property system design impacts reservation economies, but land tenure choices also communicate important community values about the relationships of people to their neighbors and about the importance of the land itself. In Indian Country, land preservation and self-governance may be goals as important as – or in some cases even more important than – economic development.[10]

---

but includes other types of property, including personal property rights to goods and intellectual property in new ideas.

[5]   Thomas W. Merrill & Henry E. Smith, *The Morality of Property*, 48 Wм. & Mary L. Rev. 1849, 1850 (2007) (emphasizing importance of efficient communication of property rights for asset transfers).

[6]   *See, e.g.,* R. H. Coase, *The Problem of Social Cost*, 3 J.L. & Econ. 1 (1960); Harold Demsetz, *Toward a Theory of Property Rights*, 57 Am. Econ. Rev. 347, 350–53 (1967); Hernando de Soto, The Mystery of Capital: Why Capitalism Triumphs in the West and Fails Everywhere Else (2000); Abraham Bell & Gideon Parchomovsky, *A Theory of Property*, 90 Cornell L. Rev. 531, 538 (2005) (emphasizing importance of stable property rights in increasing asset values).

[7]   *See generally* Jessica A. Shoemaker, *Complexity's Shadow: American Indian Property, Sovereignty, and the Future*, 115 Mich. L. Rev. 487 (2017).

[8]   *E.g.,* Terry L. Anderson, *Epilogue* to Unlocking the Wealth of Indian Nations (2016); Naomi Schaefer Riley, The New Trail of Tears: How Washington Is Destroying American Indians (2016); Terry L. Anderson & Dean Lueck, *Land Tenure and Agricultural Productivity on Indian Reservations*, 35 J.L. & Econ. 427, 427–28 (1992). Some tribes, however, are successful even within these land constraints. *E.g.,* Terry Anderson, *The Wealth of (Indian) Nations*, Hoover Inst. (October 25, 2016), www.hoover.org /research/wealth-indian-nations-1 (describing how the members of the Southern Ute Tribe "are each worth millions and receive dividends every year" from a $4 billion growth fund).

[9]   *E.g.,* Judith V. Royster, *The Legacy of Allotment*, 27 Ariz. St. L.J. 1 (1995).

[10] Kristen A. Carpenter and Angela R. Riley, *Privatizing the Reservation?*, 71 Stan. L. Rev. (forthcoming 2019).

Despite widely acknowledged perils, reservation property systems have been largely stuck in the current position for decades, with an expensive and heavy-handed federal bureaucracy and, elsewhere, a pervasive lack of clarity about who – tribal, state, or federal government – gets to govern where and what in Indian Country.[11] It is primarily this complexity and on-the-ground uncertainty that can make it more expensive and difficult to do business in Indian Country than outside it. But for entrepreneurs, uncertainty is often the ideal landscape of opportunity and the space where the best and most creative development work can occur. This chapter's ambition is to begin to consider not only how tribal governments' own specific land reform strategies could help create a better legal landscape that is more conducive for entrepreneurship, but also, perhaps even more importantly, how greater entrepreneurial energy could also be translated to build more fundamentally transformative reservation property systems for the future from the ground up.[12]

I THE STATUS OF RESERVATION LANDS

Lands within federally recognized Indian reservations in the United States are owned and governed in unique ways. There is no single reservation property system that applies uniformly across all reservation territories, and even within a single reservation's exterior boundaries, individual parcels are often subject to a complex mix of different property rules, set by different and sometimes overlapping jurisdictions. Federal law, supported by international norms, explicitly recognizes the retained, inherent sovereignty of Indian nations, but property governance within reservation boundaries remains one of the most difficult-to-decipher, heavily regulated, and complex domains of modern federal Indian law.[13]

Three separate sovereigns – tribal, state, and federal governments – all coexist within reservation boundaries, and the balance of jurisdiction as between these three is often contested and uncertain. Reservation lands are owned by both Indians and non-Indians and held in both specialized federal trust statuses and more typical (at least in Western legal traditions) fee-simple statuses.[14] Who governs where often varies parcel by parcel (or property right by property right) and depends on often-

---

[11]   Kevin Gover, *An Indian Trust for the Twenty-First Century*, 46 NAT. RESOURCES J. 317, 319, 350 (2006) (identifying federal trust land management as one of last major areas of federal Indian policy that has not been radically reformed to meet goal of tribal self-determination).

[12]   Of course, the project of property system change and land reform is complex. In related forthcoming work, I explore more deeply these challenges and chart a more detailed trajectory for wider tribally driven land reform possibilities. *See* Jessica A. Shoemaker, *Transforming Property: Reclaiming Modern Indigenous Land Tenures*, 107 CALIF. L. REV. (forthcoming 2019).

[13]   *See generally* United Nations Declaration on the Rights of Indigenous Peoples, G.A. Res. 61/295, U.N. Doc. A/RES/61/295 (September 13, 2007); Allan Erbsen, *Constitutional Spaces*, 95 MINN. L. REV. 1168, 1253–58 (2011) (describing "vexing" challenges of concurrent jurisdictions in reservation territories).

[14]   *See* FELIX S. COHEN, COHEN'S HANDBOOK OF FEDERAL INDIAN LAW §§ 15.02–.03, at 995–99, § 15.04[5], at 1015, § 16.03[1], at 1071 (Nell Jessup Newton ed., 2012) [hereinafter COHEN HANDBOOK].

invisible factors such as the identity of the owner and the land's legal tenure status. This means that even adjacent reservation lands that appear perfectly physically identical may be subject to entirely different ownership rules and regulated by different governments, creating what many call a "checkerboard" of land tenure and governance across reservation spaces.[15] Anyone seeking to use, possess, or otherwise develop a specific piece of property within reservation boundaries must first navigate these complex legal systems to determine which sets of rules even apply, and the final answer often remains nuanced and unsettled.[16]

Within these spaces, tribal nations and individual Indian landowners own approximately 56 million acres in the special federal trust status.[17] Trust lands are held in a bifurcated state. The federal government holds underlying title for the benefit of individual Indian or tribal owners. The federal government, as trustee, performs administrative and land management tasks with respect to these lands and imposes a near-complete restraint on alienation. The exact contours of these federal management processes are technical and vary based on numerous factors, including whether the land is held in trust for individuals (individual trust lands or allotments) or the tribe itself (tribal trust lands). In general, allotted lands are more heavily regulated than tribal lands, though both are subject to comprehensive federal control. With respect to allotments, the federal government still oversees and, in many cases, preapproves nearly every individual land use decision and transaction.[18] In comparison, there has been some trend to try to streamline more aspects of the tribal trust tenure status and to increase, to a degree, tribal governments' autonomy over these land use decisions.[19] Many reservation territories are also subject to other individualized land management rules for their specific trust lands, either because of unique historical contexts or other more modern negotiated legislative arrangements.[20]

The rules for fee lands within reservation boundaries can be even more nuanced. Fee lands may be owned by the tribal government directly, by outside state or federal authorities, by individual Indians (including both members and nonmembers of the governing tribe), and non-Indians who are typically not enfranchised in tribal

---

[15] *See, e.g.*, Solem v. Bartlett, 465 U.S. 463, 471 n. 12 (1984) (describing "checkerboard" land tenure patterns).

[16] For a fuller discussion of these complex property jurisdiction issues, *see* Jessica A. Shoemaker, *Emulsified Property*, 43 Pepp. L. Rev. 945 (2016).

[17] *See* U.S. Dep't of the Interior, Initial Implementation Plan: Land Buy-Back Program for Tribal Nations 6 (December 18, 2012), www.doi.gov/sites/doi.gov/files/migrated/buybackprogram/about/upload/Initial-Implementation-Plan-508_v2.pdf [hereinafter Buy-Back Plan]. These figures are limited to the lower forty-eight states. Alaska in particular is subject to unique land tenure patterns, which are not the subject of this work.

[18] For a fuller discussion of these individual allotment issues, *see* Jessica A. Shoemaker, *No Sticks in My Bundle: Rethinking the Indian Land Tenure Problem*, 63 U. Kan. L. Rev. 383 (2015).

[19] *See, e.g., infra* n. 35 and accompanying text.

[20] *E.g.*, Cohen Handbook, *supra* n. 14, at § 15.03 (discussing unique Indian-owned "restricted fee" status that currently exists only in certain parts of the country).

governments at all. Decisions about who governs which fee properties are often dependent on the specific identity of the owner and, sometimes, also the general character of the area in which the property is located.[21] For example, tribal governments may have significant authority over member-owned fee lands, but the state still likely taxes, and possibly keeps records for, those lands. If the tribe itself owns fee lands, the tribe's sovereign immunity may further limit the reach of the state government. On the other hand, the state likely has significantly more jurisdiction over non-Indian-owned fee lands, but even this is contested and may depend on other jurisdictional factors.[22]

II SPECIFIC LAND TENURE CHALLENGES FOR ENTREPRENEURSHIP AND SAMPLE SOLUTION STRATEGIES

Focusing on land tenure specifically, this section analyzes the primary ways that this current property system design impacts private sector economic development in reservation spaces. This discussion goes beyond a simple "more" versus "less" private property debate and analyzes in greater detail the specific obstacles created by current system design, including unique aspects of the federal trust tenure status and the multilayered and hard-to-read land governance model overall. Understanding the substance of these specific challenges is one step forward for more targeted solutions, and in that spirit, some sample tribally driven strategies for land-based efforts that better promote robust and diversified economies are also included.

At the same time, it is important to recognize that these land tenure issues are even larger and more complex than can be fully covered here. Property systems serve many varied goals and are adaptable and dynamic across numerous metrics.[23] The land tenure challenges in Indian Country are immense and extend beyond economic concerns. Uncertain, overlapping, or checkerboard governance schemes, for example, impact not only the ability of entrepreneurs to efficiently enter reservation markets but also limit tribal governments' abilities to manage physical landscapes cohesively for other purposes, including environmental and cultural preservation. In addition, there are numerous other layers of legal issues imbedded in any land reform discussion, including the parameters and significance of tribal sovereignty,

---

[21] *See* Brendale v. Confederated Tribes and Bands of Yakima Nation, 492 U.S. 408, 423–25, 428–32 (1989) (plurality opinion resulting in bifurcated zoning authority within reservation territories based on degree of "Indian character" of area to be zoned, not individual parcel ownership).

[22] *See* Shoemaker, *supra* n. 16.

[23] *See, e.g.*, Mirit Eyal-Cohen, *Through the Lens of Innovation*, 43 Fla. St. U. L. Rev. 951, 954 (2016) (exploring how more versus less property choice is less clear in intellectual property context where secure ownership can encourage entrepreneurship by incentivizing inventors who reap rewards of their work or, simultaneously, hinder future development by limiting the degree to which other innovators can build on or improve prior work); *see also* Michael Trebilcock and Paul-Erik Veel, *Property Rights and Development: The Contingent Case for Formalization*, 30 U. Pa. J. Int'l L. 397 (2008) (reflecting need for context-specific analysis of the benefits, if any, of property formalization).

the federal trust responsibility, the rights of current owners, and the cultural values imbedded in land tenure design. This section focuses specifically on the relationship between modern land tenure rules and the project of promoting more private sector entrepreneurship, but in Section III I also explore how entrepreneurship may be a catalyst for further entry into this necessary – but so complex – project of a wider, tribally driven land reform process for a fuller array of local concerns.

A Transfer Restraints

The current federal restraint against alienation of trust assets is the most immediate limitation on economic development in Indian Country.[24] Free property transferability is generally important to facilitate efficient transfers of resources to more productive users (including individual entrepreneurs) and to encourage investment (so that investors are secure in their rights to cash out future returns through asset sales).[25] For trust lands, however, the federal government significantly limits these kinds of flexible transfers. Under modern default rules, no trust lands can be directly transferred – including not only outright for-value sales but also intrafamily gifts and most other encumbrances (such as leases or mortgages) – without federal pre-approval and individualized oversight. This means that even when an entrepreneur can access necessary property rights given these constraints, traditional options for investor returns – including the future sale of improved assets – are not easily available or, in some cases, even possible.[26]

This modern alienation restraint, however, is important because it helps ensure a preserved land base for future generations of Indigenous governance. Modern rules requiring persistent Indian property ownership as a prerequisite to many self-governance rights even within reservation territories make this especially necessary.[27] The breadth of the modern restraint is notable. Although the federal government has moved more recently toward some more flexible tribal leasing options (which have spurred some important housing and related developments), more flexibility is possible.[28] In the future, for example, tribal governments may lobby for other optional, alternative arrangements that could preserve underlying trust title for land preservation and jurisdictional purposes, but simultaneously allow more flexible transfers "on top of" the trust interest. Sample avenues for this kind of future reform could include more expedited or less restricted intertribal or

---

[24] E.g., Gavin Clarkson & Alisha Murphy, *Tribal Leakage: How the Curse of Trust Land Impedes Tribal Economic Self-Sustainability*, 12 J.L. Econ & Pol'y 177 (2016).

[25] *Cf. supra* nn. 4–6 and accompanying text.

[26] 25 U.S.C. § 177 (2012); *see also* Cohen Handbook, *supra* n. 14, at § 15.06.

[27] *See* Malcolm Lavoie, *Why Restrain Alienation of Indigenous Lands?*, 49 U.B.C. L. Rev. 997, 1054–56 (2016).

[28] Randall Akee, *Checkerboards and Coase: The Effect of Property Institutions on Efficiency in Housing Markets*, 52 J.L. & Econ. 395 (2009) (demonstrating in specific context the significant value of federal long-term leasing authorities to trust land development as compared to fee-simple properties).

intratribal transfers; more tribal government autonomy and direct oversight of its own alienation decisions; and/or a loosened alienation restraint for certain subsidiary transfers of interests less than full title (e.g., allowing even longer-term flexible leases or more alienable possessory interests, like assignments, that could exist on top of the underlying trust title).[29]

B Credit Barriers

Relatedly, these categorical restraints on land transfer also impact access to credit and capital in Indian Country. Anti-alienation rules mean that, for most Indian entrepreneurs, their greatest source of potential wealth (land) is also not available to be used for collateral to secure private credit. Private lenders are unlikely to offer mortgages or other credit where the proposed collateral – trust land – cannot be directly foreclosed upon (i.e., transferred to the lender) in the case of default.[30] Increasingly, new models of lending, including direct loans from tribal governments, federal loan-guarantee programs, and new innovations in leasehold mortgage mechanisms, are all producing growth in the amount of credit flowing into reservation territories, and this is a promising ongoing strategy for addressing this credit challenge.[31]

C Regulatory Costs

Next, the layer of bureaucratic administration that touches almost every land use or management decision involving trust properties also adds unique cost to entrepreneurial activities on trust lands.[32] The default rule is still that the federal government continues to oversee nearly every aspect of trust land use, from leases to nonowners to an individual co-owner's own use during his or life.[33] Federal land management procedures tend to be dense, time-consuming, and require a high degree of technical expertise to navigate.[34] For example, although there are now numerous

---

[29] For example, the Ninth Circuit recently held that this overall alienation restraint prevented the Chemehuevi Indian Tribe from assigning an interest in tribal lands that could be transferred during life or at death at the direction of the assignee. Chemehuevi Indian Tribe v. Jewell, 767 F.3d 900 (9th Cir. 2014).

[30] *See* Miriam Jorgensen, ACCESS TO CAPITAL AND CREDIT IN NATIVE COMMUNITIES 47–48 (2016), https://nni .arizona.edu/application/files/8914/6386/8578/Accessing_Capital_and_Credit_in_Native_Communities .pdf [hereinafter ACCESS TO CAPITAL].

[31] *See id.* at 48–51 (profiling success of particular HUD home loan guarantee programs), 57 (noting leasehold mortgage option in Indian Country).

[32] *See, e.g.*, Robert J. Miller, *Economic Development in Indian Country: Will Capitalism or Socialism Succeed?*, 80 OR. L. REV. 757, 851–52 (2001) (blaming "cumbersome and inefficient federal bureaucracy" and trust status for hindering reservation economic development); Robert McCarthy, *The Bureau of Indian Affairs and the Federal Trust Obligation to American Indians*, 19 BYU J. PUB. L. 1, 62–67 (2004) (cataloging modern BIA land management regime).

[33] *See infra* Part II.F.

[34] *See, e.g.*, 25 C.F.R. Pt. 162 (2018) (Indian leasing, with subparts with special rules for agricultural leases, homesite leases, business leases, energy leases, and other nonspecific nonagricultural leases);

exceptions to this general rule of federal oversight and approval,[35] simply accounting for all of those exceptions – and then making the threshold determination whether such an exception applies and, if so, what occurs in its place – can be an expensive additional step in every land-based entrepreneurial activity.[36]

The Bureau of Indian Affairs (BIA) has also historically been terrible at managing these interests and performing these functions. In addition to claims that the BIA has mismanaged trust assets, there has often been a lengthy backlog and delay in BIA functions.[37] For example, it is the federal government's responsibility to maintain ownership records for trust assets, but in some cases it has taken the BIA more than a year simply to produce a report of who owns what interests in the trust land it manages.[38] The federal government also recently paid out billions of dollars in settlements stemming from lawsuits claiming it failed to live up to its trust respon-sibilities on these lands, including an inability in some cases to ever account accurately for who owns what.[39] All of these additional layers of federal government review and approval can add cost, delay, and uncertainty to every transaction involving trust lands.

Many tribes have had success taking over some of these land management functions through self-determination contracts with the federal government, but the scope and flexibility of tribal decision-making under these contracts remain limited.[40] Still, studies show that when tribal governments take over BIA realty functions – including land title and records – they are able to proceed much more expeditiously and advantageously than the federal agencies did.[41]

---

    25 C.F.R. Pt. 167 (2018) (grazing permits); 25 C.F.R. Pt. 169 (2018) (rights of way); 25 C.F.R. Pt. 211 (2018) (tribal mineral development); 25 C.F.R. Pt. 212 (2018) (individual mineral development).

[35]   For example, the HEARTH Act permits tribal leasing of tribal trust lands without any federal intervention provided that the tribal leasing regulations have themselves first been preapproved by the Department of the Interior. HEARTH Act of 2012, Pub. L. No. 112-151, § 2(h), 126 Stat. 1150, 1151 (codified at 25 U.S.C. § 415 (2012)).

[36]   *Cf.* Shoemaker, *supra* n. 7, at 522–31 (discussing challenge of hyper-categorizing these property variables).

[37]   *E.g.,* David D. Haddock & Robert J. Miller, *Can a Sovereign Protect Investors from Itself? Tribal Institutions to Spur Reservation Investment,* 8 J. SMALL & EMERGING BUS. L. 173, 213 (2004) (describing a more-than-one hundred-year staff backlog and the "glacial pace of BIA title searches" as a limit on economic development activities within reservation boundaries).

[38]   ACCESS TO CAPITAL, *supra* n. 30, at 62.

[39]   *See* Cobell v. Salazar, 573 F.3d 808, 809 (D.C. Cir. 2009); Armen H. Merjian, *An Unbroken Chain of Injustice: The Dawes Act, Native American Trusts, and* Cobell v. Salazar, 46 GONZ. L. REV. 609 (2011) (detailing history of *Cobell* litigation and its ultimate settlement).

[40]   *See, e.g.,* Matthew B. Krepps, *Can Tribes Manage Their Own Resources? The 638 Program and American Indian Forestry,* in WHAT CAN TRIBES DO? STRATEGIES AND INSTITUTIONS IN AMERICAN INDIAN ECONOMIC DEVELOPMENT 182 (Stephen Cornell & Joseph P. Kalt eds., 1992); Shoemaker, *supra* n. 12.

[41]   *E.g.,* ACCESS TO CAPITAL, *supra* n. 30, at 52; *see also* Judith V. Royster, *Practical Sovereignty, Political Sovereignty, and the Indian Tribal Energy Development and Self-Determination Act,* 12 LEWIS & CLARK L. REV. 1065, 1069–70 (2008).

D Group Rights

For the promotion of private sector economies in particular, the initial allocation of resources in Indian Country can also be a challenge. The vast majority of trust lands within the United States are owned directly by tribal governments, with only 11 million of the approximately 56 million trust acres held by individuals. This number may be further decreasing because of an ongoing $1.9 billion effort to buy back from willing sellers individual co-ownership interests and consolidate them into tribal ownership.[42]

The pervasiveness of tribal ownership has caused some to complain that land is inefficiently held in "common" ownership. This is not quite accurate. Tribal resources are not an unorganized open-access commons but rather are managed and regulated through governmental institutions – the federal government as trustee of the underlying title and the tribal government as owner and, to varying degrees, also sovereign. But to the extent any individual entrepreneur wants to conduct business on, use, or locate on tribal lands, some governmental permission or rights transfer is required. This can occur in numerous forms – from customary use rights to assignments, permits, or leases – but this is one step that always has to be navigated.[43] In addition, to the extent the tribe allocates tribal rights to an individual, federal limits on the subsequent transferability of those allocated interests persist, limiting the flexibility and in some cases value of the transferred subinterest.[44] Nonetheless, with strategic and creative action, tribal governments can continue to push boundaries to reduce entry costs and get land rights allocated, as appropriate, to entrepreneurial individuals more quickly and flexibly, pursuant to tribal economic visions.

For example, tribal governments can quickly and strategically use specific subcategories of land interests (like assignments, permits, and certain corporate assets) that have recently been removed from some federal oversight,[45] make their own direct allocations of any tribally owned fee interests, and otherwise prioritize beneficial, entrepreneurial land uses through their own land management policies, which the BIA is often obliged to enforce.[46]

E Tax and Tribal Revenue Issues

The reality of the trust status means that tribal government efforts to secure revenue from traditional government sources such as property tax are often not realistic, and

---

[42] *See* Buy-Back Plan, *supra* n. 17, at 1.

[43] *See* Miller, *supra* n. 32, at 802–06.

[44] Chemehuevi, 767 F.3d at 906; *see supra* Part II.A.

[45] E.g., 25 C.F.R. § 84.004 (2018) (listing limited class of encumbrances permitted on tribal lands without Secretarial approval); 25 C.F.R. § 162.207(a) (2018) (discussing tribal land assignments).

[46] 25 U.S.C. § 3712 (2012) (provision of American Indian Agricultural Resource Management Act of 1993 that requires BIA to abide by tribal management priorities on all Indian-owned agricultural lands, allowing tribes to give preference to individual Indian users in ways that can be creatively designed to support individual Indians' own agricultural endeavors).

in some cases private entrepreneurs in Indian Country face the unique (and invest-
ment-deterring) risk of dual taxation from both state and tribal authorities.[47] This puts
tribal governments in a bind as tax revenues are often needed for numerous projects,
including the ambitious task of rebuilding fundamental land-based institutions. After
years of this complexity, rebuilding new tribal property institutions – such as tribal
recording systems for nontrust interests, planning departments, and effective mechanisms for resolving landowner disputes and conflicts – is highly expensive and requires
significant capacity but is also incredibly important for the larger project of creating
a stable, efficient landscape for future land-based decision-making and, in some cases,
entrepreneurship. Tribal governments have to navigate these issues carefully.

F Individual Co-Ownership Limits

For individual Indian entrepreneurs, the roughly 11 million acres of individual trust
allotments that remain within reservation territories should in theory be a significant
resource for the development of private sector economies, but the specific property rules
that govern these properties are also uniquely difficult for entrepreneurship. To begin,
for complex historical reasons, many of those allotted lands are now in a fractionated or
shared ownership state. The average individual trust allotment has more than thirty-one
co-owners,[48] and even in the best circumstances, this high degree of co-ownership (or
fractionation) creates coordination challenges that can reduce the value of these assets.
To the extent co-owners' consent or agreement must be assembled for unified actions
involving these lands, this is a significant barrier to secure land uses.

More generally, the federal government's special rules for allotted land uses
are even more restrictive in challenging ways. Outside of a reservation, any individual
co-owner of jointly owned fee-simple property could make direct use and possession
of their own land as a primary incident of their undivided co-ownership and use
these possession rights for informal access to important spaces for entrepreneurial
activity.[49] Individual Indian co-owners of allotments, however, are uniquely
restricted and cannot make direct use or possess of their own property without
a formal, BIA-approved lease from their co-owners. This means that even individual
Indian co-owners must navigate the federal bureaucracy and pay fair market value rent
for their possession of their own land, regardless of whether their other co-owners have
actually asserted any interest in making use of the land themselves.[50]

---

[47] *See* ACCESS TO CAPITAL, *supra* n. 30, at 38 (describing tribal governments' opportunities and challenges
in developing tax revenue potentials); Erik M. Jensen, *Taxation and Doing Business in Indian
Country*, 60 ME. L. REV. 1, 3 (2008) (exploring overlapping tax authorities in Indian Country and
discussing impacts on tribal economies).

[48] *See* BUY-BACK PLAN, *supra* n. 17, at 6 (providing fractionation data as of November 2012).

[49] *See generally* 7 RICHARD R. POWELL, POWELL ON REAL PROPERTY §§ 50.01[1], 50.03[1][a] (Michael Allan
Wolf ed., 2013).

[50] 25 C.F.R. § 162.005 (2018); *see also* Goodwin v. Pac. Reg'l Dir., Bureau of Indian Affairs, 60 I.B.I.A. 46,
47 (2015) (holding Indian co-owner in trespass for possession of her own allotment where she failed to

Allotments are predominantly governed and mediated through this encompassing federal regulatory structure, and tribal governments tend to have only limited authority over the basic incidents of Indian ownership of these trust allotments. Although the federal leasing regime is in place because of asserted federal obligations to manage these assets for the best interests of individual owners, more than 60 percent of these jointly owned lands are idle or generating no income, perhaps creating another missed opportunity for more direct individual entrepreneurship.[51] This is one of the most difficult challenges for Indian self-governance and prosperity.[52]

G Complex and Uncertain Governance

Likewise, looking more widely across entire reservation territories, the overall prevalence of jurisdictional complexity and uncertainty is another primary challenge for economic development in Indian Country. This uncertainty takes many forms and often stems from the persistence of so many fundamentally unsettled questions of law (such as who gets to zone where or the scope of any given sovereign's taxing or eminent-domain authority) and the ad hoc nature of most jurisdictional allocations in Indian Country.[53] In numerous property-related domains, tremendous uncertainty characterizes issues including who has what rights to use or possess lands, what those rights mean, and especially how one can enforce those rights or resolve disputes as among the three separate sovereigns and their various institutional arrangements.

As just one example, consider that even within jointly owned allotments today, co-owners now frequently own undivided interests in the same land in different tenure statuses – so one co-owner may own one share of the land in trust, the tribe may own a share in tribal trust status, and others may own the rest of the undivided interests in the land in state-regulated fee. This mixed-tenure ownership (or emulsified) status creates co-owners with incongruent rights to each other, defined by different jurisdictions, and with no single tribunal with unified jurisdiction over all interests to resolve disputes, partition interests, or navigate incongruences.[54] As another example, consider the fact that within reservation spaces permanent improvements on trust lands are uniquely classified as personal property in fee, while the underlying land is held in trust. This means that in

---

receive permission from co-owners or BIA and failed to pay rent for that possession of her own property); Shoemaker, *supra* n. 18.

[51] *See* BUY-BACK PLAN, *supra* n. 17, at 6–7; *see also* Shoemaker, *supra* n. 18 (discussing these allotment issues in greater detail).

[52] *See* Kevin K. Washburn, *What the Future Holds: The Changing Landscape of Federal Indian Policy*, 130 HARV. L. REV. F. 200, 230–31 (2017).

[53] *See, e.g.*, Peter H. Schuck, *Legal Complexity: Some Causes, Consequences, and Cures*, 42 DUKE L.J. 1, 4 (1992).

[54] *E.g.*, Shoemaker, *supra* n. 16.

Indian Country a house or business structure may be recorded, taxed, probated, and governed by a different jurisdiction with different property-law institutions and rules than the land on which it sits.[55]

The complexity of these "who governs where and what" issues makes legal outcomes difficult to predict, and this uncertainty or ambiguity can increase the costs of any bargain in Indian Country. There is a significant information cost to transacting within reservation spaces, given the uncertainty of how these rights are defined and who governs what.[56] Entrepreneurs must analyze these complex governance questions, often anticipating alternative scenarios based on different possible jurisdictional rules, and this adds to the cost – and potentially the risk – of any transaction in Indian Country.

H Lack of Cultural Fit

Finally, to the extent the modern federal system has been imposed in a top-down way and derived from external sources, a lack of local cultural fit can also have negative consequences for economic development.[57] It is difficult to measure or reach specific conclusions about the degree to which current land tenure systems do "fit" modern Indigenous preferences and cultures. Robert Miller, for example, has articulated in more detail the many instances in which Indigenous legal traditions did historically include private rights to specific resources, whether it be one's personal home or the fruits of a farming enterprise.[58] Nonetheless, the lack of flexible local choice in modern system design – as well as the fundamental lack of cohesive, contiguous tribal jurisdiction across full reservation territories – is a persistent challenge.

III NEXT STEPS: EMBRACING THE ENTREPRENEURIAL SKILL SET AND CHANGING LEGAL LANDSCAPE MORE BOLDLY

Changing something as complicated and deeply entrenched as a land tenure system, especially one that has at least three overlapping layers of governance and includes

---

[55] Indian Trust Management Reform – Implementation of Statutory Changes, 76 Fed. Reg. 7500, 7501 (February. 10, 2011) (codified at 25 C.F.R. pt. 15 (2012)) (describing permanent improvements on trust land as personal property in fee).

[56] *E.g.*, Stewart E. Sterk, *Property Rules, Liability Rules, and Uncertainty About Property Rights*, 106 Mich. L. Rev. 1285, 1288 (2008) (exploring significant information costs as parties seek to translate even clear property rules to concrete applications and determinations of actual scope of rights on the ground); *see also* Abraham Bell & Gideon Parchomovsky, *Property Lost in Translation*, 80 U. Chi. L. Rev. 515, 553 (2013) (identifying "translation costs" imposed whenever multiple discrete property systems must speak across each other, using different norms and languages).

[57] Jamie Baxter, *Storytelling, Social Movements, and the 'Evolution' of Indigenous Land Tenure*, 18 AILR 65, 65 (2014) (collecting sources).

[58] *E.g.*, Robert J. Miller, Reservation "Capitalism": Economic Development in Indian Country 9–23 (2012); Robert J. Miller, *Sovereign Resilience: Reviving Private Sector Economic Institutions in Indian Country*, 2018 BYU L. Rev. (forthcoming 2019) (manuscript at Part III), https://papers.ssrn.com/sol3/papers.cfm?abstract_id=3214206 [hereinafter Miller, *Sovereign Resilience*].

already-allocated private resource rights, is daunting at best. The above discussion of specific property-related obstacles for reservation entrepreneurship, however, immediately reveals several land-specific strategies that tribal governments can deploy (and many are deploying) even within current frameworks to create more flexible opportunities for innovative entrepreneurial action. These include tribal strategies to expedite direct allocations of tribal land use rights to individual entrepreneurs[59] and for tribes to take over or even eliminate some federal administrative functions in order to streamline land management procedures as much as possible.[60] Others have also posited that tribal governments might more intentionally use other land authorities – such as existing zoning and planning powers – to create hub-style spaces of concentrated entrepreneurial activity, allowing for targeted investments in physical and technological infrastructure and facilitating innovation through the concentrated energy of multiple entrepreneurs in close physical proximity to each other.[61] Likewise, numerous tribal governments and advocates are taking direct action to support specific local entrepreneurial projects, with creative credit tools, direct grant programs, and creative training and enterprise incubation models.[62]

What this analysis also reaffirms, however, is that some of the most difficult land tenure challenges – including the pattern of uncertain and inconsistent governance across entire reservation spaces, the persistent and pervasive fractionation of individual trust allotments, and the inability of tribal governments to more fully reflect a range of social and cultural values across entire reservation landscapes – are not amenable to simple solutions. Ultimately, the entire system needs to be rebuilt, and a long-term process of tribal governments recovering, and sustaining, complete and cohesive property governance systems across entire reservation spaces is fully possible, though difficult.[63] At their best, property law and norms are adaptive and respond, iteratively and over time, to evolving land ethics and resource demands. Numerous specific, on-the-ground, resource-related interactions lead to an essential accumulation of local knowledge that is ultimately translated to congruent legal change.[64]

One of the greatest challenges of reservation property systems, however, has been the prescriptive top-down way in which federal property rules have been overlaid on reservation territories and, to the extent tribal self-governance has been promoted, it has been forced through similarly regimented and categorical decision-making. Reservation property systems have lost a lot of the kind of flexible local innovation

---

[59] *See supra* nn. 45–46 and accompanying text.
[60] *See supra* nn. 35, 40–41 and accompanying text.
[61] *See generally* Miller, *Sovereign Resilience, supra* n. 58, at 34–37.
[62] *See, e.g., supra* nn. 30–31 and accompanying text.
[63] This is a big claim. I support it in much more detail in the articles cited at footnotes 7 and 12.
[64] *See, e.g.,* Yun-chien Chang & Richard A. Epstein, *Introduction to Spontaneous Order and Emergence of New Systems of Property,* 100 Iowa L. Rev. 2249 (2015); Eduardo Moises Penalver & Sonia K. Katyal, Property Outlaws: How Squatters, Pirates, and Protesters Improve the Law of Ownership (2010).

and experimentation that characterizes the most vibrant property systems. Instead, reservation property regimes are highly formalized and rigid when it comes to trust property and a murky mess almost everywhere else.

Ultimately, this is a cue for entrepreneurs. The best entrepreneurs are nimble thinkers who can navigate complex systems – and even entrenched institutional barriers – creatively.[65] Successful entrepreneurs tend to possess a unique openness to ambiguity and a willingness (and ability) to manage uncertainty.[66] As a result, entrepreneurs also tend to thrive in environments that allow for flexible decision-making – where the outcomes are not preordained or rigidly defined.[67]

The best hope for getting reservation land tenure systems "un-stuck" may be more bold and ambitious entrepreneurial action – both by tribal governments themselves acting in more entrepreneurial ways and, where possible, by giving entrepreneurs themselves the space to navigate this terrain and imagine new land use landscapes and institutions. Thus, one way to think about the intersection of land tenure and entrepreneurship is not only how land reforms can promote a more flexible ecosystem for creative individual enterprise but also how entrepreneurs can help find (and stretch) the ambiguous spaces where greater reservation-level iterative experimentation and evolution in land tenure itself can occur.[68]

There are many domains of tribal self-governance in which tribal governments are proactively being bold, entrepreneurial actors themselves – filling gaps and pushing boundaries by navigating and even exploiting uncertainty in who governs where in entrepreneurial ways.[69] The same strategies can apply to land reform, and individual entrepreneurs' efforts can help move land reform discussions from prescriptive and abstract to responsive and specific. Focusing on resource challenges in the context of specific entrepreneurial ambitions can help build, through an accumulation of concrete experiences, a much more responsive, strategic, engaged, and participatory agenda for future land reforms. Reservation territories have the potential to become

---

[65]   For example, at least some empirical work shows that reducing transaction costs to enter business enterprises – a step that would logically make entrepreneurship easier and more profitable – has only a modest, if any, effect on overall entrepreneurship and that other psychological and social factors are more significant. *See* Licht, *supra* n. 4, at 854; *see also* Simeon Djankov et al., *The Regulation of Entry*, 117 Q. J. ECON. 1 (2002).

[66]   *See, e.g.,* Licht, *supra* n. 4, at 819, 822 (identifying openness to uncertainty and change as key defining traits of entrepreneurs); *see also* Eyal-Cohen, *supra* n. 23, at 979 ("Entrepreneurs are unique in their ability to handle uncertainties and ambiguous probabilities.").

[67]   *See* D. Gordon Smith & Masako Ueda, *Law & Entrepreneurship: Do Courts Matter?*, 1 ENTREPRENEURIAL BUS. L.J. 353 (2006) (finding better entrepreneurial activity in common-law than civil-law countries and conjecturing that more frequent modification of law through judicial intervention encourages entrepreneurship); *see also* Eyal-Cohen, *supra* n. 23, at 958 (exploring the paradox that law imposes order when entrepreneurs most need autonomy and flexibility).

[68]   *See also* Srinivas Sridharan et al., *Transformative Subsistence Entrepreneurship: A Study in India*, J. MACROMARKETING 1–19 (2014) (exploring other dimensions of transformative change that can be achieved by community-minded entrepreneurs).

[69]   For a discussion of these kinds of strategies, *see, e.g.,* Lance Morgan, *The Rise of Tribes and the Fall of Federal Indian Law*, 49 ARIZ. ST. L.J. 115 (2017).

important laboratories of new property system designs, and what this process needs most are brave local actors creating space for innovation and creativity and, over time, helping to accumulate emergent land use models that can be translated into more formalized legal change. Promoting individual entrepreneurs through a range of policy mechanisms – including land tenure policies but also other supports[70] – may do as much to diversify reservation economies as it does to the complementary project of rebuilding local tribal land governance regimes.

---

[70] For example, although real property is important, other legal spheres shape economies too, including tax, financial regulation, contracts, torts, and education. *See* Zoltan J. Acs & Laszlo Szerb, *Entrepreneurship, Economic Growth and Public Policy*, 28 SMALL BUS. ECON. 109, 113–16 (2007).

4

Right-Sizing Use Rights: Navajo Land, Bureaucracy, and Home

Ezra Rosser

I INTRODUCTION

The Navajo Nation controls over 17 million acres of land and is larger than the state of West Virginia.[1] Nonetheless, it is difficult for tribal members to find land on which to build a house, much less get formal approval for a homesite. The inability of the Navajo Nation to gain control of reservation land management, coupled with a strong deference to the status quo, is holding back tribal economic growth and hurting tribal members. Ironies abound. Traditionally, Diné (the Navajo word for themselves) land rights were based on, and dependent on, actual use. Today marginal land rights tied to grazing claims effectively block development; families with use rights to tribal trust land are able to freeze out newcomers, exercising a more complete right to exclude than would be the case if the reservation had a functioning land market.

Changing how tribal members think about land and how the tribe governs land will not be easy. The existing structure is built on a long history of trauma and struggle. Prior to their dealings with the United States, the Diné had to defend their lands against incursions and takings by other tribes and by the Spanish. The rise of the United States as a Western military power resulted in the Navajo people's removal from their traditional lands and their "long walk" to imprisonment in 1864. The tribe's triumphant return following the 1868 Treaty of Bosque Redondo underscored the devastating effects of removal and affirmed the deep connection tribal members have to Navajo Country. Though largely spared the devastation of allotment, non-Indian interest in Diné resources would play a significant role in shaping the Navajo Nation over the twentieth century. In 1922, the U.S. Secretary of the Interior created the Navajo Business Council in order to certify U.S. government-negotiated mineral leases on the Navajo reservation. During the New Deal, spurred by concerns about protecting tribal rangeland and reducing erosion, the federal government imposed a system of livestock reduction that stripped Navajo families of considerable wealth and ignored the way sheep, goats, and horses had become part of Diné lifeways and the

---

[1] NAVAJO LAND DEPARTMENT, NAVAJO NATION LANDS AND LEASES (March 13, 2015), www
.dinehbikeyah.org/docs/title/NN_Lands_and_Leases-2016.pdf.

Diné identity.[2] The Diné endured and survived as a people in part by holding fast to their land. Given this history, it is not surprising that the existing structure of land rights has calcified, that land reform proposals face almost visceral opposition, and that the very idea of land reform makes many Diné nervous.

This chapter does not present a fully fleshed out vision of Navajo land reform. As a non-Indian academic who no longer even lives on the reservation, I fear that such a chapter would be both inappropriate and wrongly divorced from the Diné experience. The vision for the future of land management and land rights on the Navajo Nation ultimately must come from the Diné. Non-Indian "experts" and governments have a lengthy history of experimenting with reservation land policy (often with the goal of moving tribal resources into non-Indian hands), which means that even "friendly" advice should be greeted with skepticism. Fortunately, the self-determination era is now in its mature period and, even though tribes and the federal government continue to hold reservation land in joint trust, tribes have considerable power over land regulation. The Navajo Nation today has the power to set its own course.

The goals of this chapter are modest. Using the tribe's 2016 effort to implement a new homesite lease process as a case in point, it aims to show why land reform is necessary on the Navajo reservation and to suggest paths forward for the Navajo Nation government. There will be costs associated with reform, but there are costs to the status quo as well. At present, preferences for grazing and customary use rights unreflective of the relative importance of the wage economy trump the needs of tribal members interested in nonagricultural opportunities. Whether the Diné are able to transition to a more flexible structure of property rights in land will depend on both the vision that elected and community-based Navajo leaders offer and the degree to which there is collective buy-in for transformation. The politics of change, including the question of how to respond to those tribal members who suffer real or perceived losses as a result of change, is fraught and has largely stalled meaningful reform since the 1950s. The chapter concludes by arguing that continuing to put such a heavy thumb on the scale in favor of grazing and customary use rights represents a break from the traditional Diné emphasis on *use* as the basis for, and limitation upon, property rights. By returning to traditional understandings of land rights and by "right-sizing" use rights, the Navajo Nation can reassert its rights over the public domain, freeing up space for economic growth and improving the lives of tribal members who want to make the reservation home.

II COLLECTIVE AND INDIVIDUAL USE RIGHTS

Traditionally, Diné land rights were tied to clustered familial groups and grounded in use. Extended family units herded and farmed together, and land rights were

---

[2] For an excellent history of the tribe's relationship to animals, especially sheep, *see* Marsha Weisiger, Dreaming of Sheep in Navajo Country (2009).

allocated among families in the same area according to their use of land. Land was not held separately from use; land that was not being used was available to others. As a study of Navajo land use observed, "Navajo individual tenure differed from the American capitalist form of private ownership in two ways, both holdovers from communal tenure. Anyone could take land from someone who claimed it but did not use it, and land in general could never be bought or sold."[3] A recent comprehensive report on Navajo land reform by Diné Policy Institute highlighted traditional importance of use, noting, "There was rarely a permanence to any one family's control of land. If a family moved on, another family could move in and occupy the land."[4] Similarly, the Navajo Supreme Court has emphasized that an "aspect of traditional Navajo land tenure is the principle that one must use it or lose it."[5]

In part, this use-based system worked because the tribe was able to release population and resource pressure through raids on ranchers to the east and expansion into unused lands to the west.[6] It also worked because the tribe did not have a central government. Rather than the top-down structure familiar to European American colonizers, Diné governance was diffuse, based on loose affiliations, shared culture and shared beliefs, a common language, and a robust clan system. This is not to suggest, as outsiders might assume, that the tribe was not sovereign or that land use regulation is a foreign concept to the Diné, only that Diné governance was largely local and able to account for changes in land use at the family or clan level.

The tribe's four-year internment at Fort Sumner and negotiated return to the Diné homeland that culminated with the 1868 Treaty helped form a unique Diné identity and provided a foundation for subsequent centralization of authority within the tribe. Following the treaty, the Diné moved onto the new reservation but did not stay there. They spread out, claiming grazing land far removed from the original reservation, which was too small to support the rapidly growing tribe.[7] Through

---

[3] KLARA B. KELLEY & PETER M. WHITELEY, NAVAJOLAND: FAMILY SETTLEMENT AND LAND USE 84 (1989). *See also* LAWRENCE DAVID WEISS, DEVELOPMENT OF CAPITALISM IN THE NAVAJO NATION: A POLITICAL-ECONOMIC HISTORY 29 (1984) ("Land was not a commodity, but rather use was based on a system of traditional use-rights, where the ability to productively use land gave the user de facto control over it."); *Id.* at 32–33 ("Land for grazing and growing crops was not a commodity to be bought and sold. It was used by a family, to be used by others on the basis of reciprocal use agreements in times of visiting or stress, or it could be permanently used by another if the original owner permanently abandoned it for some reason.").

[4] DINÉ POLICY INSTITUTE, LAND REFORM IN THE NAVAJO NATION: POSSIBILITIES OF RENEWAL FOR OUR PEOPLE 8 (2017), http://hooghan.dinecollege.edu/institutes/docs/Land%20Reform%20In%20Navajo%20Nation.pdf.

[5] Begay v. Keedah, 6 Nav. R. 416, 421 (Nav.Sup.Ct.1991).

[6] *See* KLARA B. KELLEY, NAVAJO LAND USE: AN ETHNOARCHAEOLOGICAL STUDY 19 (1986) ("The growing herds of ricos like Narbona perhaps forced not only pobres, but also the ambitious children of ricos, to colonize new land, most of which was to the west.").

[7] *See* ANDREW NEEDHAM, POWERLINES: PHOENIX AND THE MAKING OF THE MODERN SOUTHWEST 43 (2016) ("Sheep also allowed Navajos to mount the most successful response to conquest of any group of Indians in the nineteenth century.").

successive land grants and set-asides, the reservation spread out with them, growing from 3.5 million acres to the current total of 17 million acres.[8] Although from Western eyes this expansion was made possible through the actions and sympathy of Washington, from a Diné perspective, the expansion was the result of Diné assertions of their right to land within their four sacred mountains.

The modern Navajo Nation can be traced to the establishment of the Navajo Business Council in 1922, which as noted, was created by the U.S. government in order to approve reservation oil leases. The council, later known as the Navajo Nation Council, occupied an awkward position between tribal members and the U.S. government. When the Roosevelt administration insisted on livestock reduction, the council reluctantly went along, but when it was time for the Diné people to approve a new form of government put forward by Washington as part of the Indian Reorganization Act, they voiced their dissatisfaction by rejecting the proposal. After World War II, the federal government stepped back from livestock reduction. From that moment to the present, notwithstanding the continued role the federal government plays in directing resources to the tribe and policing selective land use elements, control over small-scale development – farming, grazing, and homesites – largely has been in the hands of the tribal government.

Since the end of livestock reduction, relatively little attention has been paid to routine land governance challenges. Interest in exploiting reservation resources by corporations and by the federal government opened the Navajo Nation to uranium and coal mining. The resulting flow of royalties from mining, as well as from oil and gas leases, fueled the rise of the Navajo Nation's bureaucracy and supported well-paid jobs in Window Rock. When monied outside interests sought access to the rich coal of Black Mesa and made plans to build and operate power plants just off the reservation to serve burgeoning markets in Albuquerque, Las Vegas, Los Angeles, and Phoenix, the U.S. government and the Navajo Nation came together to make it happen.[9] Meanwhile, lower-level problems associated with lengthy title searches, overlapping grazing and customary rights, and limited availability of land for locally focused development festered.

One of the clearest indictors of the need for land reform is the strong linkage between landholding and wealth among the Diné – a linkage that both created and sustained economic inequality among Navajo Nation citizens even as it reversed direction over time. In 1863–64, the Diné were defeated militarily by army units under the leadership of Kit Carson, whose brutal scorched-earth campaign against the Diné in 1863–64 involved burning down crops and orchards and destroying wells. Thousands of tribal members had no choice but to surrender and were forced to march on the Long Walk to Fort Sumner. But the Diné were not totally separated

---

[8] *See* AUBREY W. WILLIAMS, JR., NAVAJO POLITICAL PROCESS 18 (1970).

[9] For an excellent history of the development of power plants on or near the reservation and their role in facilitating the growth of non-Indian cities, *see* ANDREW NEEDHAM, POWERLINES: PHOENIX AND THE MAKING OF THE MODERN SOUTHWEST (2016).

from their traditional homeland. Some families avoided the army by hiding in the Chuska mountain range, while others slipped out of internment at Bosque Redondo. The successful negotiation of the 1868 treaty allowed the Diné to return to their homeland, but their return was not easy. Not only was the federal government slow to deliver promised herd animals to tribal members, but Diné who had managed to evade or escape confinement claimed much of the best grazing land. Nevertheless, many Diné thrived and some families amassed impressive herds. Herd size, land holdings, wealth, and political power were closely linked. Two generations after the Diné people's return to their homeland, Henry Chee Dodge had the most sheep, the biggest individual bank account, and controlled the largest amount of reservation land. Not surprisingly, he became the first Chairman of the Navajo Business Council. Inequality was a fact of Diné life and family wealth was closely tied to familial land holdings.

But just as merchant capitalism undermined feudalism and the security of the landed elite in Europe, so too the wage economy has disrupted the connection between land and inequality in Diné society. Today, formal sector employment, not control over land, is the primary driver of income and wealth among Navajo reservation residents. Grazing permits and herd size still matter, but a job with a mining company or with the Navajo Nation government pays significantly more than a family can make selling their sheep or wool. Diné made a similar rural to urban move that the rest of the United States' population made over the last one hundred years, but for Diné that move often meant leaving their extended families' traditional lands and moving to the towns – Chinle, Kayenta, Shiprock, Tuba City, and Window Rock – that are the reservation equivalent of cities. Financial wealth is concentrated in these towns, especially in Window Rock, but many members of this new Diné elite are land poor; having left their ancestral lands, they have a hard time getting access to even small lots. In contrast, those Diné who still live in remote parts of the reservation often control vast amounts of land but live well below the poverty line. In many cases, these individuals are the parents and grandparents of those who moved to a reservation town or to a border town for career purposes. This inverse relationship between land and inequality suggests there is an opportunity for land reform and that at least a subset of tribal members would support such an effort.

III LAND PRIVATIZATION

Although privatization of land rights is often the prescriptive preference of outsiders – particularly economists – looking at reservations, this "solution" is an ill fit for the Navajo Nation.[10] First, while land privatization can take many forms and need not

---

[10]   For two critical responses to proposals to privatize Indian land as a reservation development strategy, *see* Robert J. Miller, *Sovereign Resilience: Reviving Private Sector Economic Institutions in Indian Country*, 2018 BYU LAW REV. 1331, 1386–97 (2019); Kristen A. Carpenter & Angela R. Riley, *Privatizing the Reservation?*, 71 STAN. L. REV. 791 (2019).

aim to recreate the off-reservation land market, it nonetheless would be a dramatic break from the ways that the Diné traditionally and culturally think of land rights. Second, land privatization could threaten the tribe's continued vitality and the basic survival of very low-income Diné families. Families that for generations have scraped out a livelihood based on subsistence farming and animal husbandry might find it difficult to resist selling their land to access much-needed cash income. It also might be difficult for such families to pay any privatization-associated land taxes, which could jeopardize ongoing ownership even if they did not *choose* to sell the land. Of course, if the price is right and the family is able to transition to the wage economy or start a new business, things could work out – yet the substantial risk remains that privatization writ large would make many families who sold their land or were pushed off their land by taxes even more vulnerable.

The idea that reservations should be broken up and parceled out in fee simple chunks is not new; the federal government imposed a version of privatization during the allotment era, with disastrous consequences for tribes subjected to the policy.[11] By allowing non-Indians to purchase land from Indian allottees and by opening up "surplus" land to non-Indian settlement, allotment significantly reduced tribal land holdings and fundamentally reshaped reservation life.[12] For some tribes, whole areas became predominantly non-Indian, while other tribes were left with checkerboard areas that mixed trust land with land held in fee simple and in other forms.[13] The Navajo Nation largely was spared allotment's devastating effects because non-Indians were less covetous of Diné land at the time and there was recognition that the tribal land base was inadequate given the size of the tribe and the nature of the land.[14]

---

[11] *See* Ezra Rosser, *Anticipating de Soto: Allotment of Indian Reservations and the Dangers of Land-Titling,* in HERNANDO DE SOTO AND PROPERTY IN A MARKET ECONOMY 61–75 (D. Benjamin Barros ed., 2010) (discussing the dangers of land titling in light of allotment).

[12] *See* Judith V. Royster, *The Legacy of Allotment,* 27 ARIZ. ST. L.J. 1 (1995); Ann E. Tweedy, *Unjustifiable Expectations: Laying to Rest the Ghosts of Allotment Era Settlers,* 36 SEATTLE U. L. REV. 129, 133–37 (2012).

[13] For an excellent overview of the complexity of Indian land tenure, which is partially a result of allotment, *see* Jessica A. Shoemaker, *Complexity's Shadow: American Indian Property, Sovereignty, and the Future,* 115 MICH. L. REV. 487 (2017). For more on the U.S. Supreme Court's concerns about checkerboarding, *see* Ezra Rosser, *Protecting Non-Indians from Harm?: The Property Consequences of Indians,* 87 ORE. L. REV. 175 (2008).

[14] *See, e.g.,* LAWRENCE DAVID WEISS, DEVELOPMENT OF CAPITALISM IN THE NAVAJO NATION: A POLITICAL-ECONOMIC HISTORY 61 (1984) ("Given the inadequacy of reservation land for land-extensive stock-raising activity and given the significant population growth of the period, there was a great deal of pressure from the Navajo to expand the reservation. The lack of Anglo mineral claims, homesteaders, and corporate herders in the vicinity in the first few decades after the return made such formal expansion possible."); Jessica A. Shoemaker, *No Sticks in My Bundle: Rethinking the Indian Land Tenure Problem,* 63 KAN. L. REV. 383, 440 (2014) ("For example, the tribes of the arid southwest largely escaped allotment because, in that climate and landscape, federal officials acknowledged that 'tribes such as the Navajo had to live communally to survive,' and '[t]hese nomadic herdsmen who followed the grass and rain could not exist on 80 or even 320 acres.' Therefore, the Navajo today still operate with some of their own indigenous property systems and tenure rules on remaining reservation

At first blush, the creation of limited land markets through the selective privatization of land might appear to be a middle ground between problematic continuation of the status quo and the attendant risks of full-bore privatization. But details matter. The most basic requirement people concerned about possible loss of the tribal land base are likely to agree upon is that that sales only take place between Navajo Nation citizens. This intratribal limitation sounds simple, but given the Navajo Nation's requirement of one-quarter blood quantum for citizenship, it quickly can become complex and require line drawing that either challenges the intratribal limitation on sales or challenges rights held through descent.[15] Consider a child raised on the reservation whose biological parents are a non-Indian and a Navajo Nation citizen with one-quarter blood quantum. Even if the tribal member "owned" the family land under the partial privatization scheme in some sort of "tribal fee" arrangement, should the child be allowed to come into ownership of the land when his or her parents die?

The complexity only increases when details of a partial land privatization structure are considered. Diné families are likely to have quite different experiences of any partial privatization program that takes the form of a right, held by either individuals or families as units, to sell a subset of their traditional use rights. Depending on how the partial alienation right is defined, the amount of land to which families hold rights, and the proximity of salable lands to more developed areas, some families would experience a windfall from privatization not available to differently situated families. A family with extensive grazing or customary use lands allowed to convert a sizeable portion of their holdings – where "a sizeable portion" could be defined either as a large percentage of a family's entire holdings or all acres above a defined amount of land – into tribal fee land could benefit disproportionately. Families holding land within easy commuting distance of border towns or reservation population centers, especially Window Rock, stand to gain the most financially from privatization. Remote agricultural land, even land that has not been destroyed by overgrazing, is likely to be worth only a fraction of the value of land close to formal sector jobs. On the other hand, if privatization is accomplished by a central tribal authority simply "taking" land and then offering it for sale, the costs of

---

lands."); Caleb Michael Bush, Land, Conflict and the "Net of Incorporation": Capitalism's Uneven Expansion into the Navajo Indian Reservation, 1860–2000, at 6 (unpublished PhD diss., Binghamton University, State University of New York, 2005) ("Ultimately, the barren quality was the reason why so much land was given over to the Navajos; such land was not much good for anything, it seemed, so why not give it to the Indians clamoring for more land?"); *Winning the Peace*, in Between Sacred Mountains: Navajo Stories and Lessons from the Land 146 (Sam Bingham et al. eds., 1982) ("How did the Navajo win back in peacetime land that they lost in war? The won it with livestock. Sheep and cattle held land that guns and arrows could not.").

[15]   For a rich history of Navajo blood quantum requirements, *see* Paul Spruhan, *The Origins, Current Status, and Future Prospects of Blood Quantum as the Definition of Membership in the Navajo Nation*, 8 Tribal L.J. 1 (2007).

privatization are likely to fall disproportionately on those families that control larger amounts of land.

Divergence in the benefits and costs across Diné families creates harm that must be taken into account, whatever the theoretical advantages of land privatization. Inattention to the winners and losers of partial privatization not only will reshape the tribe and the Diné community in ways that are not "fair" (to use an English word) and not keeping with "k'e" or "hozho" (to use Navajo concepts of kinship and balance) but also increase the political difficulty of land reform.[16] From a neoclassical economics perspective, changes that increase overall welfare should be made so long as those who benefit from the change can theoretically compensate the losers. Though this principle, the Kaldor-Hicks efficiency criterion, has been questioned by scholars who emphasize societal values not captured by efficiency and by alternative schools of economics, it nonetheless plays a significant role in state and federal policy. Nevertheless, such changes, if made under the banner of land privatization, are not a good fit for the Navajo Nation. As Robert Miller explained in a recent article, land privatization "is not guaranteed to be a better solution than traditional Indian institutions, or even the best solution to economic development issues in Indian country. Moreover, the argument ignores historical and cultural principles."[17]

Though land privatization is likely a nonstarter in most respects, that does not mean that the Navajo Nation is out of options when it comes to land reform. It is beyond the scope of this chapter to explore all facets of land reform, but the homesite lease process is one area where there is considerable space for improvement in how tribal members experience reservation life. The home is the center of family life on and off the reservation, so it is perhaps not surprising that the Navajo Nation's most significant effort in recent years to push land reform came in the form of an effort to modernize and internalize tribal homesite leasing.

IV HOMESITE LEASE REFORM

On October 4, 2016, the Navajo Nation Council approved "Homesite Lease Regulations 2016" (HLR 2016), a bill prepared by the Division of Natural Resources Navajo Land Department. The previous regulations dated from 1993 and an update was sorely needed. According to the findings of the council resolution approving the changes, the amendments "will benefit qualified applicants who are seeking housing assistance and/or utility infrastructure assistance."[18] In part, HLR

---

[16] For a much more complete discussion of the meaning and significance of hozho and k'e, *see* RAY AUSTIN, NAVAJO COURTS AND NAVAJO COMMON LAW: A TRADITION OF TRIBAL SELF-GOVERNANCE (2009).

[17] Miller, Sovereign Resilience, *supra* note 10, at 1391.

[18] Homesite Lease Regulations 2016, Resolution of the Resources and Development Committee of the 23rd Navajo Nation Council—Second Year 2016, "An Action Relating to Resources and Development; Approving the Amendments to the Navajo Nation Homesite Lease Regulations,"

2016 simply memorialized and formalized the sovereign authority under "the Navajo Nation General Leasing Regulations of 2013, which authorizes the Navajo Nation to issue leases, except [M]ineral Leases and Rights-of-way, without the approval of the Secretary [of the Interior]."[19] The ability of the Navajo Nation to "unilaterally issue [l]eases" was confirmed by the Secretary of the Interior under the Navajo Nation Trust Land Leasing Act of 2000, 25 U.S.C. § 415(e).[20] For decades, tribes rightly complained that Bureau of Indian Affairs (BIA) red tape, in particular title search delays, hampered development. Bypassing the BIA is a central feature of HLR 2016 and reflects the extent to which, after more than a century of the federal government exercising a heavy hand, the Navajo Nation now sits in the driver's seat when it comes to land use regulation on the reservation.

At first glance, HLR 2016 does not demand too much from tribal members seeking a homesite lease. Though the regulations provide for a homesite *lease* rather than outright ownership, the monthly rental rate is only $1.00 for a renewable seventy-five-year lease term.[21] HLR 2016 did not include a provision for incremental increases in the rental rate, which presumably would be a good idea when contemplating a seventy-five-year lease agreement between the tribe and tribal members, but it nevertheless cracks open an important door for the tribal government. Ever since the formation of the Navajo Business Council, the bulk of funding for the Navajo Nation government came from royalties from gas, oil, uranium, and coal leases. But the shuttering of the coal-fired power plants on and near the reservation has led to a gradual withdrawal of extractive industry companies from the Navajo Nation. Some mines and power plants are still limping along, but the writing is on the wall.[22] For its own survival, the Navajo Nation needs to find alternative ways of generating revenue. Though $1.00 a month will not do all that much, homesite lease rental payments in the future might play a role similar to that of property taxes in the budgets of off-reservation local governments.

The problem with the homesite lease process envisioned by HLR 2016 is that it fails to recognize the significant limits on the ability of the tribe to implement its provisions – the process is cumbersome, the depth of reservation poverty makes it difficult to tax or collect fees from tribal members, and the process invites political pushback by placing the central government between Diné families and land they have long considered "theirs."

RDCO-74-16, Section One (E). Note: The Homesite Lease Regulations 2016 are available here: www .dinehbikeyah.org/docs/homesite/Homesite_Lease_Regulations_2016.pdf.

[19] Homesite Lease Regulations 2016, *supra* note 18, at § 2.01.

[20] *See* Homesite Lease Regulations 2016, *supra* note 18, at § 1.01.

[21] Homesite Lease Regulations 2016, *supra* note 18, at §§ 6.01, 7.01.

[22] *See* Andrew Curley, "The Navajo Nation's Coal Economy Was Built to Be Exploited," High Country News, June 28, 2017.

In order to help tribal members understand what is required to get a homesite lease, the Land Department prepared a flowchart detailing the steps applicants have to follow.[23] After obtaining the application packet, applicants must:

(1) Contact their Grazing Official / Land Board Member in order to identify the coordinates of the homesite location with a handheld GPS unit and identify grazing permittees with rights over the area for consent of the homesite location.

(2) Submit the completed Homesite Lease (HSL) application with a $30 money order payable to the tribe.

(3) Submit a completed Homesite Biological Clearance Form (HSBCF) so that Navajo Fish and Wildlife can complete the Biological Resource Compliance Form.

(4) Hire a private archaeologist to conduct a cultural investigation that is then sent to the Navajo Heritage & Historical Preservation Department so that a Cultural Resource Compliance Form can be completed.

(5) Hire a certified land surveyor to conduct a legal survey plat of the proposed homesite to be submitted to the Navajo Land Department.

(6) Collect all these forms and send them to the General Land Development Department for Environmental Review.

(7) Submit a completed packet to the Navajo Land Department for review by the department's director on behalf of the Navajo Nation; the packet must include (a) the Homesite Lease; (b) Certificate of Indian Blood (and Marriage License, if applicable); (c) Archaeological Inventory Report Compliance Form; (d) Biological Resource Compliance Form; (e) Cultural Resource Compliance Form; (f) Environmental Review Letter; (g) Certified Legal Survey Plat and TOPO Maps.

(8) If approved, pay $12.00 to the tribe to release the homesite lease to the applicant.

Every step in the process presented above can be justified – environmental reviews are important, archaeological artifacts matter, surveys set the boundaries of the leased land – but the end result is a complex multistage process. For some tribal members, particularly those whose primary language is Navajo and who may not read or write in either English or Navajo, the layers of written submissions that must be given to different offices, sequentially, serve as a significant barrier. As one letter writer noted about HLR 2016, "[s]ubmitting at least 10 forms for clearances by everyone but your mother (oh, wait you need that, too), and waiting up to ten years is not acceptable."[24]

The process is also expensive. While the listed $42 in application and lease-release fees are modest, the fee schedule also includes a $350 resurvey fee, and, for tribal

---

[23] 2017 Homesite Lease NN200RL Flowchart. Note: The list of requirements that follows is also taken from this flowchart with some slight language modifications made for the purpose of readability.

[24] Denee Bix, Letter to the Editor, "A Place to Call Home," Navajo Times, October 20, 2016, https://navajotimes.com/opinion/letters/letters-land-kids-future/.

members who need adjustment to an existing homesite lease, a $1,000 fee for a half-acre adjustment and a $2,000 fee for a full acre adjustment.[25] Additionally, applicants must hire a private archaeologist and a certified land surveyor. Such expenses virtually close the door to obtaining a formally recognized homesite lease on tribal members living at or below the poverty line.

These complexity and cost challenges of HLR 2016's homesite lease process are compounded by practical limits on the Navajo Nation's authority over tribal members. Though the Secretary of the Interior and the Navajo Nation Council agree that the tribe has authority to unilaterally lease trust land, such authority means relatively little if tribal members do not feel bound by land use regulations promulgated by the central tribal government. As *The Navajo Times* reported, "When the five compliance officers for the new home site regulations are hired, they will face a daunting task – enforcing laws that nearly everyone on the Navajo Nation is violating."[26] Resistance to tribal authority need not be overt; a simple belief that the tribe is unlikely to enforce lease regulations against tribal members out of compliance is enough to undermine the tribe's ability to require that people follow the homesite lease process. HLR 2016 is not just about formalizing existing rights; it also imposes costly fines on tribal members for unauthorized improvements. Significantly, HLR 2016 provides for a $200 monthly fine for illegal parking of a trailer or mobile home, and the same hefty fine for storage sheds or corrals constructed without a permit.[27] These fees may make sense in urban areas or even in developing rural areas, but strike against long-standing norms on the reservation, where informal housing abounds (and is even traditional), permits are virtually unheard of, and animals often are kept close to the home. Beyond that, depending on their circumstances and connection to the land, some tribal members may think that having to apply for permission to live on land that has "belonged" to their family for generations is an unfair imposition by Window Rock.

Perhaps not surprisingly, when HLR 2016 was rolled out, it met grassroots resistance. Western Navajo Agency Council pushed back with a resolution that argued that tribal members were neither adequately consulted nor given a meaningful chance to participate.[28] The strongly worded resolution accused the Resources and Development Committee of continuing "a regime of authoritarian paternalistic

---

[25] Homesite Lease Regulations 2016, *supra* note 18, at Exhibit F: Homesite Lease Application Fee; Penalties and Fines Fee Schedule.

[26] Cindy Yurth, "Chapter Officials, Residents Worried About New Home Site Regs," NAVAJO TIMES, August 10, 2017, https://navajotimes.com/reznews/chapter-officials-residents-worried-about-new-home-site-regs/.

[27] *Id.*

[28] Western Navajo Agency Council, "Demanding the Repeal of Amendments to the Navajo Nation Homesite Lease Regulations Approved by the Resources and Development Committee on October 4th, 2016 Via Resolution # RDCO-74-16; Calling upon All Diné Chapters to Jointly Develop a Foundational Document Based on the Principles, Laws and Teachings Embedded in Diné Traditional Fundamental Law on the Use of Diné Bikéyah on Which All Navajo Nation Land Use Laws Must Be Based," Resolution No: WCAC18-03-NB8, March 17, 2018. [Note: I serve as chairman of the board of a nonprofit, Indian Grassroots Support, whose executive director was

policies and laws originally initiated years ago by the federal government to control the Diné ... the central Navajo Nation government has copied and applied this attitude and behavior towards their own people." Western Navajo Agency Council also argued that the Local Governance Act of 1998 requires chapter-level participation in homesite lease approval and the drafting of tribal land use regulations. "Everything here is going against k'e," complained Marvin Chee, an attendee at a homesite lease public hearing.[29]

Part of the pushback the new homesite lease process encountered can be traced to the love/hate relationship the Diné have with their central government. Recent scandals, involving widespread corruption among members of the Navajo Nation Council, raise questions about whether the Navajo Nation is using its funds appropriately.[30] A letter to the editor published by *The Navajo Times* linked HLR 2016 to these problems, asserting that "[t]he current home-site lease regulations are intended to harass and intimidate Diné to force them to pay fees to a greedy and corrupt Navajo Nation government."[31] On the other hand, the tribal government is the largest employer on the reservation and Diné voters so far have seemed willing to reelect politicians proven to have abused their power. Just as voter reactions to dysfunction in Washington, D.C. are divided, so too is Diné opinion about dysfunction in Window Rock.

The Navajo Nation's effort to assert authority and impose order through the new homesite lease process most likely was undertaken for good reasons even if today it is unclear whether the tribe will succeed in imposing a top-down structure. From a planning perspective, it is prohibitively expensive for the tribe to be in a reactionary position constantly. When tribal members drag a trailer to land they choose, place it where they want, and then complain because of poor road maintenance or lack of utilities such as water and electricity, the tribal government is placed in an untenable position. Similarly, in the absence of meaningful land use regulations, when one family builds a compound without permission on land claimed by another family, disputes arise that are needlessly complicated and difficult to resolve. A set of Navajo

consulted in connection with the resolution, but I was not involved in any way in this resolution or in its contents, though other board members did contribute.]

29 Cindy Yurth, "Halona on Homesite Regs: 'We're Going to Use K'e,'" Navajo Times, August 24, 2017, https://navajotimes.com/reznews/halona-on-homesite-regs-were-going-to-use-ke/.

30 For more on the abuse of power and corruption scandals involving the Navajo Nation Council, *see* Ezra Rosser, Exploiting the Fifth World: Navajo Land and Economic Development (forthcoming Univ. of Chicago Press).

31 Western Navajo Agency Council, "Demanding the Repeal of Amendments to the Navajo Nation Homesite Lease Regulations Approved by the Resources and Development Committee on October 4th, 2016 Via Resolution # RDCO-74-16; Calling upon All Diné Chapters to Jointly Develop a Foundational Document Based on the Principles, Laws and Teachings Embedded in Diné Traditional Fundamental Law on the Use of Diné Bikéyah on Which All Navajo Nation Land Use Laws Must Be Based," Resolution No: WCAC18-03-NB8, March 17, 2018. [Note: I serve as chairman of the board of a nonprofit, Indian Grassroots Support, that was consulted in connection with the resolution, but I was not involved in any way in this resolution or in its contents, though other board members did contribute.]

Nation homesite leasing procedures not only furthers tribal sovereignty but, by cutting out the federal government and related BIA red tape, should also speed up the lease approval process.

Off reservation, land use regulation and its attendant permits, fines, and fees are an ordinary part of local governance as it relates to homesite acquisition and home-ownership, and they are arguably a necessary part of tribal governance as well. For its part, the Land Department's hope is to raise enough revenue to pay for five compliance officers, a modest staff given the size of the reservation. HLR 2016 represents a first step down a path of land taxation, a path that may or may not be appropriate given that the Diné are largely unaccustomed to having to make such payments. But as extractive industry royalty funds dry up, the Navajo Nation government arguably has little choice; it must diversify its revenue even if that means moving from taxing large outside corporations to taxing on-reservation activities of tribal members.

V BUREAUCRACY AND CONTROL

Alone, homesite lease regulatory reform will do little to free up land or reallocate unused land. Though traditionally land rights were tied to use, grazing rights today often exist more in theory, or on paper, than in practice. For a variety of reasons – everything from deterioration of the range and the expense of raising animals to changing traditions and the loss of labor as younger family members opt for the wage economy – it is not uncommon that extensive claims to land are not supported by the behavior of the family or families asserting their grazing rights. This is not to suggest that the land has additional carrying capacity – much of the reservation is at risk of further deterioration and desertification – just that some assertions of grazing rights that block newcomers or development, including new homesites, may be based primarily on historical memory and not recent use. For many Diné families, identity and land rights are closely intertwined.

More comprehensive land reform on the Navajo reservation will not be easy. As challenging as homesite lease reform has proven to be, homesite leases are low-hanging fruit compared to grazing and customary use rights. It is beyond the scope of this chapter to explore grazing and customary use rights fully,[32] but homesite leases, land use for small-scale commercial purposes, and grazing rights are all linked. The 2017 comprehensive land reform report published by The Diné Policy Institute, a research entity located within Diné College, makes this clear:

> [W]e voice the collective complaint of everyday Navajo people and speak to our tribal government and elected officials, give us land reform. We need to break up

---

[32]   I am addressing grazing and customary use rights in a forthcoming article that in many ways is a companion to this chapter. *See* Ezra Rosser, *Reclaiming the Navajo Range: Resolving the Conflict Between Grazing Rights and Development*, U. CONN. L. REV. (forthcoming 2019).

the concentration of land from a few users and provide access to all Navajo people. More importantly, we need to move away from the unsustainable permitting system we have inherited (or that was mandated) from the Bureau of Indian Affairs and reclaim sovereignty over our land ... We call for a new permitting system that focuses on the needs of livestock owners and frees up everything else for other forms of development. In the end, we argue for a renewal of Navajo community life through land policy.[33]

In this light, the Navajo Nation's attempt to bring the homesite lease process entirely within the tribe and to establish centrally dictated approval requirements is a natural first move when it comes to land reform.

One way to think about the past two decades of reservation land use reform efforts is as a series of policies that aimed to free up land for development. Of course, when the stakes are high enough, as in the case of large-scale extractive industry and power generation, grazing and customary use rights claims are no barriers to development.[34] But it is often difficult for tribal members who want to engage in smaller scale (including individual) residential and commercial development to find available land that they can obtain a right to use.[35] The Local Governance Act of 1998 (LGA) attempted to solve the problem by explicitly granting broad governance authority, including authority over land, to the Navajo Nation's 110 local chapters. But the transformative potential of the LGA was limited by the requirement that chapters go through an expensive certification process and by the limited administrative capacity of many chapters. In theory a local community could set aside land for development under the LGA, but the politics are complicated. Even for certified chapters, Window Rock retains a significant oversight role. More importantly, chapters tend to be controlled by residents with deep roots in the community who are fiercely protective of their traditional grazing and customary use rights. Kayenta Township, the only reservation town structured as an independent municipality, showed how governance rules can create space for development when it got permission to withdraw more than 3,600 acres of Navajo trust land for the establishment of the township.[36] Kayenta's authority at times is subject to challenges from Window Rock. But even if that were not the case, Kayenta Township has a unique form of governance and local land use control that has not been replicated elsewhere on the reservation.

---

[33] DINÉ POLICY INSTITUTE, LAND REFORM IN THE NAVAJO NATION: POSSIBILITIES OF RENEWAL FOR OUR PEOPLE 6 (2017), http://hooghan.dinecollege.edu/institutes/docs/Land%20Reform%20In%20Navajo%20Nation.pdf.

[34] *See generally* Ezra Rosser, *Ahistorical Indians and Reservation Resources*, 40 ENVTL. L. 437 (2010) (discussing the Navajo Nation's proposed Desert Rock mine-mouth power plant).

[35] *See* ROBERT J. MILLER, RESERVATION "CAPITALISM": ECONOMIC DEVELOPMENT IN INDIAN COUNTRY 121 (2012).

[36] Kayenta Township, Township History, http://kayentatownship-nsn.gov/Home/index.php/2-uncate gorised/14-township-history.

It is up to the Diné to decide for themselves the right balance between local control and centralized land management. What should be uncontroversial is that reform is needed. There are lots of issues (fines, fees, and tribal bureaucratic red tape) with the most recent effort to tackle homesite leasing. Resolving the issues might require moving past HLR 2016. It may be that meaningful reform must begin at the chapter level and then work its way to Window Rock. Or, it may be that until tribal members are presented with a comprehensive land reform package, they will reject piecemeal efforts. But what is certain is that there are significant costs associated with letting the status quo remain unchallenged.

VI CONCLUSION

My own view – which should be discounted and treated with some skepticism because of my outsider status – is that the Navajo Nation needs to find a way to right-size existing grazing and customary use claims as a way to free up land for residential and small-scale commercial development. There is enough land that the tribe need not infringe on the use rights of those Diné families who are actually using their land; simply returning to the idea that land not being used can be claimed by others in the community will go a long way. A heavy-handed way to do this would be to impose a sufficiently high per-acre tax on rangeland, such that tribal members might be conservative when asserting land claims. Such an approach would be controversial and invite a backlash. It may be that that is a price that has to be paid, but I am not convinced such a top-down approach is required. One of the most remarkable things about the Navajo Nation today is the continued vitality of what Charles Wilkinson called "measured separatism," what might colloquially be labeled tribal identity.[37] The Navajo Nation remains overwhelming Diné in ways that are both readily apparent and more subtle. Even though the Navajo Nation Council and the Navajo Nation Supreme Court have battled in recent years over the place of Navajo fundamental law in the courts,[38] reservation life in many ways continues to reflect the importance of connections and mutual interdependence. I have to believe that if those Diné harmed by the high degree of deference given to grazing and customary use rights raise their voices, showing how they are being locked out of homesites and the reservation itself, then collectively the Diné will seek rather than resist land reform.

---

[37] CHARLES F. WILKINSON, AMERICAN INDIANS, TIME, AND THE LAW 22 (1987).
[38] *See* Ezra Rosser, *Displacing the Judiciary: Customary Law and the Threat of a Defensive Tribal Council*, 34 AM. INDIAN L. REV. 379 (2011)

5

Access to Credit in Indian Country: The Promise of Secured Transaction Systems in Creating Strong Economies

Patrice H. Kunesh and Benjamin D. Horowitz

I INTRODUCTION

Access to credit is a cornerstone of market economies. Governments need it to fund infrastructure, consumers require it to purchase goods and services, and entrepreneurs must have it to get their projects off the ground and expand their businesses. The strongest economies rely on a robust credit and recourse system in which multiple lenders compete over customers under a clearly defined set of rules.

The United States' economy is strong and resilient because many of its residents have easy access to affordable credit. Affordable credit, however, is not universally accessible nationwide. In Indian Country, lender misperceptions, compounded by the long shadow of historic legalized discrimination and postcolonial institutions, often resulted in prohibitively expensive or nonexistent credit prospects for aspiring entrepreneurs.

Even still, for two decades, economic growth in Indian Country has outpaced economic growth in the United States.[1] But given the persistent lag in economic well-being between Indian Country and the United States, policymakers at all levels – tribal, local, state, and federal – and lenders of all sizes need to address Indian Country's credit deficit.

While no one tribe can unilaterally reverse the legacy of the past, as sovereign nations with powers of self-governance, tribes do have the power to support and encourage the flow of credit into their communities by creating the legal infrastructure necessary to protect lenders and borrowers in business transactions: a comprehensive secured transaction system (STS).

This chapter examines the history and components of the STS in the United States, developed under the Uniform Commercial Code, and then examines adoption of the Model Tribal Secured Transaction Act in Indian Country. The authors

---

[1] Miriam Jorgensen and Randall K. Q. Akee. 2017. *Access to Capital and Credit in Native Communities: A Data Review*, digital version. Tucson, AZ: Native Nations Institute. nni.arizona.edu/publications-resources/publications/papers/accessing-capital-and-credit-native-communities-data-review.

97

present an argument for the real value and strong impacts that STSs have on improving access to credit in Native communities across the country.

II SECURED LOANS AND SECURED TRANSACTION SYSTEMS: AN OVERVIEW

A *Typical Categories of Credit*

Modern market economies typically feature three types of loans, each characterized by the type of collateral involved. While the focus of this chapter is on secured loans, all three loan types are presented here to highlight the unique features of secured loans.

Unsecured loans do not require any collateral. For example, when a customer swipes their credit card at a retail store, they are rarely required to provide any collateral to the store or their credit card company. If a borrower defaults, the consequences commonly are higher interest rates and fees, as well as low credit ratings. However, the borrower's personal or real property is not at risk.

Collateral reduces lenders' risk by having borrowers provide an interest in real estate or personal property as recourse. Collateral offers some protection to a lender in the case of default, meaning that the lender's recourse is to use the property (e.g., see below on mortgage loans) to recoup the amount owed. In developed market economies, the consequences of default and lenders' resulting rights to collateral are well-defined in law and by contracts.

Mortgage loans use real property as collateral. Real property includes land and the things that are attached to it, like buildings. If a borrower defaults on a mortgage loan, creditors generally can foreclose on the loan and take possession of the land and the building that sits upon it.

Secured loans allow debtors to offer personal property as collateral. Personal property is essentially any property that is not real property. Personal property need not be a physical object. For example, it could be intellectual property, a business's accounts receivable, or licensing rights. Many secured loans made in support of economic development fall under a subcategory of secured loans known as *secured transactions*.

B *Secured Transactions & Consent*

Secured transactions differ from other secured loans for one important reason: the lender–borrower relationship is consensually created. This may not be the case in other secured loans. For example, most state laws in the United States authorize putting a lien on a car once a mechanic begins to work on it, even without the explicit consent of the car's owner. This means that the mechanic's work on the car is securitized by the vehicle until the owner pays the mechanic for the services rendered.

Compare this statutorily created lien to a lien on the same car due to a borrower's outstanding auto loan from a dealership. In the loan scenario, the borrower consented to the lien through a contract creating the lender–borrower relationship. The lending of money by the car dealer through an agreement and secured by the car itself is an example of a secured transaction.

C Secured Transactions: Possessory Interests

Secured transactions create a *security interest* in a borrower's personal property in favor of a creditor. The security interest gives the lender certain rights in the event of a default. There are two types of security interests, possessory and nonpossessory, each defined by who retains control of the property during the contract period.

A *possessory security interest* occurs when the personal property involved is actually given over to the lender to hold until the terms of the agreement are satisfied. Pawn shops are a common venue for creation of a possessory security interest. For example, when Joe takes a piece of jewelry into Mary's Pawn Shop to acquire money to start up his business, the two agree on terms of repayment. If Joe fails to repay the loan on those terms, Mary may be entitled to sell Joe's jewelry to offset the loan balance. When Mary sells Joe's jewelry, she would have to pay him any proceeds from the sale that exceed the loan balance.

More common in the marketplace are secured transactions involving a *nonpossessory security interest*. Such transactions occur when a borrower retains possession and use of their collateral. Suppose Joe needed cash to offset a temporary reduction in operating revenue at his leatherworking shop. Joe approaches Mary's bank and takes out a loan, offering some of his tools and supply of raw materials as collateral.

Joe maintains ownership of his tools and materials, allowing his business to continue making money as he repays his loan. If he fails to repay his debt, Mary's bank may take the collateral and sell it. In that event, as with possessory security interests, the bank would be required to pay Joe proceeds from the sale beyond the remaining balance of the loan.

III COMPONENTS OF SECURED TRANSACTION SYSTEMS

In modern economies, secured transactions are facilitated by tripartite *secured transaction systems*. The three key components are: (1) a system of laws that establishes reasonably similar rules across jurisdictions; (2) a reliable and transparent lien filing system; and (3) mechanisms for resolving contract disputes. This chapter discusses STS components and manifestations in the United States and in Indian Country.

A Secured Transaction Laws

When two consenting parties agree to a secured loan, the rules governing the transaction are defined by the relevant jurisdiction's *secured transaction laws*. These laws establish a standardized framework for interactions between creditors and debtors. Secured transaction laws govern:

- how borrowers may give a security interest in collateral;
- lenders' rights relative to third parties, like other lenders;
- remedies available to lenders in cases of borrower default; and
- protections available to borrowers, ensuring lenders' remedies are fairly applied.

B   Lien Filing Systems

After the parties create a contract secured by collateral (a secured transaction), they file it with a public agent in a central registry who then records it within a searchable database. This filing accomplishes two main objectives. It puts the world on notice of the lien, establishing the time of filing for priority purposes (i.e., whether this lender's interest in the collateral occurred before or after another lender's interest in the same collateral). The filing also enables lenders to research potential new borrowers to determine the borrower's preexisting secured indebtedness to other parties. Recording the collateral secured by the contract in a central registry is vital to efficient dispute resolution, particularly when a borrower defaults after creating multiple security interests in a single piece of personal property.

C Contract Enforcement Mechanisms

In addition to the terms of a contract, secured transaction laws lay out the recourse accorded to the lender in the event of a loan default, as well as the protections a borrower has against their creditor. The laws would not be very effective, however, without a broader system to adjudicate disputes and ensure that remedies are available to both borrowers and creditors. Such a system includes a forum for dispute resolution, typically a court with impartial judges to resolve contractual disputes and remedies for enforcing these decisions, such as recourse to the collateral. To be most effective and facilitate the course of business, this judicial and enforcement system must be accessible, timely, and consistent.

IV MARKET BENEFITS OF SECURED TRANSACTION SYSTEMS

Interest rates associated with a loan reflect a combination of factors, including perceived risks to the lender and the degree of loan market competition. When secured transaction laws are reasonably standardized across jurisdictions, transaction costs are lowered because lenders need not invest time in learning different systems. In addition, a comprehensive STS provides lenders with clear options for recourse, allowing lenders to better manage their risk and resulting in more favorable terms for borrowers. In a competitive lending market, the lower cost and risk that lenders face as a result of an STS tends to lead to better loan terms for borrowers.

Importantly, STSs provide more certainty for lenders that disputes between a creditor and a debtor will be resolved quickly and predictably. This is particularly important when personal property is involved in a loan – personal property is often mobile and subject to rapid deterioration as compared to real property.

In addition to increasing the efficiency of conflict resolution, establishing a system for enforcing remedies and recourse enhances the likelihood that the terms of a contract with a debtor will be satisfied. For example, in the United States, lenders know that a transparent, impartial judicial system is available to adjudicate any disputes and, furthermore, that those court rulings and decrees will be honored when necessary.

Research suggests that even the seemingly simple service provided by a lien filing system can have a large impact on access to credit for small firms. For example, a 2013 World Bank study of seventy-three countries found that the introduction of a lien filing system increased the share of businesses with access to credit by eight percentage points. After a country introduced a lien filing system, credit also became cheaper – interest rates tended to decline while their repayment period increased. Small enterprises appeared to benefit more than large ones. The study further suggests that giving lenders information about their potential clients greatly increases their ability to gauge the riskiness of a loan.[2]

In the international arena, Albania offers one example on the potential impact of STS implementation. After passing a new collateral law and creating a collateral registry, the interest rate for loans went down by five percentage points, and the interest rate spread between loans and deposits decreased by more than 40 percent.[3]

---

[2] Inessa Love, María Soledad Martínez Pería, Sandeep Singh. 2013. Collateral Registries for Movable Assets: Does Their Introduction Spur Firms' Access to Bank Finance? Policy Research Working Paper No. 6477. Washington, DC: World Bank. https://openknowledge.worldbank.org/handle/10986/15839.

[3] Fintrac, Inc. 2013. State of the Evidence: Finance and Movable Collateral. Washington, DC: USAID. http://eatproject.org/docs/State_of_the_Evidence_Finance_Movable_Collateralz.pdf.

V SECURED TRANSACTION SYSTEMS IN THE UNITED STATES

A *Developing Standard Secured Transaction Laws Across the States*

In the United States, the system of secured transaction laws is determined mainly by state governments. As recently as the middle of the twentieth century, states operated under significantly different secured transaction laws. Advocates for a more unified system argued that the patchwork of secured transaction laws limited the nation from reaching its full economic potential.

State lawmakers began to worry that the federal government would intervene in secured transaction law, reducing the power of state legislatures. They began working with the Uniform Law Commission (ULC), a nonprofit association made up of lawyers and judges whose aim is to harmonize laws across the states, to devise a solution.

The ULC organized the National Conference of Commissioners on Uniform State Law (NCCUSL). Members of the NCCUSL spent more than a decade developing a legal framework for secured transactions that would prove amenable to state legislators and business leaders alike. The end result was the Uniform Commercial Code (UCC).

The UCC creates rules that cover everything from warehouse receipts to commercial leases. Article 9 of the UCC covers secured transactions. Fourteen years after its drafting, the UCC had been adopted by every state in the United States. Puerto Rico and the U.S. Virgin Islands also operate under the UCC.

Each jurisdiction adapted the UCC to meet its particular legal and cultural needs. Rather than creating identical laws in every state and territory, the UCC sets up certain reasonably similar expectations for lenders within each jurisdiction. Because governments' modifications did not stray from certain core principles, policymakers are able to meet the needs of their constituents while providing a predictable business environment for transactions made across political boundaries.

The UCC is not a static set of laws. Periodically, the ULC reviews the code and reflects on any unintended consequences from prior versions as well as any perceived new needs for businesses, creditors, borrowers, or consumers. Revisions are proposed and scrutinized by a committee of practitioners and academics and then the code is formally updated. State lawmakers follow suit by reviewing and updating their own laws to reflect the suggested changes from the UCC.

VI SECURED TRANSACTION SYSTEMS IN INDIAN COUNTRY

Ready access to secured transaction laws and the recording system is vital to the strength of the marketplace and flow of business. State secured transaction laws can be found on their legislative websites. Many tribal legal codes and laws, however, are not publicly available. Of the 573 federally recognized tribes, a large number have adopted some form of a commercial or business code, but how many have adopted a secured transaction law is unknown. Also unavailable is the range of remedies and recourse available to lenders and borrowers through a tribal judicial system. Without a publicly available resource to access tribal laws, court decisions, and recordings, STSs in Indian Country fail to achieve their full potential for spurring economic development.

If a tribe has not enacted an STS, credit can still be extended, but it will come with higher transaction costs. Furthermore, the absence of a court system and governing law lead lenders to perceive greater risk and unobtainable recourse. These factors result in higher interest rates and less advantageous loan terms for borrowers. The lack of an established STS also may lead to a denial of credit altogether.

For example, when an STS is in place, often all that is needed to establish an enforceable secured transaction is a boilerplate contract. Behind that contract is the secured transaction law of that particular jurisdiction that delineates the consequences in the event of borrower default or lender fraud. Without the backdrop of an STS, the parties instead must come to an agreement on a wide range of circumstances and consequences. A contract must delineate process and procedures to resolve issues surrounding a potential default and spell out the steps to obtain adequate recourse, such as repossession of the goods or equipment. This scenario makes the transaction more complicated and requires more due diligence, ultimately increasing the contract's cost. The burden falls heavily on smaller businesses, since the costs of contract writing tend to be relatively fixed (i.e., the same for big or small loans) and thus difficult to absorb in the case of a small loan.

In Indian Country, many Native American businesses and consumers have difficulty getting affordable credit. Tribal governments can help address this capital deficit by enacting laws and establishing remedies that address the perception of greater risks and unobtainable recourse – the two most challenging issues to attracting capital and credit in their communities. Indeed, some scholars have argued that STSs may be more important in Indian Country than elsewhere, particularly due to the difficulties Native communities face in using real estate as collateral. Not only is trust land difficult to use as collateral, but reservation lands may not be valued as high as fee land.[4]

Data clearly support the need for increased access to credit in Indian Country. Native American entrepreneurs are more likely to rely on credit cards to finance their start-ups and less likely to use bank financing.[5] A recent survey of Native

[4] Miriam Jorgensen. 2016. Access to Capital and Credit in Native Communities. Tucson, AZ: Native Nations Institute. https://nni.arizona.edu/application/files/8914/6386/8578/Accessing_Capital_and_Credit_in_Native_Communities.pdf.

[5] Miriam Jorgensen and Randall K. Q. Akee. 2017. Access to Capital and Credit in Native Communities: A Data Review, digital version. Tucson, AZ: Native Nations Institute. nni.arizona.edu/publications-resources/publications/papers/accessing-capital-and-credit-native-communities-data-review.

American Community Development Financial Institutions found that demand for credit within the communities they served was significantly greater than they could meet.[6] And anecdotes from Indian Country economic development practitioners abound: when lenders do show an interest in lending to Native-owned businesses, they frequently offer terms at higher rates and lower repayment periods than they offer off the reservation.

The rest of this section details efforts to adapt the three parts of an STS to fit the needs and circumstances of Indian Country.

A *Secured Transaction Laws in Indian Country*

In 2001, recognizing the need for increased access to credit in Indian Country, the ULC tasked the Committee on Liaison with Native American Tribes with drafting a model tribal secured transaction act (MTSTA) that could more easily be adopted by tribes across the country. While some tribes had enacted commercial codes or adopted state secured transaction laws, the MTSTA would offer the broad secured transaction framework familiar to most lenders. It would also provide a model that tribes could adapt to their own needs.

Several tribes contributed to the MTSTA's drafting over the next three years. These included the Sac and Fox, Cherokee, Navajo, Chitimacha, Oneida, Chickasaw, and Crow nations, the Confederated Tribes of Warm Springs, the Little Traverse Bay Bands of Odawa Indians, and several California rancherias.[7] The result of these efforts was the MTSTA and an accompanying Implementation Guide. Several years later, owing to the changes in the ULC, the ULC again convened an advisory group to update the MTSTA and bring it into conformity with changes to the UCC's Article 9. These changes were finalized in 2017, along with an updated Implementation Guide.

The MTSTA addresses an array of lending and business issues concerning tribal and reservation transactions. Many of the early tribal secured transaction laws applied only to dealings with tribal governments or tribally owned enterprises. At the height of gaming development, most tribes had developed some form of lender recourse system for their financing of casino facilities. However, laws that pertain only to tribally owned businesses are inadequate to be considered as a complete secured transaction system. Such laws do not address the entire needs of the community's private economy or provide for the recourse needed for individual transactions. Likewise, tribal laws that replicate state law without consideration for

---

[6] Michou Kokodoko. 2017. Findings from the 2017 Native CDFI Survey: Industry Opportunities and Limitations. Federal Reserve Bank of Minneapolis. www.minneapolisfed.org/indiancountry/research-and-articles/cicd-working-paper-series/findings-from-the-2017-native-cdfi-survey-industry-opportunities-and-limitations.

[7] National Conference of Commissioners on Uniform State Laws. 2005. Implementation Guide and Commentary to the Model Tribal Secured Transactions Act. Chicago, IL. www.uniformlaws.org/.

unique tribal institutions are insufficient because they lack an essential imprimatur of tribal culture and values. Thus, tribes should consider establishing a tribally appropriate legal system for contract enforcement that covers all entities doing business on the reservation.

In drafting a model law for Indian Country, committee members did their best to balance the strengths of the standard UCC with key concerns raised by the tribes. Some ways in which the standard secured transaction law has been modified to better address the unique needs of Indian Country are discussed below.

B Repossession

Under Article 9 of the UCC, lenders are permitted to unilaterally take possession of collateral if a borrower fails to meet the terms of their contract and if repossession does not threaten the law and order of the community. For example, if someone fails to repay their car loan, a lender can repossess the car and tow it away so long as there is a reasonable expectation that doing so will not result in a violent confrontation or be contested by the borrower.

Several tribes expressed concerns about permitting this approach to repossession in their communities.

One of the most important roles of tribes as sovereign governments is to maintain public safety within their communities, much of which involves controlling entry onto the reservation. Allowing lenders access to the reservation to repossess a car without setting up a forum for tribal borrowers to receive adequate notice from a lender and have an opportunity to offer a cure could raise public safety concerns. It also could implicate fair treatment of tribal citizens by lenders.

With these issues of sovereignty and safety in mind, the MTSTA was drafted so that a tribe could elect to permit lenders to repossess their collateral only by processing their claim through the tribe's legal system. By doing so, the MTSTA makes it more likely that the goals of the UCC in protecting borrowers are met – that is, that lenders will be required to provide adequate notice of default to a borrower, and that a borrower will be allowed an opportunity to be heard and offer a cure for their default. It also recognizes the sovereign authority and jurisdiction of tribes over activities on their reservations.

C Artisans and Consignment

Many artisans supply their wares to stores without receiving payment in advance. When an artisan's goods are sold, the store then passes some of the revenue along to the artisan; if a good goes unsold, it is returned to its maker. This arrangement constitutes a type of secured transaction called consignment.

Article 9 requires artists to file a secured transaction when they give their goods to a store if the value of the goods exceeds a certain amount. This requirement is intended as a protection for the artisan. For example, suppose Kim provides $5,000 worth of beadwork to Joe's art gallery on consignment. Joe hits hard times and takes out a loan from a bank for operating capital, offering up his gallery's inventory as collateral. If Joe fails to fulfill the terms of his loan, and the bank moves to repossess his inventory, Kim's art is at risk. A secured transaction filing by Kim will give her standing to repossess her inventory rather than the bank. Kim also would have this right if her goods were valued at less than the amount required for a lien filing under a jurisdiction's secured transaction law, but would not need a secured transaction filing to exercise this right.

During the drafting of the MTSTA, several tribes commented on the particular importance of consignment options for many tribal members. Native arts and crafts can represent a significant source of income for members of many tribes, both as primary and supplementary income. Tribal leaders were concerned that if the MTSTA were adopted by a tribe with the same limits as in the UCC, such as requiring a lien filing for relatively low consignment amounts, many artisans would be unaware of the new rules and be exposed to having their goods repossessed by a lender who had an interest in the inventory of another vendor. Artisans would need time and education to adapt to the new system. As a result, the MTSTA allows tribes to set a higher threshold for filing a secured transaction in a consignment.

D   Limiting Allowable Personal Property as Collateral (Sacred Objects)

Another important issue raised during the drafting of the MTSTA concerned sacred cultural objects that could be used by individual tribal members as collateral. These objects generally are considered cultural patrimony, including human remains and funerary objects. Such objects possess unique and enduring cultural, traditional, or historical importance to a tribe.

American Indian and Alaska Native peoples have a substantial interest in protecting, accessing, and controlling their cultural resources. Access to and usage of these cultural resources are integral to the preservation of Native lifeways. Many of these resources may be protected by tribal, state, or federal laws; however, some are not. Native peoples have a significant interest in ensuring not only that their laws protect tribal culture, but also that new laws and policies are geared toward safeguarding and sustaining tribal culture as well.

Thus, although the ULC ultimately determined that the complexity of this subject is ill-suited to the boilerplate language of the MTSTA, the Implementation Guide suggests that tribal governments address cultural patrimony explicitly when adapting the MTSTA to fit their tribe's needs, including definitions of that tribe's cultural patrimony and sacred objects. Taking this lead, some tribes have adopted secured transaction laws that explicitly prohibit the use of cultural patrimony and sacred objects as collateral.

Tribes also can use secured transaction laws to spell out what will happen when cultural practices result in the exchange of personal property. For example, in some tribes, major life events or celebrations feature potlatches and giveaways, ceremonies in which a host distributes personal property to other members of their tribe or community. If the personal property given away is being used as collateral in a secured transaction, lenders and borrowers could both be put at risk. Tribes can lay out the rules for such transactions in their secured transaction laws.

In addition, tribes may decide to prevent their members from assigning security interests in other sensitive property interests. For example, per capita distributions from settlements or gaming revenue often are targeted for use as collateral or a guarantee of repayment. Per capita payments can be a onetime event or an ongoing source of income. For a host of policy reasons, a tribe may wish to limit the ability to assign per capita distributions. These reasons range from the legal understanding that per capita payments are a mere aspiration rather than a firm expectation (based on business performance), to protecting community members from unfair lending practices.

E Tribal Laws Impacting Secured Transactions

It is highly advisable for tribes to review their current laws and resolutions to determine whether any would potentially conflict or duplicate the MTSTA before adoption. Conflicting laws create confusion and could nullify important provisions. Duplications in law and processes should be clarified and organized into a coherent code or provision.

F Lien Filing Systems and Indian Country

Every state in the United States has developed a searchable database to record liens filed within its jurisdiction. Rather than duplicating the investment and work of state governments, tribal governments can avail themselves of an established and trusted system by entering into contracts with state governments to host liens filed on a reservation. The cost of such an arrangement could be on a per-filing fee basis, likely costing much less than creating a specialized local filing system.

Filing systems raise additional considerations. The UCC requires secured transactions to be filed in the state of an individual's principal residence. For businesses, the UCC requires secured transactions to be filed in the state where the company is legally formed. Tribes that adopt the MTSTA typically contract with the state within which they are geographically located to use the state lien system. Reservations that span more than one state may require dual state filing. Notwithstanding cost issues, tribal sovereignty and self-determination may factor into the consideration of developing a tribal lien system. The MTSTA addressed this issue by recognizing that tribes are the most appropriate authority to determine the appropriate filing system for transactions involving their members who reside within the reservation. Since any change from the state system has the potential to complicate the transaction for lenders, it is crucial that the tribe publish its laws and clearly articulate its filing processes, as well as those for remedies and recourse. As long as a tribe's laws and lenders' filings are readily accessible, lenders should be able to adapt their search processes to ensure they are finding any preexisting secured transactions for credit applicants.

G Tribal Enforcement of Secured Transactions

As sovereign nations, tribal leaders further need to consider their judicial and law enforcement systems along with the enactment of secured transaction laws.

1 Availability of Tribal Laws and Codes

Commercial transactions on a reservation are civil actions that generally fall under the jurisdiction of the tribe. Public accessibility to tribal law and court decisions is critical to the full expression of sovereignty, particularly when dealing with inter-jurisdictional issues such as secured transactions. According to the nonprofit Tribal Law and Policy Institute, about sixty tribes have published at least some of their courts' decisions online. About 140 tribes post their codes and laws online. Even though publicly available, these laws may not be updated on a regular basis, so due diligence with the tribe is imperative.[8]

Obviously, enacting a secured transaction law, or other complementary laws, without making such available to the general public will frustrate the tribe's goal of realizing a robust legal system. Lenders are unlikely to know what laws exist, what remedies are available, and what forum in which to seek redress on a nonperforming loan. The considerable uncertainty about tribal laws and judicial processes not only raises the cost of capital to Indian Country, but it discourages lending as well. To strengthen their legal systems and attract capital, tribes should consider establishing a system for publishing their laws and court decisions, and making them accessible for general reference and research.

2 Complementary Uniform Business Laws

The MTSTA is a robust law that defines the rights and remedies of lenders and consumers in particular transactions. To address a broader range of business transactions and activities, tribes may consider enacting a suite of complementary business

---

[8] The Tribal Law and Policy Institute maintains the Tribal Court Clearinghouse at http://tribal-institute.org/.

laws. For example, every state has a version of a uniform partnership law. If two people want to start a business together, they can fill out a short application and file it with their secretary of state. The uniform partnership law defines the rules for partners in the absence of an ad hoc contract. On a reservation without a well-developed system of business laws, the same incorporation would require drafting a lengthy document that spells out the terms of the agreement – even if the partnership is a fairly simple one. This may discourage lending and thwart business opportunities for entrepreneurs, or drive business development off-reservation.

3 Tribal Judicial Systems

As much as tribes exercise their sovereignty to make laws, they also determine how and where they are subject to suit. This often involves a waiver, or a limited waiver, of tribal sovereign immunity for actions involving the tribe itself. Waivers of tribal sovereignty immunity from suit must be clear and unequivocal, including any agreement to arbitrate a dispute. Recourse to tribal funds and other remedies against tribal property must be expressly delineated as well. For actions involving tribal members that arise on the reservation, tribal courts should be available, supported by tribal laws addressing required procedures and processes. Tribal laws also should address the enforcement of alternative resolution mechanisms such as mediation and arbitration as both are common forms of dispute resolution in contracts.

H Resources for Adopting and Implementing the MTSTA

The Implementation Guide to the MTSTA published by the ULC, along with the Federal Reserve Bank of Minneapolis, details the history of the MTSTA and explains the different components of the model act. Following the publication of the model act and the Implementation Guide, both organizations conducted outreach to tribal leaders across the United States to explain the MTSTA and the potential that a tribal STS has to improve reservations' economies.

Such outreach and teaching are critical parts of adopting the MTSTA as tribal law. For an STS to be effectively implemented, it must be well understood by the community, judges, law enforcement professionals, elected officials, and business leaders. Tribes that have adopted the MTSTA have reported initial resistance from community leaders based on inadequate information about how the MTSTA would be implemented in their community. Misperceptions around cultural values, sovereignty, and fair dealing often derail efforts to enact and enforce a robust STS.

Importantly, business and finance leaders in Indian Country play a particularly critical role in establishing the value of the MTSTA in developing the private economy among tribal entrepreneurs without sacrificing a tribe's autonomy or cultural values. These community leaders include organizations such as Indian business alliances, tribal credit programs, and Native-owned financial institutions, as well as non-Native business partners and lenders. Such advocates can help ameliorate misconceptions about the purpose and application of the MTSTA, as well as the interplay with state law. However, when looking at economic development through the lens of affordable access to credit for tribes and tribal citizens, tribes can approach the enactment of an STS with the goals of preserving cultural values, protecting tribal sovereignty, and establishing clear rights for borrowers and third parties such as cosigners or good faith purchasers.

VII CONCLUSION

Tribal governments are integrally involved in making credit more available and affordable to their citizens and on-reservation businesses. They can strengthen Indian Country credit markets by enacting laws and establishing systems to facilitate secured transactions and expand business development. Resources like the MTSTA and its Implementation Guide can go a long way toward eradicating the gap in opportunities between on- and off-reservation businesses – it is a pillar of economic development and promises opportunities to build a private economy.

ACKNOWLEDGMENTS

The authors would like to thank Richard M. Todd, Senior Advisor to the Center for Indian Country Development, for his comprehensive contributions to this chapter.

6

Tribal Economic Resurgence: Reflections from a Tribal Economic Development Practitioner

David Castillo

I INTRODUCTION

Where English canon law was used as a weapon to dispossess Native people of their lands, languages, and cultures;[1] Western-style finance as a tool has been withheld through current times for the rebuilding and resurgence of tribal nations. To this day, the overwhelming majority of tribal communities face social and economic problems arising in part from inadequate community development to support economic opportunity and the overarching challenge is a lack of access to capital.

The issue is now so entrenched that it is as if both tribes and conventional financial institutions are operating on completely different planes. The reticence tribes maintain toward the use of private capital comes in large part from a simple lack of precedent in accessing capital – we fear what we don't know or understand. That inertia is compounded by traditional lenders' compliance expectations that often require robust legal, programmatic, and administrative infrastructure that many tribal organizations and Native business owners have not yet developed. Moreover, tribal trust land has limited use as collateral and conventional bank credit standards are often inflexible. The consequent lack of capital, collateral, and credit produces a negligible economic base in Native communities.

This resulting economic climate negatively impacts development and inhibits opportunities to strengthen self-governance, social development, industry diversification, and tribal employment opportunity. Consequently, Native people remain locked in what MacArthur Award-winning writer Ta-Nahisi Coates calls compounded deprivation[2] – which can be described as the crushing effect of the shared myriad indignities affecting one group and including political disenfranchisement, health disparities, educational inequities, disproportionate rates of violent crime and incarceration, as well as unresolved historic trauma. Yet, the foundation for lifelong educational and economic equity for Native people rests in tribal governments'

---

[1] Steve Newcomb, "Five Hundred Years of Injustice: The Legacy of Fifteenth Century Religious Prejudice," NativeWeb, accessed October 23, 2018, http://ili.nativeweb.org/sdrm_art.html.

[2] Ta-Nahisi Coates, "The Black Family in the Age of Mass Incarceration," *The Atlantic* (October 2015).

ability to provide economic opportunity. To do so, private capital must be as readily accessible and in use on tribal lands as in any non-Indian community.

II THE CLINTON YEARS AND NEW TOOLS FOR BUILDING TRIBAL ECONOMIES

My work facilitating access to capital for use in tribal settings began during the Y2K scare.[3] At that time the general population was anticipating disastrous disruptions to digital technologies. Ironically, although tribal populations would remain largely unaffected due to limited modern telecommunication infrastructure on tribal lands, the digital divide still today separates tribes from access to capital and the now almost ubiquitous digital economy. Nevertheless, with the advent of a new millennia and William Jefferson Clinton in the White House, Indian Country would make significant strides in addressing barriers that have negatively affected the tribal economic landscape for too long.

During the first Clinton administration, tribal leadership helped advance a watershed piece of legislation that was signed into law as P.L. 104–330 or the Native American Housing Assistance and Self-Determination Act of 1996 (NAHASDA). NAHASDA revamped the distribution of federal funds to ensure all tribes had better access to federal housing dollars; two specific provisions carried over from previous legislation and related to loan guarantees promised new sources of capital for housing development on tribal lands. During the second Clinton administration, tribes and their allies secured another new source of funding. Specifically, the Department of Treasury Community Development Financial Institution (CDFI) Fund established what would eventually become the Native American CDFI Assistance (NACA) program for the establishment of loan funds to serve Native Americans – now known as Native CDFIs. Other federal agencies such as the Department of Energy and the Department of Health and Human Services were also advancing significant initiatives to address tribal community development during the Clinton years.

I had a front-row view of the negotiated rulemaking process for NAHASDA and I led an effort to secure approval from tribal leadership for the establishment of the first regional Native CDFI to serve tribes in Arizona.[4] Those years were filled with gatherings to draft regulatory language, to assess barriers for accessing capital on tribal lands, and to forge partnerships. Tribal leaders, and especially congressional members who sought to gain political favor with tribes, lauded the new initiatives

---

[3] "Y2K bug," Encyclopaedia Britannica, accessed October 12, 2018, www.britannica.com/technology/ Y2K-bug.

[4] First known as Arizona Tribal CDFI, then Native Home Capital, and later Native Capital Access. Also, the Hopi Credit Association and First Americans Credit Union were established prior to Native Capital Access and even prior to the establishment of NACA although both have historically served just one specific tribe.

with celebratory language memorialized in the Congressional Record.[5] I recall one congressional delegate announcing to tribes that NAHASDA would lift the yolk of paternalism and allow Native Americans an opportunity to achieve the American dream of homeownership. Lofty language aside, something seemed amiss.

At a rally in 1999 where then Secretary Cuomo of the Department of Housing and Urban Development (HUD) was announcing another promising initiative, one tribal member openly questioned the prospect of success given the dearth of precedent. He asked, "How is it that the United States can put a man on the moon but it can't get a bank on the Pine Ridge Indian Reservation?" Although today there are a handful of Native-owned banks and over seventy Native CDFIs throughout the United States,[6] there are not anywhere near the number of financial institutions serving tribes as there are banks serving non-Indian populations. Therefore, the continued impatience of tribes on the matter of access to capital and banking services is reasonable.

In another incident and during one of the first negotiated rulemaking sessions for NAHASDA, a tribal delegate recalled that the acronym for NAHASDA sounded very much like a word in his language (pronounced na-HÁÁZ-t'aa) that means one who sits and waits patiently. He recalled how tribes had indeed waited patiently but perhaps too long for the improvements the new law promised. Despite some early and scattered success stories, the waiting for much of Indian Country would continue for at least another two decades. A harbinger of the wait was forged in my mind when a banker sincerely asked me why he should go through the brain damage of doing a deal in Indian Country when he could get what he needed from the Office of the Comptroller of the Currency (i.e., bank regulator) by doing a deal with blacks or Hispanics.

The Y2K scare referenced earlier and the passage of NAHASDA are now relatively distant memories. However, the Y2K scare was a threat that never materialized. Conversely, NAHASDA and the Native CDFI program have left still too many tribes waiting for a comprehensive solution for how to bridge the capital divide that must be overcome in order for tribal governments and residents on tribal lands to break the cycle of poverty prevalent across most of Indian Country. Tribal elected leaders, tribal housing, community and economic development professionals, their public and private sector allies, and Native CDFIs continue to experiment and forge ahead. What follows below is a review of one such effort.

III MAKING UP LOST GROUND: FEDERAL, STATE, AND TRIBAL PARTNERSHIPS

In September of 2003 at the foot of Mt. Baboquivari on the Tohono O'Odham Nation, tribal elected leaders and Arizona Governor Janet Napolitano met to discuss

[5] "Native American Housing Assistance and Self Determination Act of 1996," Congressional Record – House, September 28, 1996, H11613.

[6] "Mapping Native American Financial Institutions," Federal Reserve Bank of Minneapolis, accessed October 13, 2018, www.minneapolisfed.org/indiancountry/resources/mapping-native-banks.

the issue of housing and access to credit. Tribes described the fact that cities, towns, and municipalities just on the other side of reservation boundaries had access to myriad capital sources while tribes, on the other hand, were left to rely on public sector grants. After a thoughtful, wide-ranging, and engaged discussion that remains a testament to the special government-to-government relationship that Governor Napolitano sought to honor, she offered a solution. She suggested that if banks weren't willing to make loans for projects on tribal lands, then maybe the assembled tribes should capitalize a fund and form an organization that could demonstrate how such transactions could be structured.

Shortly after the 2003 meeting, a task force of state and tribal representatives seized on an opportunity made possible by the work of a former tribal economic development director now working within the U.S. Department of the Treasury. Rodger Boyd, working as the CDFI Fund Program Manager, had conducted a nationwide series of workshops with tribal and lending industry representatives to assess the barriers to lending on tribal lands. The resulting study[7] was used to justify and request the creation of what is now known as the Native American CDFI Assistance (NACA) program. Tribes now had a vehicle to implement the governor's recommendation. Tribes, acting through the Inter Tribal Council of Arizona, approved a resolution to request funding, Governor Napolitano's administration made the first commitment of funds, the Department of the Treasury committed additional funding, and shortly thereafter it certified Arizona's first regional Native CDFI.

Slowly but surely Native CDFIs began to have more and more of a presence on the economic landscape across Indian Country. As a result, tribes and individual tribal members have more actively utilized borrowed funds from CDFIs for community development projects and entrepreneurial endeavors. Native CDFIs represent a community-driven and community-based source of capital and technical assistance that complements other resources defined and driven by the capital markets. The use of tax-exempt bond financing for community infrastructure, Low-Income Housing Tax Credits for affordable housing, and New Markets Tax Credits for economic development as well as various federally guaranteed loan products demonstrates the significant potential for the use of debt financing to improve tribal infrastructure and tribal economies. Yet, many of the transactions that community and economic development professionals consider model leveraged financing activities too often fail to replicate. As a result, these financing tools remain highly underutilized where they are needed most – in Indian Country.

One reason for the underutilization rate is the remote and rural nature of communities that make up most of Indian Country. It is difficult to attract and retain individuals with the professional experience needed to structure and manage the various financing solutions that could facilitate the sorely needed improvements for

---

[7]   "The Report of the Native American Lending Study," U.S. Department of the Treasury CDFI Fund, November 2001, accessed October 13, 2018, www.cdfifund.gov/Documents/2001_nacta_lending_study.pdf.

tribal economies. When the requisite professionals are available, the turnover in tribal governments – some in New Mexico for example change annually – severely affects a tribe's ability to maintain relationships with the various partners needed to consummate complex financial transactions. One result is the development of an industry of, mostly non-Indian, roving consultants offering a full range of specialized services for one specific financing tool or another on behalf of tribes on a regional or national basis. The costs are often much higher than an in-house effort and tribes lose out on the opportunity to build their own capacity, sophistication, and the relationships with would-be public and private sector partners. Native CDFIs could, if nothing else, help build the capacity needed to increase access to capital on tribal lands.

IV GOING WHERE BANKS FEAR TO TREAD – LESSONS LEARNED FROM LENDING ON TRIBAL LANDS

When Arizona's first regional Native CDFI was established, ten years after the passage of NAHASDA, it first attempted to address what NAHASDA alone could not fully address – the problem of reliable financing for affordable housing on tribal lands. Initial efforts to cultivate interest among tribal housing professionals made clear the extremely limited precedent for use of debt financing to fund tribal housing projects. Most tribal housing and community development entities remained exceedingly dependent on annual federal grants. As such, very little capacity had been built for tribes to engage conventional lenders without relying almost exclusively on intermediaries or consultants. More importantly, the lack of market-rate housing and therefore any semblance of a mortgage market on tribal lands began to surface the misgivings that veteran tribal housing professionals had raised, but that were muted, during the politically charged arguments for the drafting of NAHASDA and the eventual push to get it signed into law.

NAHASDA's Section 184 mortgage loan guarantee program and related lending models were presented and discussed at conferences and individually with tribal housing professionals before, during, and after the passage of the law. After passage of the law, more and more often the beleaguered practitioners would relay the difficulty of collecting even nominal rents on a consistent basis from tribal residents for existing lease-to-own programs. That fact made the prospect of collecting monthly mortgage payments over thirty years highly improbable if not impossible. The "brain damage" suggested by the banker in the early years after the passage of NAHASDA was beginning to take its toll but we carried on. One colleague commiserated with our plight by agreeing to keep banging her head against the proverbial wall with me because at some point it would start to break. She never did clarify if the break would be the wall or our heads.

The constraints of limited organizational capacity and other barriers to residential development on tribal trust lands are chronicled in numerous studies, such as those done by the Government Accountability Office.[8] As such, Arizona's first regional Native CDFI sought to take a step back from pursuing loan prospects in favor of providing technical assistance and capacity-building services. Ideally, by building an understanding of finance, tribes could become better positioned to optimally use the powerful financing tools and products that had become available. The assumption was that we could cultivate tribal lending clients over time to better address the tribal housing and community development crisis and for our own organizational stability.

Yet, even with robust capacity-building efforts directed at tribal housing and community development entities, the stark, stubborn reality is that limited employment opportunities on tribal lands mean that many tribal members often have a limited ability to pay monthly mortgages – just as tribal housing professionals had been saying all along. We pursued the deals available but lagging deal flow began to encourage a rethinking of the business model.

As it turned out, many Native CDFIs across the United States were rethinking and reformulating their approaches. Native CDFIs struggle, in part, due to the disproportionate economic distress prevalent in the remote communities they serve. However, CDFIs – by definition – are expected to serve distressed populations. The way most non-Native CDFIs find success is by filling the gaps that conventional financial institutions in their geographic areas overlook. In many cases non-Native CDFIs receive direct investments by their bank counterparts who can then claim credit from bank regulators for serving high-credit-risk populations during formal regulatory reviews.[9] However, most Native CDFIs restrict their services to the needs of their tribal members who lack access to mainstream financial institutions in the first place.

The organization's vision that private sector capital shall be as readily accessible and in use on tribal lands as in any non-Indian community remained a bright beacon, but the path was unclear. Nevertheless, we remained committed to supporting tribal government efforts to finally secure the capital resources that had been out of reach for far too long. Insight from tribal leaders, support from our governance board, collaboration with our counterparts around the country on their successes and lessons learned, and commitments from allies kept us optimistic.

V TRIBAL GOVERNMENTS AS OUR OWN BEST HOPE – LOOKING FOR HEROES

The remaining land base of tribal nations across the United States and the sovereign authority tribal governments retain to control activities within these lands provide

---

[8] "Native American Housing: Additional Actions Needed to Better Support Tribal Efforts: Report to Congressional Committees," U.S. Government Accountability Office, March 2014, accessed October 10, 2018, www.gao.gov/products/GAO-14–255.

[9] Banks must request approval from the Office of the Comptroller of the Currency for the ways in which they intend to comply with the Community Reinvestment Act of 1977, which was passed to counter past and ongoing discriminatory behavior by financial institutions.

a major foundation for rebuilding tribal economies. The ongoing development or rebuilding of viable social and economic institutions on tribal lands as well as the jobs, wages, and related benefits that flow to families residing on tribal lands is a critical element to long-term economic self-sufficiency for tribal communities. Compared to previous generations where tribal welfare initiatives were completely in the hands of the federal government, the last several decades have seen a growing critical mass of tribal government initiatives including enterprises using debt financing as an increasingly common tool to support economic growth. If the trend could continue and grow it seems tribes will surely regain a prominent seat at the table of nations. The success of the Mississippi Band of Choctaw, Ho-Chunk, Inc., and several other notable examples across Indian Country provide hope and inspiration for how tribal governments are the key to building and stimulating tribal economies. However, far from an argument for libertarian economic prescriptions that would ravage tribal lands by promoting profit-driven predatory interests, a long-term solution must value above all else local human capital – Native people and the sacred bond to their homelands.

Despite the tribal economic success stories, too many tribal governments remain heavily and often exclusively reliant on federal grants for their government operations and economic development costs. Decades of stagnant reservation economic activity make it obvious that grant funds alone are not sufficient to build vibrant economies or successfully affect the social distress in tribal communities. An exclusive reliance on public sector funding may have even exacerbated issues as tribal economic landscapes are often dominated by an institutionalized bureaucracy of social programs. One result is the regular weekend exodus to off-reservation border towns by tribal community members to find any meaningful variety of commerce, banking, and even entertainment.

Non-Indian rural communities in Appalachia, or communities in the deep inner city, also lack commercial amenities. However, by comparison one of the defining characteristics of rural tribal economies is the heavy influence of federally funded institutions as the primary source of employment. Also indicative is the palpable lack of entrepreneurial activity that scales beyond the tailgate on the side of a road or the booth at a fair or cultural event. Aside from the informal economic exchange at local social or cultural events and with some very notable exceptions, Native entrepreneurs who have had commercial success serve markets primarily outside of tribal communities. No doubt, small business opportunities such as the production and sale of high-end Native art and state minority preference or tribal preference in contracting have promoted unique opportunities for small business growth and employment. However, the pervasive and ubiquitous presence of tribal government programs, departments, and their agents seems almost to stifle the creativity and innovation that enterprising activity demands. Yet tribal governmental entities are too often maligned, and their employees are typically the very tribal residents that efforts toward a broader, more just economic environment seek to benefit.

Research on organizational design abound from which much insight is available to address the shortcomings of tribal government departments. Peter Senge's learning organization, Henry Mintzberg's review of archetypes including adhocracies and machine bureaucracies, and Frederic Laloux's path from red to teal organizations can all help assess where an organization is in its evolution. The many insights of well-known management theorists like Peter Drucker, and more recent applied research by Jim Collins, Eric Reis, Chip and Dan Heath, and specifically for Indian Country, Stephen Cornell and Joseph Kalt, all offer novel prescriptions. However, even a cursory review of these works reveals that any serious attempt to affect the efficacy of tribal departments requires a deep dive into the history, context, organizational culture, and environment under which they operate. That level of assessment and realignment, perhaps routine for Fortune 500 companies, is often considered a luxury that must wait until after tribal organizations can secure grant funding or, more likely, address the latest crisis. In lieu of a thorough organizational assessment, often the most one can do is offer an impassioned plea for tribal employees to become the heroes we seek and commit to resolve the social and economic issues that habitually confront tribal communities.

One tribal leader was overheard encouraging tribes to make strides addressing problems affecting Indian nations by stating, "If you're going to be sovereign, act sovereign!" In engagements with tribal clients our comments are slightly more nuanced but similar in intent. An emphasis on corporate goals or better key performance indicators alone may fail to address more fundamental topics such as how intergenerational trauma may uniquely affect tribal organizations as illustrated by the following excerpt from a tribal client engagement.

> During our group work yesterday, you talked about how "when there's a crisis, that's when we really come together – that's when we shine." However, many of you also confirmed that there's a real lack of a willingness to make a decision; lack of coordination between departments and divisions; a reluctance to assume authority; a perceived lack of guidance from upper management; and a longing for transformational leaders. And as I thought why this might be, I started asking questions of you and here's what I heard and the sense that I made of it.
>
> Crisis is a big part of what defines us – it can be both a strength and a weakness. It's who we've been for a long time. Historically, the Indian wars weren't that long ago – many of us have living relatives who were told stories of the atrocities firsthand from their elders. In our own families we're used to dealing with crisis and we come together like we always have since the days of the Indian wars – as a tribe, as extended family, as XYZ. However, that history of dealing with crisis, after crisis, after crisis takes a toll. To the point that no one wants to be responsible for another crisis or another failure and so you get this interesting dynamic that occurs where people say things like "that's not my problem," "I'm not responsible for that," "you worry about what your department does," "what we do at our department is none of

your business," and finally the one I heard most often, "I'm not authorized to make that decision."

Traditionally, we talk a lot about balance and order ... in the natural world, in our relationships, and within ourselves. Medicine people and spiritual leaders teach us that much of life is finding and maintaining that balance. Therefore, if crisis in part defines XYZ, how do we find balance? What role will crisis play in your activities as a manager? As XYZ? And how do we turn that quality into a strength?

This specific but common example of interaction with tribal government community development professionals suggests a single focus on economic initiatives alone is insufficient. Additional effort to recognize and address the pernicious effect of past United States–Indian policy eras is vital for long-term success of tribal community development efforts.

VI THE NEXT ERA OF UNITED STATES–INDIAN POLICY: TRIBAL ECONOMIC RESURGENCE

Vine Deloria, Jr., Donald Fixico, David E. Wilkins, Robert J. Miller, and numerous other American Indian scholars have expertly chronicled how the subjugation of Indian nations early in United States political history displaced tribal political, social, and economic institutions in favor of Western-style tribal governments and their bureaucracies. A review of these and other notable authors' works is warranted for any serious study of the matter as they clearly show that the entrenched issues are rooted as much in the conflicts of early colonization and subjugation as in more modern sources of ongoing social and economic distress in tribal communities. The expansion of federally funded programs starting in the mid-twentieth century – and their bureaucracies – has redressed some of the more damaging outcomes of colonial-era federal policy but it also has complicated tribal economic development efforts.

The United States federal government's well-intentioned but highly misguided social programs of the 1950s such as the latter years of Indian boarding schools, termination and relocation efforts, and not least of all the many federal agency initiatives that provide poverty-level welfare benefits, likely undermined the intrinsic motivation necessary for private sector activity to thrive. Instead, minimally viable tribal governments manage or co-manage housing, health, education, public safety, and numerous other programs, and in more recent decades, business enterprises as well. The result is the oft-criticized scenario where trained tribal bureaucrats and politicians guide underfunded social services as well as complex entrepreneurial efforts. Nevertheless, tribal leaders were and remain critical for the success of the various Indian self-determination policies promulgated during the 1970s and again in the 1980s that have fortunately facilitated many improvements to counter the many more maladies resulting from prior federal–Indian policy eras.

The Alaska Natives Claims Settlement Act of 1971 (P.L. 92–203) and the Indian Self-Determination and Education Assistance Act of 1975 (P.L. 93–638) laid the foundations for increased Native control of land as well as management of federally funded programs on tribal lands. Agriculture, sand and gravel, petroleum extraction as well as other occasionally showcased enterprises of various tribes across the United States were made possible by efforts resulting from the Nixon-era legislation. Never quite the political equals of states or multinational corporations, tribes nonetheless have been able to make progress toward the prospect of self-governance and economic self-sufficiency. Finally, the Indian Gaming Regulatory Act of 1988 (P.L. 100–497) heralded the advent of tribal gaming. Far from the panacea non-Indian observers might imagine, Indian gaming has made important contributions to how Indian nations are rebuilding their economies.

Mainstream financial institutions began to play a larger role as well. Sometimes as partners but more often as formidable counterparties, banks developed commercial lending teams to serve the growing volume of tribal enterprises, particularly after the passage of the Indian Gaming Regulatory Act and the resulting growth of tribal gaming. Spurred on by a new source of tribal revenues, specialty bond or tax credit financing firms helped supply funds for other capital-intensive projects. However, the same financial institutions that had eagerly pursued financing opportunities for large multimillion-dollar tribal enterprises were much less inclined to open banking centers on tribal lands or to offer consumer or small business loans to tribal citizens living on Indian reservations. Thus, the complaint issued during the earlier referenced Cuomo speech that establishing a bank on tribal lands was akin to a moonshot endeavor.

Native CDFIs were quick to form throughout the early 2000s under the new Native CDFI Program. They set to the work of addressing the long-neglected need for consumer lending and micro- and small business financing. Native CDFIs recognized that tribal member-owned businesses must be cultivated and supported to provide more and higher-paying jobs. The wages earned by tribal members and the economic activity they stimulate can help reduce the economic leakage to off-reservation border towns. We believed that economic activity could create a positive feedback loop to support the growth of tribal economies that can lead to more consistent consideration and use of financing as a tool for ongoing economic growth.

Native CDFIs are more than financial institutions looking to generate economic returns. Native CDFIs, as part of their certification by the U.S. Treasury, commit to providing community development services to more fully address the social and economic distress in the communities they serve. If the Indian Self-Determination Era policies set the foundation for tribal governments to gain momentum for enhanced self-governance, NAHASDA and NACA should allow individual tribal members to raise their standard of living and should further promote tribal economic resurgence. It's odd then that still and very often tribal members prefer pawn shops, check-cashing services, title loans, and all variety of predatory lenders that charge annualized interest rates of 700 percent and more over Native CDFIs. It is a peculiar problem indeed that begs many basic questions about human economic behavior and presents an ongoing challenge for how Native CDFIs can help usher in the next historical era of tribal economic resurgence.

VII TRANSFORMATIVE FINANCE IN A TRANSACTIONAL WORLD

Arizona's first regional Native CDFI, acting opportunistically, closed its first loan with a tribal entity in 2007. The loan presented itself after the conventional lender failed to close with the Yavapai-Apache Nation (YAN) even though the proposed financing would be 100 percent guaranteed by NAHASDA's 184 Loan Guarantee program. The bank's failure could likely be blamed on a lack of process, precedent, and enduring skepticism about making loans on tribal trust lands. Off-reservation, most lands are held in fee-simple status, allowing a lender to take possession of a property in the case of a loan default. Not so on tribal lands where state lending laws cannot be assumed to take precedent over tribal legal codes. Also, the federal government is obligated to maintain a trust responsibility over the remaining vestiges of once expansive aboriginal territories, thus complicating the process with additional layers of bureaucratic red tape. Lending on land held in trust or in other forms of restricted ownership is not a novel concept. However, the lack of robust economic activity on tribal land, in this case for homes, makes the prospect of mortgage lending dubious in the eyes of a conventional lender. Had a Native CDFI not been available in this case, another tribe would have fallen victim to the "brain damage" factor.

Tribes typically work with federal program officers who deploy federally appropriated grant funds and who offer free technical assistance when a tribe is unable to comply with federal grant requirements. Therefore, the idea of working with a bank means tribes will face the cold reality of the universally accepted standard of profit-driven transactional goals as a determinant for approval of a proposed project. Given this contrast, the challenge for Native CDFIs is how to best stimulate, partake in, and advocate for the use of debt capital to help transform the economic landscape of largely impoverished tribal communities with a history of using grant funds on an almost exclusive basis. Fortunately, this is exactly the role Native CDFIs are best suited to play so long as the capital and technological resources are made available for Native CDFIs to catch up to the very mature and heavily regulated lending industry.

Despite the YAN transaction and others taking place around Indian Country, championing the use of debt by tribes was further complicated by the need for tribal housing professionals to balance program development efforts with the immediate, often dire, needs of their community members. The process of establishing mortgage markets and the accompanying programs, policies, and procedures, the lender and new partner relations, and mostly the organizational redesign necessary to maintain low-rent housing programs, as well as creating a new numbers-driven approach to housing development that requires providing financial literacy and homebuyer education, seemed a very tall order indeed. One veteran tribal housing manager exasperated by the process exclaimed, "You yuppie Indians at tribal head-quarters think all of our people need 1,700 square-foot ranch-style homes that will take decades to build. Most of our people are just asking for some place warm to sleep at night right now!" The point lost in the debate was that tribal markets have various sectors, all of which need to be addressed to achieve a more balanced economic landscape.

Nevertheless, at the time, the initial model for Arizona's regional Native CDFI seemed one with limited prospects for success. In an effort to recommit itself to tribal housing professionals, it began providing consulting services and helped build what came to be known as the Tribal Housing Excellence Academy (THE Academy). Since it seemed most Tribally Designated Housing Entities (TDHEs) remained focused on serving the dire and basic housing needs of their most vulnerable populations, Arizona's regional Native CDFI would focus on building the capacity of progressive TDHEs and craft solutions for specific types of tribal housing projects that could make use of debt financing, with the expectation that a more typical market would emerge over time.

Both the technical assistance and training efforts were based on the fact that staff from HUD's Office of Native American Programs (ONAP) as well as the National American Indian Housing Council (NAIHC) stated that an inordinate amount of their time and resources was spent working to address ongoing problems with the implementation of NAHASDA, triaging at-risk recipients of NAHASDA's Indian Housing Block Grants (IHBG), and working to minimize enforcement actions against nonperforming TDHEs. They both expressed regret that they were unable to adequately serve those tribal entities with an interest in utilizing the various leveraged financing opportunities now available via NAHASDA.

Despite a significant effort, success through THE Academy alone would require significantly more time and resources. Cultivating enough lending prospects and deal flow to sustain even the smallest Native CDFI would likely have required a nationwide effort or much more significant financial support. Meanwhile a non-Indian private sector business had developed into a thriving practice and practical monopoly in facilitating tax credit financing for affordable housing on tribal lands. Another non-Indian business started specializing in originating federally guaranteed mortgages primarily for Native Americans living off-reservation. Transactional to the core, both efforts have been successful in affecting the affordable housing needs of Native Americans but much less so in building the capacity for tribes to find success on their own. In all fairness, that last task falls on Native communities and Native CDFIs.

Existential reflections about how to best serve tribes as a Native CDFI were informed by critics and allies alike. The founders of Craft3, a successful non-

Native CDFI in Seattle, provided significant insight. The now veteran founder provided a sobering reply to the question of what keeps him up at night after all the success his organization had experienced. He stated that the organization had set out to be transformative and for the exclusive benefit of the communities and specific industries they support. However, remaining an agent of transformational change was becoming a challenge. The larger the organization became, the more investors it had, and the more the organization incentivized its staff to perform to the standards of conventional financial institutions, the more transactional the organization was becoming. His words were daunting as back in Arizona we had been preoccupied with how to grow the balance sheet without considering how success along those lines might change the organization for the worse. Fortunately, the Great Recession of 2009[10] had caused a stir among private foundations that inspired new thinking and ultimately a new strategy for increasing access to capital for tribes.

VIII INSIGHTS FROM THE PHILANTHROPIC AND DEVELOPING WORLDS

One particularly brilliant silver lining of the Great Recession was the development of foundation- and philanthropic-led impact investment funds. These funds seek to address environmental, social, and governance (ESG)[11] issues as well as generate economic returns. Prior to the Great Recession, most private foundations sought to address various causes primarily by deploying a minimum 5 percent of their wealth through grant making. The 5 percent figure is related to the payout rule[12] derived from the tax code,[13] which sets the standard upon which foundations may claim tax-exempt status. In contrast to foundation giving, 95 percent of a foundation's assets are at work elsewhere in the economy as more typical investments. A 2007 exposé of investments held by the Bill and Melinda Gates Foundation found the benefits of their philanthropic giving were likely largely negated by the actions of the public companies in which the foundation was invested.[14] As the Great Recession took hold and private foundations started scrutinizing their own investment portfolios, very similar reckonings began, which resulted in greater consideration of ESG or impact investing by more and more foundations.

---

[10] Robert Reich, "The Great Recession, December 2007 to June 2009," last modified November 22, 2013, accessed April 24, 2019, www.federalreservehistory.org/essays/great_recession_of_200709.

[11] Georg Kell, "The Remarkable Rise of ESG," last modified July 11, 2018, accessed April 24, 2019, www.forbes.com/sites/georgkell/2018/07/11/the-remarkable-rise-of-esg/#70ef80a81695.

[12] "What is a 'Payout Requirement' for a Private Foundation?," Grantspace, accessed October 13, 2018, https://grantspace.org/resources/knowledge-base/payout/.

[13] "Taxes on Failure to Distribute Income – Private Foundations," IRS, last modified July 23, 2018, accessed April 24, 2019, www.irs.gov/charities-non-profits/private-foundations/taxes-on-failure-to-distribute-income-private-foundations.

[14] Robyn Dixon, Charles Piller, and Edmund Sanders, "Dark Cloud over Good Works of Gates Foundation," *Los Angeles Times*, January 7, 2007, accessed April 24, 2019, http://articles.latimes.com/2007/jan/07/nation/na-gatesx07.

Historically, Native American causes receive less than 0.5 percent of philanthropic giving[15] and so when a small group of foundations expressed interest in directing funds to support Native CDFIs, a new model for the work of building tribal economies began to develop. Unlike bank representatives who considered the extension of credit to tribes "brain damage," private foundation staff and trustees had already spent decades evaluating how to address severe social and economic concerns of Indigenous communities in Central and South America and many other areas of the world. Those investments, as well as those of the World Bank and International Monetary Fund, provide a rich source of data and analysis about community economic development and individual economic behavior that can inform the development of tribal economies in the United States.

In *Poor Economics: A Radical Rethinking of the Way to Fight Global Poverty*,[16] the authors thoroughly review multiple interventions. They also push back against the theoretical arguments for or against giving aid to desperately poor developing countries in the southern hemisphere as likely corrupted by political ideologies. Although the authors, who are also field researchers, offer some general prescriptions, for the most part they argue for a true empirical approach that seeks to understand the granularity of an issue. They suggest that the efficacy of popular poverty interventions by NGOs would vastly improve by independent evaluation of their efforts. Nevertheless, owing to the complex nature of human interaction, bias, and resulting unintended consequences, any intervention may still need to be refined or rethought along the way. Or as Jack Welch, who *Fortune* magazine dubbed CEO of the Century was fond of saying, "[P]ick a general direction and implement like hell!"[17]

Of course, the work of Muhammad Yunus, as memorialized in Banker to the Poor: Micro-Lending and the Battle Against World Poverty,[18] puts forward a challenge to reestablish a relationship-based economy to counter the excesses of the dominant greed-based economy. Morgan Simon, in *Real Impact: The New Economics of Social Change*,[19] chronicles how Yunus's micro-lending has been co-opted and corrupted by institutional investors. Her body of work warns and instructs how to better equip foundations seeking to impact social causes without the undue influence of extractive and exploitative practices common in the financial and corporate sectors. Although there are no shortcuts, the good news for Native CDFIs is that there is now perhaps more opportunity to affect change due to the

---

[15]   "Helping Philanthropy Address Gaps," Native Americans in Philanthropy, accessed October 13, 2018, https://nativephilanthropy.org/the-need/.
[16]   Abhijit V. Banerjee and Esther Duflo, *Poor Economics: A Radical Rethinking of the Way to Fight Global Poverty* (New York: Public Affairs, 2011).
[17]   Jack Welch, *Winning* (New York: Harper Business, 2005), 165.
[18]   Muhammad Yunus, *Banker to the Poor: Micro-Lending and the Battle Against World Poverty* (New York: Public Affairs, 1999).
[19]   Morgan Simon, Real Impact: The New Economics of Social Change (New York: Nation Books, 2017).

proximity of Native CDFIs to the issue of access to capital for tribal communities, the capital resources available through impact investors, the growing critical mass of partners, and the shared motivation to find a way past the political and economic consternation brought about and represented by the election of the forty-fifth president of the United States.

The latest strategy of Arizona's first regional Native CDFI centers on growth by acquisition. It has partnered with two other Native CDFIs to form the first known multitribal, regional Native CDFI in the nation. It is combining its assets, talents, and networks to more fully address the full spectrum of credit needs on tribal lands. That work, however, is only possible with a parallel effort of progressive tribes and tribal departments, Native small-business incubators, and over seventy Native CDFIs throughout the United States. Informed by the large body of research and work to affect change in the most economically distressed communities, encouraged by the vision of Native governance bodies, and with the substantial support of industry allies,[20] an idea discussed by tribal leaders in 2003 is now a movement. Several new strategic initiatives set to be unveiled sometime after the publication of this book promise to make a still small Native CDFI in the American Southwest into an enduring institution dedicated to the social and economic resurgence of Indian nations.

IX THE MEN WITH GUNS

Self-congratulatory language about commitments to palliative measures is the realm of politicians. An honest discussion about affecting poverty and social distress requires a more consistent, solemn, and mindful internal dialogue about the role each of us plays in our daily interactions with each other. We should also remember that although the last of the Indian wars in the United States was approximately a century ago, they continue in other parts of the Americas. The reality is that most of us with the luxury to study, read, and write on topics of poverty have managed to escape the full impact of the cruelest human behaviors that play a role in maintaining inequality. The following is just one vivid episode that I reflect upon for the sake of focusing on the work ahead.

I was in Peru less than a year after then President Alan Garcia decreed a suspension of two articles within that nation's constitution that require consultation with tribes prior to taking action that might affect their traditional homelands. Garcia was motivated by international petroleum interests and the result was an armed confrontation with several Native American tribes from the Amazon region.[21]

---

[20] Such industry allies include those managing the BIA Loan Guarantee and Insurance Program, regional and national intermediaries, others guiding new initiatives launched by several conventional financial institutions and secondary-market government-sponsored entities, and foundation partners.

[21] "2009 Peruvian Political Crisis," Wikipedia, last modified July 1, 2018, https://en.wikipedia.org/wiki/2009_Peruvian_political_crisis.

I asked a tribal leader how his tribe's situation had progressed since the conflict under the solutions offered by a local NGO. He reflected on how the lawyers had given him a piece of paper that assured him of his property rights but he noted that it was little defense against the armed men (i.e., paramilitary soldiers hired by the petrol industry) holding guns in their hands.

Quite by coincidence I met an individual at the 2018 International Funders for Indigenous Peoples conference who had a role in drafting the peace accords after the Amazon incident (i.e., massacre). He let me know that the community leadership had done the hard work and developed unity on the issues, and that currently the accords were holding and the government was reluctantly complying. He was certain that in a world with so much suffering, theirs was a good story even if it came at a great cost and even if there would be no fairy-tale ending.

Although current-day tribes in the United States have avoided the types of massacres that continue in South America, Native people across the Americas share the same hope for social and economic justice. And just like the Native people from the Amazon, I don't believe our work longs for a fairy-tale ending. Rather, our work longs for honoring the traditional kinship, family, and clan relations that Native people continue to recognize and with that the obligations we have to each other's well-being ahead of our individual self-interests. With that, the story of one Native CDFI has come, not to an end, but back to an idea, a new beginning, and a new opportunity for us to come together.

REFERENCES

Banerjee, Abhijit V. and Esther Duflo. *Poor Economics: A Radical Rethinking of the Way to Fight Global Poverty* (New York: Public Affairs, 2011).

Coates, Ta-Nahisi. "The Black Family in the Age of Mass Incarceration," *The Atlantic* (October 2015).

Congressional Record – House. "Native American Housing Assistance and Self Determination Act of 1996." September 28, 1996, p. H11613.

Dixon, Robyn, Charles Piller, and Edmund Sanders. "Dark Cloud over Good Works of Gates Foundation." *Los Angeles Times*, January 7, 2007. Accessed April 24, 2019. http://articles .latimes.com/2007/jan/07/nation/na-gatesx07.

Encyclopaedia Britannica. "Y2K bug." Accessed October 12, 2018. www.britannica.com/tech nology/Y2K-bug.

Federal Reserve Bank of Minneapolis. "Mapping Native American Financial Institutions." Accessed October 13, 2018. www.minneapolisfed.org/indiancountry/resources/mapping-native-banks.

Grantspace. "What is a 'Payout Requirement' for a Private Foundation?" Accessed October 13, 2018. https://grantspace.org/resources/knowledge-base/payout/.

IRS. "Taxes on Failure to Distribute Income – Private Foundations." Last modified July 23, 2018. Accessed April 24, 2019. www.irs.gov/charities-non-profits/private-foundations/taxes-on-failure-to-distribute-income-private-foundations.

Kell, George. "The Remarkable Rise of ESG." Last modified July 11, 2018. Accessed April 24, 2019. www.forbes.com/sites/georgkell/2018/07/11/the-remarkable-rise-of-esg/#70ef80a81695.

Native Americans in Philanthropy. "Helping Philanthropy Address Gaps." Accessed October 13, 2018. https://nativephilanthropy.org/the-need/.

Newcomb, Steve. "Five Hundred Years of Injustice: The Legacy of Fifteenth Century Religious Prejudice." NativeWeb. Reprinted from Steve Newcomb, "Five Hundred Years of Injustice," *Shaman's Drum*, Fall 1992, 18–20. Accessed October 23, 2018. http://ili .nativeweb.org/sdrm_art.html.

Reich, Robert. "The Great Recession, December 2007 to June 2009." Last modified November 22, 2013. Accessed April 24, 2019. www.federalreservehistory.org/essays/ great_recession_of_200709.

Simon, Morgan. *Real Impact: The New Economics of Social Change* (New York: Nation Books, 2017).

U.S. Department of the Treasury CDFI Fund. "The Report of the Native American Lending Study." November 2001. Accessed October 13, 2018. www.cdfifund.gov/Documents/ 2001_nacta_lending_study.pdf.

U.S. Government Accountability Office. "Native American Housing: Additional Actions Needed to Better Support Tribal Efforts: Report to Congressional Committees." March 2014. Accessed October 10, 2018. www.gao.gov/products/GAO-14-255.

Welch, Jack. *Winning* (New York: Harper Business, 2005).

Wikipedia. "2009 Peruvian Political Crisis." Last modified July 1, 2018. https://en .wikipedia.org/wiki/2009_Peruvian_political_crisis.

Yunus, Muhammad. *Banker to the Poor: Micro-Lending and the Battle Against World Poverty* (New York: Public Affairs, 1999).

PART III

Learning from Business Scholars

7

Becoming an Entrepreneur: Essentials for Any Environment

Mark C. Maletz

I CAN A CULTURE AND PRACTICE OF ENTREPRENEURSHIP BE DEVELOPED ANYWHERE, INCLUDING NATIVE AMERICAN RESERVATIONS?

There are many challenges facing prospective entrepreneurs on the reservation: tribal bureaucracy, complexities of land/site license acquisition, and difficulty in raising capital are but a few of the hurdles that reservation-based Native American entrepreneurial ventures face. But does this mean that such efforts to create new businesses are doomed to fail? To explore this question, let's begin with a particularly inhospitable environment from the past; one that successfully gave rise to hundreds of new entrepreneurial enterprises.

When the Soviet Union dissolved on December 26, 1991, it left in its place a collection of fifteen independent republics, most of which were barely able to operate as stand-alone economies, let alone serve as fertile grounds for new entrepreneurial activity. The Soviet Union had operated as a centrally planned economy, leaving little room for entrepreneurial thought or action. Then suddenly, with the stroke of a pen, it was gone. People found the course of their lives radically altered and many were at a loss as to how to rebuild their foundering new countries. Just over a decade later, during the summer of 2002, the EastWest Institute (www .eastwest.ngo) undertook an experiment to bring entrepreneurial thinking and action to the former Soviet republics by launching the Central Eurasia Leadership Academy (CELA). The inaugural CELA program took place at Koç University in Istanbul with a group of about forty participants from eight of the former Soviet republics. These participants had no track record of entrepreneurship, but all of them expressed a willingness to take risks and an interest in building new organizations in their countries (mostly in the private sector, although some were also focused on the NGO sector). While there was no culture or track record of entrepreneurship in the region, these participants served as living proof that given the right mindset and training, entrepreneurship can surface and flourish even in the most unaccommodating environments. By comparison, Native American tribal reservations, which already have some entrepreneurial activity, represent more fertile environments to expand entrepreneurial activity.

The participants attended a thoughtfully designed entrepreneurship boot camp that focused on developing an entrepreneurial mindset that could then embark on an entrepreneurial lifecycle that would give rise to new enterprises. In the time since its inception, CELA has trained hundreds of new entrepreneurs who have launched new businesses and NGOs across the former Soviet Union. And today, the CELA Academy is a key component of a stand-alone NGO: the Central Eurasia Leadership Alliance (www.celanetwork.org) – which hosted the CELA 14 Academy during the summer of 2018. Using a series of case examples, this chapter will explore the key elements required to embark on an entrepreneurial journey: operating with an entrepreneurial mindset and managing through the entrepreneurial lifecycle.

II WHAT DOES ENTREPRENEURSHIP LOOK LIKE? HOW DO ENTREPRENEURS THRIVE IN HOSTILE ENVIRONMENTS?

Case Examples of Entrepreneurship in Action

A Red Bull

In 1987, Coca-Cola and Pepsi dominated the global soft drink sector. Coca-Cola, the U.S. market leader, had more than $7.5 billion in soft drink sales in the United States alone. Launching a new business in the drink sector that might compete with powerful incumbents like Coca-Cola and Pepsi could only be classified as highly risky – particularly given the considerable resources that these incumbents could deploy should they see a new entrant as a competitive threat. Against this backdrop, Dietrich Mateschitz launched Red Bull in his native Austria in 1987. Knowing that Coke and Pepsi prided themselves on being family-friendly brands, Mateschitz positioned Red Bull as an edgy energy drink and happily embraced a variety of "adrenaline junkies" as core consumers (e.g., snowboarders and windsurfers). As an entrepreneur, Mateschitz knew better than to take on Coca-Cola and Pepsi directly – he correctly determined that neither incumbent would care much, at least initially, about a new energy drink consumed by adrenaline junkies. His risk management strategy was to occupy a subsector that the incumbents wouldn't care about. He created the impression of an amped-up beverage – while the reality was that a can of Red Bull had roughly the same amount of caffeine as a single cup of coffee. And, when rumors began to circulate about Red Bull being made from bulls' testicles, Mateschitz chose not to deny them – since these rumors added to the mystique of his new brand.

In 2001, three Swedes died after consuming Red Bull (two after mixing it with vodka and the third after drinking several cans of Red Bull after a workout). Companies like Coca-Cola and Pepsi would have mounted a PR campaign in response to calm fears and try to assure the public that their products were very sage. Not so Red Bull – which seemed content to let the public think that their product had risks, the implicit message being that if you live life to the fullest and on the edge, there are risks – but, if you want to play it safe and live on your couch, you could drink Coke or Pepsi.

Mateschitz's strategy of focusing on a niche that Coca-Cola and Pepsi would be reticent to enter (where it would take years for either company to make the decision to enter the subsector in a substantial way) paid off, and by 2001, Red Bull controlled about two-thirds of the energy drink market in the United States. The energy drink market ($275 million in total) was less than 1 percent of the carbonated soft drink market in the United States (so, not only was the energy drink market a challenging one for family-friendly brands like Coke and Pepsi, it was tiny compared to their core market, which made it difficult for either company to want to risk their brand image for such a small niche market). Ultimately, both incumbents entered the energy drink market, but Mateschitz had years to build his entrepreneurial business.

B Softsoap

In 1977, the U.S. bar soap sector had retail sales of about $1.5 billion and a product that was the ultimate commodity. The sector was dominated by huge incumbents like Procter & Gamble, Armour-Dial, Colgate-Palmolive, and Lever Brothers, with large marketing budgets, strong brand recognition, and well-established relationships with retailers. And, the sector had experienced little growth or innovation for years. In such an environment, only an entrepreneur would even consider entering this market. Robert Taylor, founder of Minnetonka Corporation (founded 1964, sold soaps and other personal care products to department and specialty stores) saw an opportunity to enter the broader soap market with a differentiated product, still soap, but in liquid rather than bar form – dispensed in a pump bottle. He called his new product Softsoap and spent $30 million on marketing this new product. To be clear, liquid soap itself wasn't innovative – the first patent for liquid soap was issued to William Sheppard back in 1865.

As an entrepreneur, Taylor knew that he had to protect his new product from competition from the large incumbents who controlled the sector and who could spend ten times what he could on marketing without hesitation. He chose two key strategies to delay the incumbents. First, he positioned Softsoap as an alternative to bar soap – why would anyone want a messy dissolving bar of soap when they could have a clean and hygienic bottle with a use-as-needed pump? This positioning caused the incumbents to pause and analyze the situation. Jumping on the liquid soap bandwagon could result in cannibalization of their $1.5 billion sector – and Softsoap was only projecting $70 million of revenue for their new product. And, to further complicate matters, if all of the incumbents shifted to liquid soap, their market share positions would be up for grabs – some could lose significant market share, something that all incumbents feared. The second strategy focused on buying Softsoap time to establish itself as a dominant brand in the sector. Taylor knew that there were only two manufacturers capable of producing pumps in needed quantities for the new liquid soap dispensers – and he contracted for the rights to 100 million pumps – blocking competitors for at least a year. He knew that any of the incumbents would build manufacturing capacity to make these pumps, but that it would take time. The combination of these two strategies gave Minnetonka the time that it needed, and by 1985, it was the leading brand in what had become a $100 million market.

C Uber

In 2008, taxi and limo companies dominated the ride-for-hire sector. These companies had strong protections against new entrants (in the form of regulatory barriers and, in many key markets, medallions limiting the total supply of ride-for-hire vehicles). But the sector also had huge customer service challenges – taxis in particular were widely viewed as dirty, unreliable, and unpleasant. And, the more one needed a ride (e.g., during rain or snow), the harder it was to find one. Not only were customers highly dissatisfied, taxi drivers were as well (driving a taxi was one of the least desirable and least safe jobs anywhere). Much as was true of the energy drink and soap sectors, the ride-for-hire sector seemed like one worth avoiding. And yet, two serial entrepreneurs (Travis Kalanick and Garrett Camp) found a way to enter this sector after struggling to find a taxi in the snow in Paris (ironically, while looking for their next entrepreneurial business opportunity).

Kalanick and Camp understood that consumers had evolved over time – they had a deep understanding of the trends reshaping consumer behavior. These trends included widespread use of smartphones (one might even call it an addiction), with smartphones being used increasingly to manage all aspects of one's life. They also included a growing desire for both instant gratification and transparency along with an increasing preference for a cashless society and a growing reliance on crowd-sourced reputation systems (consider the Amazon product and Trip Advisor service rating systems). The service model used by taxis hadn't evolved and didn't align with any of these trends in consumer behavior, except that some taxis accepted credit cards (typically when the cities within which they operated required this as a matter of regulation or law). The Uber application conceived by Kalanick and Camp aligned with all of these trends – from running on smartphones, to ensuring an adequate supply of cars so that pick-ups could occur within minutes with high reliability, to graphically showing the movement of the car coming to pick the customer up, to operating both without the need for cash and without the need to have a credit card on hand (since it was registered to the customer's Uber account), to providing real-time crowdsourced ratings for all drivers (and to serve the analogous needs of the drivers, of all customers).

Kalanick and Camp designed a disruptive business model that was fundamentally different from the business model used by taxis. This new business model included smartphone integration, GPS tracking (and therefore transparency), and embedded payment and reputation systems. They designed this model to eliminate or minimize friction. For example, it was remarkably easy for riders and drivers to sign up. The Uber algorithms/system ensured that drivers would be available as needed and would show up within minutes (the widely disliked surge pricing actually helped with this) and pricing was used to fine-tune supply and demand. The integrated GPS provided transparency for riders and guidance for drivers (to reduce the issues with drivers getting lost or stuck in traffic). The automated payment system meant that riders and drivers didn't have to deal with payments. And, the simple rating system eliminated the need for a rules-based system to govern behavior. In fact, the simple fact the riders and drivers knew that they were being rated tended to improve the behavior of both – and in those cases where this didn't work, the rating system enabled Uber to remove undesirable drivers and enabled drivers to avoid undesirable riders.

Uber built a new business model that aligned with trends in consumer behavior, was disruptive, and reduced or eliminated friction, but Kalanick and Camp went even further by embedding two significant positive feedback loops in their model. The first was a scale/satisfaction cycle that aggressively drove increases in both driver and rider populations (more drivers translated to greater availability and shorter wait times, and more passengers translated to less downtime and more revenue for drivers – so both drivers and riders were more satisfied). And, the second was the rating system/quality control feedback loop that ensured that both drivers and riders had a better experience. As an aside, there have been many questions about why Uber enters a new market so aggressively, often ignoring existing rules and regulations, and complaints about the surge pricing model. The aggressive market entry is intended to "jump-start" the scale/satisfaction feedback loop in a new market and the surge pricing is intended to ensure adequate supply during times of high demand.

Kalanick and Camp developed a disruptive business model that became so popular that when New York City Mayor Bill de Blasio tried to shut down Uber, the mass outcry from passengers was so great that the mayor had to back down. The entrepreneurs had successfully launched a new business that radically transformed the ride-for-hire sector and that changed both driver and passenger behavior (drivers who started out thinking that driving for Uber would be a short-term gig found that they appreciated the extra discretionary income and continued driving for far longer than the drivers had imagined and passengers ended up using Uber for rides that they would never have even considered using a taxi for – many even deciding to abandon car ownership).

III MARKET ENTRY STRATEGIES

While entrepreneurs can enter any industry/sector/market where they see opportunity, as the above examples illustrate, there are some heuristics that tend to shape the market entry strategies employed by entrepreneurs. The first involves seeing opportunity where others cannot – especially opportunities that enable one to change the nature of the market/playing field. The entrepreneurs in each of the above examples do this with their new businesses. Mateschitz enters a market where the natural assumption is that the dominant incumbents will manage market expansion and will crush anyone who gets in their way. Taylor enters a market with little growth or innovation, but where the game is played for market share with huge marketing budgets. And, Kalanick and Camp enter a market with strong barriers to entry and where the conventional rules of the game require high up-front capital (to buy vehicles and sometimes medallions as well). Instead, they build an asset-lite model where they don't have to own any vehicles or medallions.

A second heuristic involves developing a deeper understanding of market dynamics and consumer preferences than existing market players. Again, each of the entrepreneurs in the three case examples accomplish this. Mateschitz sees a subsegment of the market that includes adrenaline junkies who want a product that captures their imagination and risk-taking self-image. He also sees a subsegment of potential consumers who want to be part of the "in crowd" and he therefore focuses selling his new product where the in crowds gather and where the product can be connected with colorful locals. Taylor understands the limitations of bar soap and understands the subsegments of consumers who would be drawn to liquid soap. He's even happy to see his consumers remain buyers of bar soap – for example, using bar soap in the shower and liquid soap in more public areas (e.g., a guest bathroom). And, Kalanick and Camp understand the frustrations with taxis and the new trends in consumer behavior and build a new business designed to shift consumers to their model based on addressing many of the limitations of taxis and leveraging the new trends in consumer behavior.

A third heuristic is a tendency to begin with an attractive niche and to attack this niche in a way that flies under the radar of large, entrenched incumbents. Both Mateschitz and Taylor do this – starting small and with subsegments of consumers who the large incumbents could lose without really even noticing (at least initially). Kalanick and Camp do not employ this heuristic, but it's a conscious choice, because their scale/satisfaction feedback loop requires scale. And, a fourth heuristics involves constructing new forms of barriers to entry – both business and reputation/culture oriented. Mateschitz constructs a kind of reputational/cultural barrier to entry by going after a subsegment of consumers and a risk profile that causes Coca-Cola and Pepsi to pause, neither wanting to put their family friendly image at risk. Taylor constructs a barrier to entry that is both business oriented (by buying 100 million pumps and locking out competition for about a year) and reputational/cultural (by positioning liquid soap as a better option than bar soap, thereby raising cannibalization risks for the incumbents). Kalanick and Camp construct a barrier to entry that is based on aggressive growth and achievement of scale, knowing that competitors would have to achieve similar scale to be effective in managing the supply/demand challenges of the business. In all three cases, competitors could and did surface, but these barriers gave all three entrepreneurial businesses a "head start."

IV AN ENTREPRENEURIAL MINDSET

Understanding What It Takes to Be a Successful Entrepreneur

We've talked about the nature of entrepreneurial businesses and how entrepreneurs can launch new businesses to compete against strong incumbents in challenging or hostile market environments. In the remainder of the chapter, we'll talk about what it takes to be a successful entrepreneur – beginning with an entrepreneurial mindset and ending with managing through the entrepreneurial lifecycle.

A Opportunity Focus

An entrepreneurial mindset begins with an unrelenting focus on identifying and pursuing new business opportunities. Imagine walking into your bathroom and picking up a bar of soap, only to find that it's slimy and half disintegrated. For most people, this would be a frustrating experience – one better forgotten as the disgusting bar of soap is discarded and a new one opened to replace it. But for an entrepreneur like Robert Taylor, this kind of experience would present itself as a potential opportunity – raising the question of what could replace the bar of soap to eliminate this kind of situation. More generally, every time an entrepreneur experiences a product failure or customer service disappointment, they naturally reflect on this experience and ask the question: "What could replace such a failure with a higher probability of success?" For example, in the world of financial services, one of the most regularly disappointing and frustrating experiences is applying for a mortgage. The process is slow and complicated and entirely lacks transparency – there's no way to know how long it will take or what the outcome will be. Years ago, one astute financial institution (Commerce Bank) decided to largely eliminate mortgages from the products that it offered its clients – they knew that they couldn't be sure that their mortgage application process would be any better than that of their competition and were happy to see their customers work with their competitors in an area where their customers were sure to be frustrated and unhappy – thereby making Commerce Bank look that much better (their customer service experience in the areas of other banking products was world class). Commerce couldn't offer the kind of mortgage product that an entrepreneurial business might develop, so they didn't even try. In contrast, Quicken Loans took a more entrepreneurial route and entered the online mortgage space with a commitment to "make mortgages simple" and "put the power in your hands." The result was Rocket Mortgage (launched in 2016), one of the first fully online mortgage products and by 2018, Quicken Loans had become the nation's largest mortgage lender.

There's another chapter in the Quicken Loans story that provides further evidence of an opportunity focus. What is today Quicken Loans was originally Rock Financial, founded in 1985 by three entrepreneurs, Dan Gilbert, Gary Gilbert, and Lindsay Gross. In 1999, Intuit (which made financial products like QuickBooks, TurboTax, and Quicken) purchased Rock Financial for $532 million and renamed the company Quicken Loans. In 2002, Dan Gilbert saw an opportunity and led a small group of private investors in the repurchase of Quicken Loans back from Intuit – for only $64 million. Interestingly, Intuit, in its early days, had been highly entrepreneurial when it was founded in the early 1980s as a seven-person start-up. Incumbents in the personal financial software sector focused on competing on product features and their products grew more feature rich but also more complex with each release. As a result, these products were very difficult to use and master, and a majority of users found that they only used a small subset of the features available in a product. Intuit knew that it couldn't compete on features, so instead, developed a product with only the most frequently used/important features and made their product highly intuitive and easy to learn and use. In this way, Intuit saw opportunity in a shortcoming of the incumbent products in the space and managed to capitalize on this to shift the playing field (from features to ease of use) – and became the market leader in the space that they had helped to redefine.

B Deep Understanding of Risks and a Willingness to Take Risk Based on This Understanding

Entrepreneurs are often characterized as natural risk takers, individuals who are drawn to making big bets and taking on significant risk. This is, in fact, a mischaracterization. Great entrepreneurs are comfortable taking risk based on a deep understanding of the risk and ways to manage it. The fact that entrepreneurs typically have a better understanding of risk than their peers can lead their peers to believe that these entrepreneurs are taking on greater risk than they are – which enables the entrepreneurs to act in ways that their peers could not or would not. Consider, for example, Robert Taylor's situation after he had secured 100 million worth of pump production – making it impossible for others to enter the pump bottle-dispensed liquid soap market for at least a year. This knowledge could enable Taylor to make what might seem like risky pricing decisions in a world where competitors could quickly enter the market and undercut his prices. But, since Taylor knew that he had at least a year free of significant competitive pressures, he could make more aggressive pricing decisions than would seem appropriate to those without the knowledge of his 100 million pump agreement. While great entrepreneurs often begin with a focus on opportunities, before they commit to pursuing any specific opportunity, they always develop a deep understanding of the risks associated with the opportunity and ways to reduce or eliminate at least some of these risks.

Sometimes risks can be offset. For example, a strong first mover advantage, coupled with a commitment to rapidly improve an early product, can help to offset technical risks with that product. When Apple first introduced the iPhone, one could have argued that the product wasn't really ready – it was too expensive, operated with a closed architecture in an environment that was clearly moving toward open architectures, and had no enterprise connectivity (which effectively eliminated corporate buyers from considering the first iPhone). Within four months, Apple reduced the price and within eight months, it shifted to an open architecture and added enterprise connectivity. Apple fully understood the technical risks associated with the first iPhone release but had a rapid/iterative follow-on release schedule that enabled them to overcome these risks and enter the market with what became a dominant product.

C Embracing the Long View, Coupled with a Willingness to Adapt

Entrepreneurs naturally embrace the long view and play the "long game" with a willingness to adapt over time. The Apple iPhone launch (described above) is one example of this behavior. Those mobile phone manufacturers operating with a short timeframe/horizon would have waited until the iPhone was "ready" for market – figuring that they had to get it right from the beginning, that they essentially had only one shot. Apple knew that consumers buy in predictable waves, beginning with early adopters, and that they had more than enough time to refine their new phone before the more mature buying wave would begin.

Another example of operating with a long view is Amazon when it decided to enter the toy market. Today, most of us think of Amazon as the dominant retailer in the toy market, but when Amazon made the decision to enter this market, Toys "R" Us was the dominant player. Amazon developed a ten-year partnership agreement with Toys "R" Us in which Toys "R" Us owned and managed the toy inventory (which they considered their core competency) and Amazon handled the co-branded website and customer service. Amazon understood that with a ten-year horizon, they would have ample time to learn what they needed to know about toy buying. And, Amazon understood that by managing customer service on behalf of this partnership, they would ultimately own the customer relationships. The partnership limited the ability of Toys "R" Us to compete against Amazon and even before the end of the ten years, Amazon emerged as the dominant retailer in the toy market.

Adaptability is a key complement to embracing the long view. Most entrepreneurs realize (or learn) that what they think the future holds is often wrong, and their ability to adapt (quickly) ensures their long-term survival. One of the early players in the artificial intelligence sector (a company named Inference) built an engine that could be used to develop expert systems (software capable of reasoning and performing tasks typically performed by human experts). Their founders were convinced that there was a market for the engine that they had developed. What they learned was there was a much bigger market for expert systems and they adapted their business model to focus more on developing expert systems for corporate clients than on selling their engine. In making this shift, they had to be willing to realize less revenue from engine sales while revenue from expert system develop-ment projects grew (this was complicated by the fact that the sales cycle for these expert system development projects was longer than the sales cycle for the engine). Their long view enabled them to commit to this shift, which resulted in a more profitable business over time.

D A Relentless Focus on Excellence – Both Service and Operational

Most businesses talk about providing excellent customer service (exceeding custo-mer expectations) and operating efficiently – but for far too many of these businesses, these are more like slogans than core operating principles. A key factor in the inability of these businesses to achieve excellence in both of these dimensions is the lack of an "owner mindset" among the executives responsible for organizational performance in the customer service and operational dimensions. It's not that these executives don't care, but they care at the level of delivering "best efforts," which is a very different standard than the level of care that someone who feels like an owner of the business (and therefore fully responsible and accountable for the performance of the business) experiences. Almost by definition, entrepreneurs operate with an owner mindset because at least in the early stages, these entrepreneurs are the owners. They typically see the business as an extension of themselves – and therefore want the business to achieve excellence in its interactions with customers and in the way that it operates internally. And, because most entrepreneurial businesses are resource constrained (particularly with respect to cash flow), the entrepreneurs who launch these businesses are highly cost conscious and care deeply about cost control.

Commerce Bank (mentioned in Section IV.A.1) is a great example of customer service achieving levels of service and satisfaction that are distinctive and represent a genuine competitive advantage. Similar to the way in which most ride-for-hire customers were historically dissatisfied with taxis, most bank customers were histori-cally dissatisfied with banks. In fact, for most customers, they had so little confidence any bank could rise above the rest, they often chose to stay with banks that they were not satisfied with. Most customers felt that the cost of switching to another bank wasn't worth it, since any other bank would likely be equally bad. The term "banker's hours" came to refer to short working hours (something like 10 to 3) that meant that bankers were never available when you needed them. Nowhere was this more the case than New York City – with a bank on almost every corner, all closed when a majority of customers were off work and needing to visit a bank. Against this backdrop, Vernon Hill founded Commerce Bank in 1973 as a small community bank in southern New Jersey and playing the long game, expanded into New York City (along with Pennsylvania and Delaware). Commerce branches were open from 7:30am to 8:00pm during the week with modified hours on the weekend. And if a branch was in a busy location or if there was a local event that might require bank access later, a branch's drive-through window might stay open as late as midnight. Commerce even had a ten-minute rule requiring branches to open ten minutes before the posted opening time and to stay open until ten minutes after the posted closing time. Commerce recruited employees based first on attitude – friendly, outgoing, service oriented. The bank kept their product offering simple (far fewer products and less complexity) so that in the attitude versus aptitude dimensions, they could focus more on attitude (while other banks typically focused largely on the aptitude needed to handle the complexity of their product set). The result was that while all other banks chose to compete on products, Commerce competed on service – and achieved the highest levels of customer service ever seen in the banking sector. Interestingly, they funded this customer service excellence by offering the lowest interest rates on deposits of any bank in the region – not apologetically, but proudly. Customers who chose Commerce were choosing and valuing customer service over range of products or interest rates (and, this policy tended to repel price/interest rate-sensitive customers who were typically less loyal). The Commerce operating model emphasized delivering and recognizing excellence in customer service. Every employee could give peers WOW! stickers when they observed a colleague delivering excellent service. In many organizations, this kind of model would lead to collusion ("I'll give you a sticker if you return the favor"), but at Commerce, because employees were hired for attitude and a commitment to service excellence, this model provided for informal recognition that was highly valued and not abused. The unprecedented levels of customer satisfaction led to growth rates (of customers and deposits) that were far greater than any peer institution in the region.

The other dimension of excellence that entrepreneurs focus on (almost as an obsession) is operational excellence and cost management. Entrepreneurs understand the importance of managing cash flow, being highly cost efficient, and having the opportunity to optimize return on investment through both driving revenue (which customer service excellence fully facilitates) and minimizing expenses (which the cost-conscious focus ensures). As an example, consider an investment bank based in Brazil (BTG Pactual). The bank went public in 2012, but unlike all other banks that had been partnerships and chose to go public (including Goldman Sachs in 1999), BTG Pactual chose to maintain their partnership, with partner equity remaining at book value (rather than trading up to market value at the time of the IPO). To be elected a BTG Pactual partner required an entrepreneurial spirit and a track record of performance, client service, and cost consciousness. Unlike their counterparts at other investment banks who often traveled in luxury (limos, first-class airfare, suites at five-star hotels), BTG Pactual partners were extraordinarily cost conscious – traveling in taxis, coach-class seats on airplanes, and regular hotel rooms at three-star hotels). Moreover, at the time of the IPO, when senior executives at other banks were enjoying meals costing hundreds of dollars, BTG Pactual partners limited their meal costs to something like $50 per day. It's not that the firm couldn't afford to spend more – by the time of the IPO, BTG Pactual was valued at several billion dollars. It's that they chose to remain true to their entrepreneurial, cost-conscious culture.

E Creating a Meritocratic Culture

A meritocratic culture is one where people are selected, assessed, and rewarded entirely on the basis of their ability and performance. Creating such a culture requires highly effective performance and talent management processes and practices – especially because it's so easy to believe that one is being meritocratic when in fact, one is influenced by biases (often not even fully recognized). For example, for years, symphony orchestras were comprised entirely or largely of white men. New orchestra player selection was typically performed by a panel of experienced musicians who were tasked with finding the best possible performer for each role – based on interviews, listening to individuals perform, and trying to assess "fit" with the orchestra (recognizing that performing in a symphony orchestra is as much about teamwork as it is about individual capability). These panels routinely selected substantially more white men for open roles than women or people of color. Then, what seemed like a minor change to the selection process was made. Instead of being able to see candidates as they performed, the panels listened to these performances while the candidates played from behind a curtain – so that the panels could not determine the gender or race of the candidates. With this single modification, far more women and people of color were selected for open roles. The panels were not intentionally biased and believed that they were meritocratic, but were clearly influenced by unrecognized biases. For this reason, while most organizations claim to want to be meritocratic and many claim to have succeeded in this aspiration, a great many are not actually meritocratic.

To determine whether an organization is genuinely meritocratic, one has to first assess the quality and effectiveness of the organization's performance and talent management processes and practices – to see if they're sufficiently rigorous and to see if there's any likelihood of embedded bias. One then has to determine the extent to which the organization embraces these processes and practices – making them the core mechanisms by which people in the organization are selected, assessed, developed, promoted, and rewarded. For far too many organizations, the formal people management processes look adequate to supporting a meritocratic culture, but fall short in their implementation and adoption across the organization.

An example of an organization with a highly meritocratic culture is the consulting firm McKinsey & Company. All employees, from junior associates to senior partners, undergo regular and rigorous performance evaluation processes – that include 360-

degree input from an employee's manager, peers, and (if the employee manages others) subordinates along with input from clients with whom the employee interacts. And, to ensure that the meritocracy begins at the top of the organization, all partners undergo regular performance evaluations that are even more rigorous than the evaluations used with other employees. This includes a panel process whereby every partner is evaluated by other partners who haven't worked with the partner being evaluated (to help to minimize any bias that could result from the evaluator knowing or having a relationship with the person being evaluated). In a consulting firm where all partners are responsible for client service, revenue generation, and engagement management, investing this kind of time in the performance evaluation process signals the importance of this process and the meritocratic culture that it supports.

F Being Willing to Fail Fast and Learn from Failure Without Assigning Blame

Entrepreneurs live with two often contradictory beliefs. The first belief is that the opportunity that they've chosen to pursue is highly likely to result in a very profitable business and that they know enough to have a clear sense of what this business will look like (once they've committed to the opportunity). Without this belief, an entrepreneur shouldn't pursue the opportunity – since entrepreneurial start-ups require tremendous time and effort and a firm belief in the value of the opportunity. This belief is also important because it lets entrepreneurs recruit others who can buy into the excitement that the entrepreneur feels. Almost nobody would want to get involved with a start-up where the founder says that he or she doesn't know what the business will look like. The other belief is that the path to success almost always includes elements of failure – that there are important lessons in this failure – and that the resulting business will be even more successful based on applying these lessons. Generally, entrepreneurs keep this second belief mostly to themselves – knowing that it's difficult to excite others about a vision that includes a reasonable likelihood of some failure. But, at the same time, entrepreneurs have to build an environment that has a high degree of tolerance for failure and a commitment to learn from failure rather than assign blame or punishment for the failure. In this way, failure is best seen as a part of the journey toward success. And, every time that a failure occurs, the way in which the entrepreneurial leader and leadership team respond to the failure signals how the organization really feels about failure. Truly accepting failure means accepting it every time it occurs. Even occasional lapses where failure is punished can signal that failure really isn't tolerated. Of course, this is subject to some natural constraints. A recurring failure where the people involved fail to learn from their mistakes should not be accepted – nor should failures that result from taking risks that were far too large for the organization. The entrepreneurial leader of BTG Pactual is fond of saying that he's comfortable if employees take a risk and "crash the car if passengers are wearing seatbelts and not being reckless," but not if employees "crash the plane." In addition, failures that result from inadequate

TABLE 7.1: *Key elements of an entrepreneurial mindset*

Opportunity focus
Deep understanding of risks and a willingness to take risk based on this understanding
Embracing the long view, coupled with a willingness to adapt
A relentless focus on excellence – both service and operational
Creating a meritocratic culture
Being willing to fail fast and learn from failure without assigning blame

thought or effort (i.e., failures that could have been avoided had those involved taken more care, thought, or effort) should also not be accepted. One other important characteristic of the willingness to accept failure is the preference to "fail fast" – which means that entrepreneurs are generally willing to recognize failure sooner than most business leaders (who either demand more data and analysis than is necessary or become too invested in pushing for success to be comfortable with failure).

Consider a leading corporate example of willingness to fail in pursuit of innovative business opportunities (an example of corporate entrepreneurship), 3M. The 3M journey toward corporate innovation and entrepreneurship began back in 1914 when William McKnight became general manager of the company and instituted a philosophy of "listen to anyone with an idea." This philosophy spawned the 3M 15 percent rule, which allows employees to spend 15 percent of their work time on experimental efforts that could result in new products for the company. One famous example of this in action was the Post-it Note innovation. But, interestingly, the Post-it Note was preceded by a failure. A 3M scientist, Spencer Silver, had been working to develop a new, strong adhesive. That effort failed and the result was a very weak adhesive. Then, a colleague of Silver, 3M scientist Art Fry, used his 15 percent time to see if he could apply Silver's adhesive to the back of a piece of paper. He thought he was building the "perfect bookmark." He tested his new invention with some of the secretarial staff for senior leaders at 3M, who loved the new Post-it Notes – so much so, that when Fry had finished the pilot, many of the secretaries didn't want to return the samples and instead, wanted a larger supply, having found the Post-it Notes to be so useful. Silver's "failure" proved to be the essential ingredient in a hugely successful new product for 3M.

V THE ENTREPRENEURIAL LIFECYCLE

Effectively Managing Through All Stages of the Lifecycle

For the remainder of the chapter, let's assume that you either naturally operate with an entrepreneurial mindset or that you've committed to adopting this mindset in preparation for identifying and launching an entrepreneurial venture.

Imagine that it's the late 1990s and you've just had an MRI done at a major research hospital. The technician who worked with you to take the MRI is on break and you start up a conversation. You're hoping to get the technician to tell you what she saw (something she's not supposed to do), but you end up getting an interesting history of medical imaging:

- Until the late 1970s, all medical images were produced in hard-copy form. This involved multiple roles and handoffs and was quite costly. It was estimated that for a simple x-ray image, the total cost was in excess of $30 (and sometimes much higher). And, to make matters worse, a nontrivial number of x-rays were misplaced or lost – which in some cases put patients at risk and in all cases frustrated both patients and physicians.
- In the late 1970s, networking and digital imaging had progressed sufficiently so that hospitals could shift from physical to digital medical imaging. A new approach called PACS (Picture Archiving and Communication System) was introduced to manage these medical images. PACS required significant capital expenditure – including a dedicated network for use by PACS and dedicated reading rooms with specialized hardware/monitors to read the images. Radiologists would then go to these dedicated reading rooms to read the medical images. While far less expensive than physical images (roughly $10 for an x-ray versus $30 for a physical x-ray copy), given the number of medical images at a hospital, the PACS costs did amount to a significant expense item (in addition to the very substantial up-front capital cost and ongoing licensing and maintenance costs).
- By the time of your visit, all hospitals operated highly reliable and robust intranets – completely separate from the PACS networks.

As your technician's break was coming to an end, you asked to see a radiology reading room. In the room, you saw several radiologists reviewing images on the room's monitors – and couldn't help but wonder why they had to go to a reading room when they all had large, comfortable offices with large computer monitors.

A Opportunity Identification

The first, and ongoing, stage of the entrepreneurial lifecycle is opportunity identi-fication. Given the opportunity focus of the entrepreneurial mindset, looking for new opportunities is something that entrepreneurs should be doing constantly. Every product or service failure, every unmet customer need, every emerging trend in consumer behavior and preference, could give rise to a new business opportunity.

In the case of the medical imaging situation described above, you might ask yourself if there's an opportunity to replace PACS with something that could run on the existing intranets within hospitals. This could eliminate the need for a dedicated

PACS network (something that the IT department would presumably appreciate, since it would eliminate the need to maintain two separate networks within the hospital) and could let radiologists read medical images from the comfort of their own offices. It would also eliminate the need for dedicated reading rooms and for all of the associated hardware (freeing up capital for allocation to other medical equipment or facility needs).

Once an opportunity has been identified, there are two key trains of thought to pursue. The first involves the feasibility of pursuing the opportunity and the second involves understanding the economics, market, and likely impact should the opportunity prove to be feasible.

To address the feasibility question for the medical imaging question, you would have to find subject matter experts who could determine whether medical images could be delivered to a radiologist's office computer over the hospital's existing intranet and whether the radiologist could then effectively read and interpret the image on his or her computer monitor. In the late 1990s, conventional wisdom would indicate that this wouldn't work – the images were too numerous and too large for the existing intranet to manage and radiologists required the complete image without any compression (since compression resulted in image distortions that would reduce the radiologist's ability to correctly read and interpret the image). PACS vendors, serving their own interests, fully supported the view that only dedicated networks could handle the bandwidth requirements of hospital-wide medical imaging. But, remembering that entrepreneurs always take a long view, you could hold on to this opportunity until either technology advances enabled hospital intranets to handle the bandwidth requirements of medical images or something else changed. As an entrepreneur, you wouldn't just put the idea in a "future file drawer," but rather, you would regularly scan to see if something changed to make the idea feasible. Doing so over time would let you uncover some interesting research out of the University of Pittsburgh Medical Center (UPMC). UPMC researchers discovered that while radiologists were unwilling to read compressed images and thought that they needed the entire image before they began reading it, in reality, they did a kind of preliminary high-level scan of the image followed by "deep dives" into areas of interest. This meant that rather than requiring the entire image in full resolution at the start, a high-level view of the image with a real-time ability to deep dive into an area in full resolution would suffice. While hospital intranets couldn't manage the delivery of all images in full resolution, they could manage the delivery of images that could be read using this deep-dive approach. The research opened the door to a technical solution that would work across existing hospital intranets – and identified a potential source of technical resources that could be approached as part of pursuing this opportunity.

To address the economics/market/impact question you would start with the economics of the PACS market, which surpassed $500 million in annual revenue by the mid-1990s. You would also find various projections indicating that the market

TABLE 7.2: *Opportunity identification questions*

What are the most significant trends in consumer behaviors and preferences on the reservation and are there new products or services that would align with these trends?
Do you see unmet needs or customer service deficiencies on the reservation that could be addressed by an entrepreneurial start-up?
What do tribal members who have lived off of the reservation for a period of time miss most if they return to living on the reservation?
What are the most common reasons people travel to businesses that are based outside of the reservation, and could any of these be replicated on the reservation – perhaps with a greater focus on tribal members as customers?
Are there products or services that are useful, but not fully aligned with the cultural values of your tribe – and if so, which could be redesigned to be a better fit with your cultural values?
Are there long-standing products or services on the reservation that could be significantly upgraded or improved based on new technologies?

would surpass $1 billion by the mid-2000s. So, the market potential for your opportunity, positioned as a replacement for PACS, would be more than sufficient to consider pursuing this opportunity. In terms of impact, some financial analysis would suggest that your product could bring the cost per image down from $10 for an x-ray to something on the order of $1 per x-ray – and without the need for up-front capital investment in hardware or networking. The other part of the impact analysis would determine that both radiologists (who would be able to read images using your approach in their offices) and hospital IT departments (who would no longer have to maintain dedicated PACS networks or reading rooms) would likely be strong supporters of your new approach.

So, having determined that your opportunity is both technically feasible (albeit with real work still to be done) and attractive with respect to economics/market/impact, you're ready to proceed to the next stage in the entrepreneurial lifecycle!

By the way, the medical imaging opportunity that we've been discussing was a real opportunity in the late 1990s and resulted in the launch of a new start-up (Stentor) in 1998. In 2005, Royal Philips Electronics acquired Stentor for $280 million.

Opportunity identification can take place in any environment, including the reservation. Table 7.2 raises some questions that might help to identify potential opportunities on the reservation.

B Formation of an Entrepreneurial Leadership Team

In the Red Bull, Softsoap, and Uber examples discussed in Section II, we focused on the founding entrepreneurs of these three companies. In fact, it's natural to associate a new entrepreneurial business with its founding entrepreneur(s). But, the reality, particularly for successful entrepreneurial businesses, is that the founding entrepreneur assembles a team capable of achieving high performance and delivering results as a team. In forming and leading this entrepreneurial leadership team, there are several things that have to be in place for the team to achieve high performance. And, if all of these things are in place, the team also develops a higher degree of trust than most teams.

1 SHARED OBJECTIVES AND VISION. The team has to have a clearly articulated shared vision of what they want to accomplish as a team. Teams often believe that they have this, but a simple exercise can demonstrate the extent to which the vision is genuinely shared across the team. Interview each team member individually and ask them to articulate the vision in just a couple of minutes. Videotape these interviews, and then watch all of them, one after another. In listening to the videos, assess whether each team member is saying essentially the same thing, or whether there are material differences in the visions that they articulate. The vision can certainly change, and with entrepreneurial ventures, the vision is in fact likely to change over time. But, the key to an effective team is that at any specific point in time, team members should share a common vision.

2 COMPLEMENTARY SKILLS – WITH DIVERSITY. High-performing teams are comprised of members with complementary skills – an essential factor in ensuring that the team is "more than the sum of its parts." And, the set of skills represented by the team has to be aligned with the nature of the work (and vision) that the team will pursue. Teams also achieve greater performance when there's diversity among team members, in a variety of dimensions (including gender and race, background, problem-solving approaches, and diversity of thought). Entrepreneurs can fall into the trap of recruiting a team in their image – since such a team can readily embrace the entrepreneur's vision – but while this may seem appealing initially, it leads to suboptimal team performance and business results.

3 EFFECTIVE TEAM PROCESS, INCLUDING ROLES AND NORMS. Entrepreneurial teams tend to be task focused. With limited resources and big visions/agendas, it's all too easy to focus on getting work done. But great teams protect time to also focus on team process – which helps to ensure that the tasks being worked on are the right ones. As part of this process focus, these teams establish clear roles and team norms. Many teams establish roles and norms early in the formation of the team, but great teams regularly revisit roles and norms (and team process more generally) to make sure that they remain relevant or that they're updated as needed.

4 OPEN COMMUNICATION. Most teams express an interest in "open communication" but this is far harder to achieve than to state. It means that when most of the team is in agreement, but there are dissenting members, the team is committed to make the time to hear dissenting opinions with the real possibility that the team might shift direction based on these opinions. To achieve high performance, a team

has to be highly transparent in its actions (a form of openness with respect to communication) and has to ensure that all members are listened to (and, importantly, feel heard). Many of the highest-performing teams talk about an "obligation to dissent" – as a step beyond a willingness to listen to dissenting opinions.

5 MUTUAL ACCOUNTABILITY. Mutual accountability is the result of team members holding themselves and one another accountable for things that they commit to do on behalf of the team. In teams with a culture and practice of mutual accountability, team members can focus on their responsibilities, comfortable in the knowledge that their colleagues on the team will do the same. And, when mutual accountability is a core characteristic of the team, it's accompanied by a culture of trust among the team members.

6 COMMITMENT TO LEARNING AND REFLECTION. High-performing teams make the time to pause and reflect – ensuring that they're pursuing the right vision and working on the right things. And, they do this routinely, not just infrequently. This reflection contributes to a learning culture for the team – since reflection can surface issues, concerns, and failures – all of which can lead to learning and improvement. This team attribute aligns nicely with the willingness to fail attribute of the entrepreneurial mindset.

C Obtaining Needed Resources

Once the leadership team is in place and has established a preliminary vision for the new enterprise, they have to work to identify and obtain the resources (e.g., human, financial, technological, etc.) needed to pursue the vision. In the case of the medical imaging business (Stentor), the leadership team had to obtain capital (from venture capitalists) and several kinds of specialists. Some of these specialists were immediately obvious – for example, researchers from UPMC (who had conducted the breakthrough research on which the company's medical imaging application would be based) and information technology subject matter experts (in the areas of imaging and user interface design for medical applications to be used by physicians). Other resource needs only became clear over time. For example, as the Stentor project progressed, it became clear that there was a significant need for project managers who were experienced in working with information technology departments in the hospital setting – since these departments served as gatekeepers for the hospital's information resources and could either support or block vendors offering new applications. The important takeaway here is that obtaining needed resources begins as soon as the entrepreneurial leadership team is in place, but it continues throughout the remainder of the entrepreneurial lifecycle – since changes in vision and direction for the business often elicit the need for new and different resources.

D Business Development

With the leadership team and needed resources in place, the new business can transition to the business development stage – which includes prototyping the products or services that the new business will bring to market and then testing these prototypes with pilot initiatives. This stage has to be approached with an iterative orientation – iterating between prototypes and pilots to see how the market responds. While these iterations are taking place, the company should also begin building both brand awareness and market anticipation for their new products and services. As the business development stage progresses, these products and services should become more robust and increasingly more ready for full launch.

E Launch

When the prototypes and pilots of the business development stage have achieved a sufficiently high probability of market adoption, the business enters the launch stage where it commits to and implements a go-to-market strategy. Product and service iteration can continue during the launch stage, but the primary focus of this stage is managing the market adoption for the company's new products and services and ensuring sufficient sales and profitability to transform the company into a viable economic entity. With a successful launch of the company's products and services, the company establishes these products and services as its core business and is then ready to move to expansion of this core.

F Expansion

McKinsey & Company developed a model of Three Horizons of Growth. The first horizon is the maintenance and defense of the core business. The second horizon is the nurturing of emerging business – often business that is adjacent to the core business (e.g., a sneaker retailer deciding to develop a line of sports clothing). And, the third horizon is the creation of entirely new business. Most large companies focus most of their attention on horizon 1, some on horizon 2, and a relatively small amount on horizon 3. The nature of entrepreneurial businesses shifts this pattern, at least initially – with entrepreneurs creating something entirely new (horizon 3). This then becomes the core of a new business (which effectively makes it horizon 1 for the new business). The leadership team then has to manage expansion across all three horizons: continuing to defend and expand the core business, finding natural extensions and adjacencies for the core business, and finding entirely new businesses that could be housed in the same organization. The complementary skills attribute of effective leadership teams means that the team should have leaders who have strengths in (and preferences for) each of the three horizons. It is common to find that the entrepreneurial founder is often most comfortable with horizon 3 activities.

G Reinvention

Reinvention can apply to entrepreneurs and to the businesses that they create. In the case of entrepreneurs, reinvention typically begins with the entrepreneur exiting the business that he or she founded. This exit can be the result of a liquidity event (e.g., IPO or acquisition) where shareholders conclude that it's time for the founding entrepreneur to exit or it can be the result of the entrepreneur's choosing to exit – typically because he or she feels ready to do something new. In either case, reinvention starts with a return to the opportunity identification stage of the entrepreneurial lifecycle.

Entrepreneurial business reinvention is typically a response to a business that has either reached its natural end of life (where the market for the product or service is on a decline curve that will ultimately result in the obsolescence of the product or service) or never really took off. Sometimes, the best outcome is letting the business die, so that something new can emerge in its place (in keeping with the tolerance of failure component of the entrepreneurial mindset), but sometimes, it's worth salvaging elements of the business and returning to the opportunity identification stage of the entrepreneurial lifecycle, armed with the potentially viable building blocks from the failing or failed business.

In either case, reinvention leads back to the opportunity identification stage of the entrepreneurial lifecycle – and the lifecycle proceeds through its stages on the journey toward something new and entrepreneurial.

Successfully navigating the seven stages of the entrepreneurial lifecycle enables entrepreneurs to pursue new business opportunities in any environment – including environments that are as generally inhospitable to business development as Native American reservations.

TABLE 7.3: *Stages of the entrepreneurial lifecycle*

Opportunity identification
Formation of an entrepreneurial leadership team
Obtaining needed resources
Business development
Launch
Expansion
Reinvention

To succeed as an entrepreneur, particularly in environments where new business development is challenging, entrepreneurs have to ensure that they can accomplish three things:

1. Operate with an entrepreneurial mindset, beginning with a consistent focus on opportunities. These opportunities must be viable in the reservation context, but the entrepreneur should make sure that he or she considers opportunities that are "out-of-the-box" (e.g., while there may be opportunities in the more conventional fast-food, hospitality, and tourism spaces, the entrepreneur shouldn't limit his or her envisioning to these spaces). Whatever the opportunity, the entrepreneur must develop a deep understanding of the risks, embrace the long view with a willingness to adapt (knowing that whatever the initial vision, it's likely to change over time), focus on service and operational excellence, create a meritocratic culture within the new enterprise that he or she launches, and ensure a willingness to fail fast, learn, and evolve.
2. Build a strong leadership team, one that has complementary skills that are well suited to the new enterprise, and that operates as a team with shared vision and goals and norms designed to enable the team to deliver on the vision and opportunity. The entrepreneur should simultaneously operate as a leader of the team, a collaborative member of the team, and a coach and talent developer for members of the team.
3. While every entrepreneur must build a meritocratic culture to succeed, in more challenging environments, the entrepreneur must ensure a dual focus while building the enterprise: delivering strong business performance and building an organizational culture tailored to supporting the business (and this culture should be aligned with the core values of the tribe). For example, for businesses with a service orientation, a fundamental focus on understanding customers and delivering service excellence should be core cultural values. These values should permeate the entire organization, not just those employees who have regular customer contact. For businesses with a production/manufacturing orientation, the culture should focus on achieving excellence in every aspect of one's work. For example, for many tribes, tribal culture embraces excellence in work done by hand (which explains why Native American jewelry is so highly prized) – and this core value could be used to foster production excellence.

If an entrepreneur can deliver on all three of these imperatives, he or she significantly increases the chances of success for the new enterprise.

8

Prototype, Validate, Pivot, Repeat: A Short, Short Course in Entrepreneurship

Daniel Stewart

If you open twenty academic textbooks and look for a definition of entrepreneurship, you will likely get twenty different versions. In other words, entrepreneurship is a concept that has no objective, generally accepted "truth" as to what it means to be an entrepreneur. Most academic definitions will include something about the exploitation of opportunities for gain. Many definitions also include the term "innovative," implying that entrepreneurs must create something disruptive in their market space to be considered entrepreneurial.

However, academic definitions of entrepreneurship don't always align with general layperson definitions. My guess is that if you walked around a public event and randomly queried twenty people on their definition of entrepreneurship, many definitions would include the terms "small business" or "business owner."[1] So, the public often thinks of business ownership and entrepreneurship as being one and the same. As it turns out, the definitions are not incompatible, especially within Native American communities. I say this because, compared to other ethnic groups, Native Americans have one of the lowest rates of private business ownership within the United States.

It merely takes a drive around a rural reservation to confirm that there are not, in general, an abundance of private businesses. My own reservation (Spokane Tribe) is in Wellpinit, Washington, a rural area on the eastern side of the state. When you drive around Wellpinit (a typical, decent-sized reservation with a population that hovers around one thousand tribal members), you notice that there are only two population centers in which a business could feasibly be located. A closer inspection reveals that most of the buildings within these areas are, in fact, government buildings that house various tribal government programs. There is some commercial activity, to be sure. For instance, you will find a nice grocery store at the center of the reservation and you will find a boating marina, gas station, and small casino at the edge of the

---

[1] Please excuse the informal tone I will often take throughout this chapter. It is my firm belief that our youngest generations, regardless of education level, must embrace entrepreneurship quickly to ensure the well-being of our tribal economies. Given the urgency of the topic, this chapter is written with the general reader in mind, with the intent that it might reach a broad audience – and quickly so.

reservation. However, even these businesses, the most highly visible on the reservation, are tribally owned. This is not to say that Spokane tribal members do not own private businesses –there are a few. What it does say is that most of the jobs on the reservation are to be had with tribal government or within a tribally owned business (which, technically, are also under the purview of the tribal government). Because there are so few privately held businesses, a tribal member who opens a private small business could, in fact, be considered a social innovator. In my mind, this makes small business ownership quite entrepreneurial within the American Indian community.

This is not to say that entrepreneurship and small business ownership are equivalent terms. Think of the relationship like this: all small business owners are entrepreneurial, but not all entrepreneurs are small business owners. In fact, entrepreneurship is a concept that applies to all sizes of organizations from the smallest to the biggest, including nonprofit and governmental organizations. This is because the process of entrepreneurship is the tool that organizations use to evolve and adapt to changes in their competitive environment. There are very few, if any, organizations that are fortunate enough to exist in a static marketplace. Thus, the adage rings true – the only constant is change. In a world of constant change, organizations have two choices to thrive. You can either imitate others who are doing well or create new ways of doing things, which includes new and innovative products and services. So, when we talk about entrepreneurship in the Native American community, we can talk about the smallest, one-person micro-ventures as well as the largest tribal organizations. Both the micro-entrepreneur and the large tribal venture will eventually need to show an entrepreneurial flair to survive.

Another reason I dislike the artificial separation of "entrepreneurship" and "small business" is this: at the heart of the business model, the entrepreneur and the small business owner both have the same issue – the need to create value for customers. I teach a sequence of entrepreneurship courses at the undergraduate and graduate levels. The core tenet we focus on in these courses is "value creation." All businesses must create enough value in their products or services that customers are willing to pay for that good. In addition, that value must be greater than a competitor's value if there is competition.

Frankly, I think value creation is a topic that is underdiscussed in Indian Country. A cursory review of the emails and social media posts I receive from various Native American business entities reveals many forums and discussions that focus on topics such as finding government contracting opportunities and legislative issues, but very few on the more microelements of establishing and growing an entrepreneurial venture. As such, in this chapter, I will review the basic elements of the entrepreneurial sequence I teach to my students, which include enrolled tribal members in Gonzaga University's unique MBA-in-American-Indian-Entrepreneurship (MBA-AIE) program. Normally, this entrepreneurship curriculum takes place over several months. So, consider this to be a short, short (perhaps the shortest ever) course in entrepreneurship.

I STEP O: IDEATE

Some entrepreneurs are lucky. Ideas are given to them and their job is to focus on the execution of that idea. For example, a tribe may have an opportunity that suddenly presents itself and it simply needs an astute management team to run with the opportunity. As such, we'll call this step "zero." Most other entrepreneurs are left to the process of ideation – the careful and deliberate process of forming a new idea. Ideation is important for entrepreneurship, since a new business may be formed around the idea. Ideation is also important for older and established organizations, since this is the process that leads to new product ventures, which potentially become the lifeblood of the organization in subsequent generations.

Ideation is daunting to many. I encounter many would-be entrepreneurs who believe that they are not creative individuals and, as such, they believe that they could never come up with a new idea that is good. It surprises many to hear that creativity is only part of the ideation process. In addition to creativity, ideation also involves imagination and innovation.

A Imagination and Innovation

One version of imagination involves reflection. Reflection helps one to see things that take time to notice. I am not suggesting that entrepreneurs need to go on literal ceremonial vision quests, but it does pay to occasionally sit quietly and observe one's surroundings. One activity that is popular with my students is to find a quiet place and journal the things they notice in five-, fifteen-, and forty-five-minute increments. This is done without moving around, just sitting peacefully. In the first five minutes, students notice structures, landscaping, and other obvious features of their surround-ings. By fifteen minutes, they notice subtle architectural patterns in buildings or maybe they catch a glimpse of a piece of artwork that they had never noticed before. By forty-five minutes, they often report discovering the sounds of the breeze moving through the trees and even the smell of the grass in which they are sitting. In other words, their minds become more finely tuned to the nature of things around them as they sit quietly and observe. Imagine what you might see if you were to sit and reflect at your place of work, or at the place where your customers use your product or service. Perhaps there will be new discoveries about your customers or your product offerings just waiting for you to take the time to notice.

Another version of imagination is the group version. Think of the initial stages of group ideation like you would a brainstorming session. One of the primary rules of brainstorming is that anything goes. It is a numbers game that is usually won with a higher number of ideas. The general idea here is that the probability of finding a good idea increases as the number of ideas generated increases. Implicit in this statement is the notion that not all the ideas that come from the group are good.

So, how do you get to the good and innovative ideas? Churn. Start throwing out ideas without judgment. Typically, the first ideas to come out of a group aren't bad, but they are typically safe and mediocre. Nobody wants to be the first person with a "crazy" or "dumb" idea. So, let those mediocre ideas get their airtime and then keep the ball rolling. As the number of ideas generated starts to accumulate, the ideas will start to become increasingly bad . . . and increasingly good, as well. This is what we call the idea curve. In the idea curve, mediocre ideas emerge first followed by a mixture of bad ideas and good ideas, followed by a mixture of even worse and even better ideas until eventually the ideas coming out are a mixture of horrible and brilliant. So, to get to the brilliant ideas, you must churn through the mediocre ideas, the bad, the good, the worse, the better, and the horrible!

Why is it that the brilliant ideas emerge last? It's partly due to risk aversion among group members – nobody wants their idea to be rejected. However, what also happens is that ideas begin to build off one another and patterns and possibilities emerge that wouldn't be seen, except for the path dependence that is created when the group starts to build upon previous ideas. New and novel combinations and syntheses emerge, based on the iteration of ideas that come before. Therefore, the bottom line is: generate lots of ideas and allow them to build on one another.

B Open Innovation

More recently, a lot of attention has been placed on the notion that many of the ideas available to an entrepreneurial organization don't even come from within that organization. This is called open innovation. Open innovation is a community-based perspective on ideation. In other words, it is possible that an organization may get good ideas from external stakeholders such as alliance partners, joint venture partners, and even end users and customers. With open innovation, an entrepreneur actively looks to the outside world for ideas that it can use, license, buy, or develop with the help of others (such as business partners, universities, or government entities). Open innovators are fond of the slogan "not invented here."

A key advantage of open innovation is speed. Rather than spending time to conduct numerous rounds of internal research and development, an organization that uses open innovation can capitalize on ideas that are already out there, just waiting to be exploited by the right organization. It may be the case that your organization is in a better spot to exploit an idea than the original owner of the idea. For instance, reservation-based tribal businesses may be able to use their location on sovereign land to create or distribute products or services that would otherwise be difficult or impossible to produce or sell off-reservation due to unique tribal commercial codes.

C Summary

Ideas may emerge from multiple levels: individuals, groups, organizations, and communities. An organization should be prepared to seek and exploit ideas at all levels. A robust process of ideation helps ensure an entrepreneurial organization produces an ample number of ideas so that at least a few of those ideas are marketable.

II STEP 1: PROTOTYPE

A *Physical Prototype*

This is usually what people think of when the term prototype is used. *If* your idea involves a physical good, then it is important to quickly start building a prototype of your idea. The key here is simplicity. Do not go overboard trying to build a perfectly functional beta model. Start with sketches and move on to simple builds, using whatever materials you might have available. If you are designing a digital product, create a quick "wireframe" prototype so people can see what the app/website might look like. The reason for speed is simple. The faster you build a prototype, even a crude one, the faster you can begin learning more about your idea, its pitfalls, and whether it truly has merit with buyers.

B *Value Proposition*

How does an organization know which ideas and products are good? Good ideas create value that others want to pay for. In other words, an idea should address a need or solve a problem *and* have a market. The short statement that you use to communicate the idea to others is known as the "value proposition." The value proposition is something that is important to all entrepreneurial ideas, whether those ideas involve a physical good or not. So, in addition to physical prototyping, consider value proposition design (VPD) to be the process of prototyping of your abstract idea. The value proposition has two main components: a) your targeted customers and b) the benefits of your product/service, which can be described in terms of "pains" and "gains."

Pains and Gains

For your product or service to sell, you must create value for your customer. Value is created when a product either provides a positive benefit that customers like or removes a negative problem that customers dislike. In other words, valuable products and services provide "gains" or remove "pains." This gains/ pains framework is the basis for determining a product's value proposition.

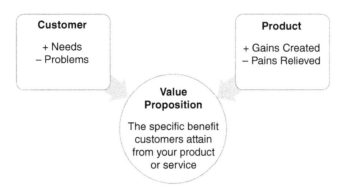

FIGURE 8.1: The value proposition

Benefits can be defined along multiple dimensions. For instance, customers usually prefer products that are a) inexpensive, b) innovative, c) high quality, d) convenient, or some combination of these attributes. Note that the value proposition is not simply a description of your product/service – it is a clear statement of specific gains or pains your product addresses for your targeted customers. A useful exercise is to fill in the chart below:

Start with identifying the needs and problems faced by your targeted customers. Then list the specific gains that will be experienced by your customer or, alternatively, the specific pains that your product will relieve. If there is a good match between customer needs and product benefits, then your product creates value for consumers. If there is not a good match, then you may be building a product or service that no one needs or wants.

C Value Propositions in Indian Country

It is worth discussing how the value proposition framework applies to Native American businesses. All products must have a perceived benefit, or the product will not sell, but it is not always clear what that benefit is. Some Native American products and services are not perceptibly different than other products sold in the competitive market. For instance, a tribally owned construction company will provide roughly the same building services to its clients as will a nontribally owned competitor in the same market (construction firms build to preexisting architectural specifications that will apply equally to all prospective builders, regardless of ownership). If products/services are not noticeably different, the Native American entrepreneur must either compete on price alone or find some way to differentiate the product. One way to differentiate products is simply by association with American Indian culture, which is an outcome of something called the culture-of-origin effect.

The Culture-of-Origin Effect

The culture-of-origin effect[2] is similar to what marketing scholars call the "country-of-origin" effect. The country-of-origin effect suggests that consumer perceptions of a good are influenced by its country of origin. Thus, attributes of the home country have a halo effect on the products emerging from that country. For example, German engineering is considered to be world-class and, as such, German automobiles benefit from the perception that German engineering is superior. Now, swap out "culture" for "country" and we can make the same argument for goods originating from specific cultures –cultural associations affect the perceived value of products emerging from that culture. In our case, American Indian businesses can leverage positive public perceptions of American Indian culture and identity as a commercial resource. Simply put, Native American identity becomes a source of cultural capital that entrepreneurs can use to help market and brand goods or services.

It is important to note that cultural identity can only remain a source of competitive advantage if cultural authenticity is protected. When cultural identity is perceived as valuable by outsiders, it becomes possible for community members to use identity as a form of capital, but noncommunity members may try to appropriate the culture for their own use. However, in most communities, there is a process of legitimation by which individuals earn the right to be recognized as authentic members of the community. The process and legalities of identifying "authentic" tribal members is a discussion for another day, so for now we will simply note that, once an authenticity threshold is met, cultural insiders can use their "insider" status to create and market authenticated goods to others. Thus, the culture-of-origin strategy is the explicit use of cultural identity *by community insiders* to increase the perceived value of their goods or services.

The direct implication for Native American entrepreneurs is this: consumer perceptions of Native American culture affect the desirability of Native American-branded goods and services. American Indian culture becomes a commercial resource when American Indian identity is invoked in the marketing of "authentic" Native American goods or services. For example, Sister Sky, a northwest U.S. company owned by two Native American sisters, brands its line of lotions and cosmetics as authentic traditional products, since the formulas used in their products have been handed down through multiple generations (www.sistersky.com). This authenticity creates value for consumers and helps to increase demand for Sister Sky's goods. All entrepreneurs who use "Made in Native America" in their marketing explicitly utilize positive cultural connotations to increase perceived customer value for their goods.

---

[2] Stewart, Daniel et al. "Native American Cultural Capital and Business Strategy: The Culture-of-Origin Effect." *American Indian Culture and Research Journal* 38.4 (2014): 127–38.

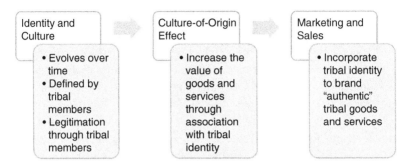

FIGURE 8.2: Culture-of-origin in Native American business strategy

There are a few noteworthy implications of using tribal culture to sell goods. As a business strategy, culture-of-origin protects tribal members from outside competition since authentic cultural identity cannot be easily imitated by outsiders (non-tribal members). However, the underlying cultural identity that is used to create value for consumers is subject to constant evolution, and, moreover, culture is under little control from any specific tribal member. As a social process, tribal culture evolves endogenously through community dynamics that are similar to crowdsourcing and open innovation (discussed in <u>Section I.B</u>).[3] Here are a few inherent issues and risks associated with using tribal culture and identity as the basis of a business strategy:

- Culture and identity are nonproprietary, which makes them difficult to protect through legal channels.
- Culture is shared within the community, which means other tribal members have the same claim to use cultural identity as you do.
- No single person controls the culture or how the culture evolves, which means other tribal members may interpret or utilize the culture differently.
- Identity-based strategies are easy to see and can be imitated by other tribal members.

Tribal communities develop their own norms, beliefs, and values over time and those values change across generations. Thus, what we consider to be authentic American Indian culture and identity is likely a bit different than what our parents (and their parents, etc.) consider to be authentic. However, no single tribal member determines the collective tribal norms and values. Culture is determined by the shared beliefs of the broader community of tribal members. Thus, a tribal entrepreneur that chooses to compete on cultural "authenticity" will need to ensure that authenticity is maintained within the bounds of evolving, community-defined

---

3   Stewart, Daniel et al. "Open Identity: The Evolution and Exploitation of Shared Cultural and Community Identity," in *Harvard Open and User Innovation Conference Book of Abstracts* (2016): 129–30.

norms and standards. Failure to do so will make it difficult for the entrepreneur to create a commercially viable good or service.

D Business Model Prototype

Once you have established a value proposition, your next task is to create a business model around that value proposition. You may be asking yourself, "Why didn't he say business *plan*?" After all, your tribal council probably wants to see a business plan and your tribal economic development entity may require a business plan before they will approve new tribal ventures. The short answer is this: a full business plan takes too long to create, and it is likely to be wrong, anyways. Formal business plans are typically full of details that outline and discuss multiple variables you need to consider to execute your idea. A lot of the information in a business plan is good information to have, but there is a key difference between established organizations (which do benefit from a business plan) and an entrepreneurial venture: an established organization executes an idea that is already known to work, while an entrepreneur is attempting to build an idea that has not been fully vetted. Hence, a business plan is great for execution of an established idea, but an entrepreneur still needs to figure out if the idea works!

In lieu of a full-fledged business plan, entrepreneurs may consider a business model canvas. A business model canvas is a simple visual representation of the way in which you intend to execute your idea. Thus, while the value proposition defines the benefits you wish to provide to your customer, the business model canvas shows how you plan on creating and delivering that value. In other words, value proposition is the "what" and the business model canvas is the "how."

Currently, the most popular canvas is Osterwalder and Pigneur's framework, which utilizes a large, single-page map of the key elements of an organization's business model.[4] The major elements of the canvas are:

- Value proposition – what is the specific benefit offered?
- Customers – who are your buyers?
- Customer relationships – what type of relationship will you establish with customers?
- Marketing and sales channels – how will you reach those customers?
- Key activities – what key *tasks* do you need to perform?
- Key resources – which *assets* are critical?
- Key partners – who will help you perform key activities and attain resources?
- Key costs – how much will this cost you?
- Revenue streams – how does this all turn into revenue?

---

[4] Osterwalder, Alexander, and Yves Pigneur. *Business Model Generation: A Handbook for Visionaries, Game Changers, and Challengers.* John Wiley & Sons, 2010.

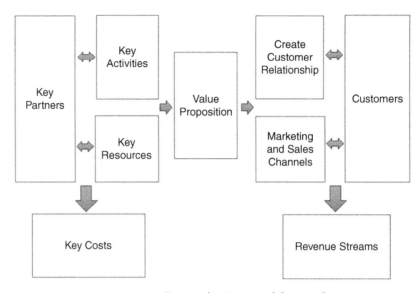

FIGURE 8.3: Generic business model canvas[5]

Figure 8.3 shows a simple and generic business model canvas. The left-hand side of the canvas focuses on building the product, or if you have a service business, creating the service. Each business has tasks it must perform (activities) and assets it must get (resources) to build the product. Examples of key activities include: research and design, manufacturing, marketing, sales, and customer service. Examples of resources include: equipment, cash, and intellectual capital. Normally, an entrepreneur will not have all of the skills, nor will it have all of the resources, it needs to be successful. Hence, it is critical to identify which other organizations or individuals the company must partner with to perform key activities or acquire key resources. Some examples of key partners include: manufacturers, subcontractors, and financial institutions. In Indian Country, I would also include tribal governments and federal agencies as potential key partners. Once a firm identifies its key activities, resources, and partners, it is then able to identify the key costs that will be incurred to get the product built or service to market.

The right-hand side of the canvas focuses on the interface with customers. A firm needs to decide the type of relationship it wants to develop with customers. When defining relationship, think in terms of depth and length. Depth is the amount of interaction required or desired by customers. Length is the time frame that the relationship is expected to last. At the simple end of the spectrum, firms do business over the Internet and never meet their customers, limiting their customer relationship to the cash-for-goods exchange at hand. For example, Amazon resellers are there to sell you a good, and following that transaction, the buyer and the seller go their separate ways

[5]   Visit www.strategyzer.com for a larger, digital version that works well for group use.

with no implied relationship beyond that sale. At the other end of the spectrum, firms develop deep customer relationships that can last years, or even decades, and the firm may even treat customers as partners in the evolution and development of the firm's product or service. For example, tribal casinos often create membership "clubs" that encourage casino guests to come back often. In return, the casino uses real feedback from its guests to help the casino improve its services and offerings.

In addition to defining the type of customer relationship, a firm must decide which sales channels to use to reach the customer. Examples include: internet, retail, wholesale, and direct sales. A firm can use multiple channels, but it is important to learn which channels customers prefer and to note if different customer segments prefer different channels. Once a firm has defined its customers and the ways in which it will reach those customers, it is then able to identify where it can expect its primary revenue streams to emerge (the bottom right block of the canvas).

Once a business model canvas is filled out, we can see the real value in using a canvas instead of a full business plan. Because the canvas is filled out with simple bullet points, it is easy to change any variable and then use the canvas to see if change in one block creates cascading change in other nearby blocks. When I use the canvas with students, we will fill out a large canvas using sticky notes. When a student wishes to prototype or brainstorm changes to their business model, we simply replace an existing sticky note with a new sticky note showing the proposed changes, and then we work outward from the changed block, gaming changes that might need to occur in adjacent or nearby blocks. As such, the business model canvas can be a powerful business prototyping tool.

Summary

Prototype your idea quickly to determine whether your product or service has merit. Physical prototyping need not be sophisticated or expensive. In addition to physical prototyping, begin creating a value proposition, a statement that describes the specific benefit that your product or service gives to customers, either by creating a positive (gain) or removing a negative (pain). A business model is the entrepreneur's general idea of how the firm will deliver its good or service. A business model canvas allows an entrepreneur to visually prototype changes to its cost structure and/or revenue streams and to analyze how changes in different elements of the business model affect profitability.

III STEP 2: VALIDATE

Once a business model is developed, it is time to validate the idea. Simply put, validation is the process of finding evidence that your idea works. This encompasses verifying both the value proposition and the business model. The canvas itself can be used for gaming hypothetical changes, but nothing replaces getting verifiable evidence that a) customers really do want the product you are offering and b) your business model can realistically be executed the way you think it should.

THINK LEAN. The failure to validate is perhaps the biggest mistake new entrepreneurs make. It is too easy for entrepreneurs to fall in love with their idea and become so enamored with the idea that they move forward too aggressively, spending precious resources on an idea that isn't proven. In entrepreneurship, it is better to follow the principle of "lean" design. Lean design is the principle of investing minimally, but quickly, in a prototype to establish a Minimum Viable Product (MVP) that can be tested with real customers before more substantial investments are made – and potentially lost. In essence, lean design is the iterative process of design, build, test, and redesign, while incorporating constant feedback from key customers and other stakeholders. Being quick to test your idea reduces the risk of losing capital on ideas that have no market or need major adaptations.

GET OUT OF THE BUILDING. Validation requires entrepreneurs to get their idea out of their imagination and into the real world. As such, validation requires learning more about potential customers and their needs. There are many possible ways to attain insights about potential customers. Here is a partial list:

- Use archival data from third parties.
- Create surveys.
- Observe customers in their environment.
- Try to impersonate your customer to gain an understanding of their needs.
- Interview the customer directly.
- Create experiments where customers can test your MVP.
- Involve customers directly in product development.

There is not a single "best" method. In fact, an entrepreneur may want to use multiple methods and triangulate the results. The main point is that the entrepreneur must be willing to go out and get customer feedback, both positive and negative, that can be incorporated into the product or service *as the product is being designed* to reduce the notable financial risks of going to market with a product that nobody wants.

POSITION YOUR PRODUCT AND COMPANY. As the core product/service idea becomes more fully vetted, it is important that the entrepreneur also validate the accompanying business model. Every element in the canvas should be verified. Are you targeting the right customers? Are you reaching them through the most effective channels? Do you have the correct skills and resources? Will you need to partner with others to help build or create a valuable product? Etc.

One important element in the business model is the identification of company-specific strengths that contribute to value creation.[6] In business, a firm-specific strength is a called a distinct competence. For a firm to create a product that

---

[6] Stewart, Daniel, "Business Strategy: Building Competitive Advantage in American Indian Firms" in Kennedy, Deanna M. et al., eds., *American Indian Business: Principles and Practices*. University of Washington Press, 2017.

consumers value enough to buy, the firm should have unique skills or possess assets that contribute value to the product. In other words, each firm should *be good at something* or *have something* unique to create uniquely valuable products. The difference can be described as "things we do" (capabilities) versus "stuff we have" (resources).

Competencies based on skill sets are referred to as "capabilities." Capabilities are skills that allow an entrepreneur to create a good that is differentiated from competing goods by quality or price, or perhaps both. For instance, a capability in manufacturing could allow a company to build higher-quality goods than its competitor. In Native American communities, an example of using unique skills would be traditional arts. Native American artists and musicians possess a skill set that is valued by consumers and is difficult for others to mimic. In other words, they have a unique (distinct) skill (competence) that allows them to create products that consumers value. For instance, good beadwork or good drumming are skills that take years, even decades, to master and consumers of these art forms would have to look far and wide to find acceptable alternatives to authentic beading or drumming.

Competencies based on unique assets are referred to as "resources." Like capabilities, resources are assets that allow an entrepreneur to create goods or services that are differentiated from competitors by price or quality. Resources may reveal themselves in many forms. Common tangible resources are cash, physical plant, property, and equipment. However, resources are often intangible. Intangible resources include valuable nonphysical assets such as intellectual capital, patents, cultural awareness, key relationships, or legal protections. Intangible assets are often more difficult to identify and quantify, but they can be just as critical for a company's success as tangible assets.

To create competitive advantage, skills and/or assets should contribute to an entrepreneur's value proposition. Using the terminology above, a firm's competencies must allow the entrepreneur to either create a gain or relieve a pain. Table 8.1

TABLE 8.1: *Examples of tribal distinct competencies*

		Customer Value	
		Pain Reliever (−)	Gain Creator (+)
Source of Tribal Distinct Competences	Resource (Asset)	• Tribal Sovereignty • Section 17 Charter	• Natural Resources • Cultural Identity • SBA 8a Status
	Capability	• Traditional Healing	• Traditional Arts

shows examples of competencies that can be used by American Indian entrepreneurs to create customer value:

Resource as Pain Reliever. Tribal sovereignty works well here. Sovereignty is a legal status that is held by tribes, but that status can create benefits for entrepreneurs. As such, this legal status falls into the "stuff we have" category instead of the "things we do" category. Tribes can use sovereign status – for example, through Section 17 charters – to create a more business-friendly environment by minimizing regulatory and/or tax burdens (both pains) for firms that wish to do business on reservation or trust lands.

Resources as Gain Creator. The most obvious example to place in this block would be true natural resources. Some tribes and tribal businesses are fortunate enough to be in geographic regions that allow for the sustainable harvesting of natural resources that have value on the open market. Another example would be the "culture-of-origin" strategy discussed above, which uses the intangible resource of tribal identity to create goods that are valued for their association with American Indian culture. The push to brand products as "Made in Native America" demonstrates the demand for products that are perceived as being culturally authentic. Cultural capital is a resource that outsiders (nontribal entrepreneurs) are not able to take advantage of. Therefore, cultural authenticity becomes a source of competitive advantage for tribal businesses.[7] A third example would be federal SBA "8a" status, since the status itself creates unique contracting opportunities and price advantages for 8a firms.

Capability as Pain Reliever. Traditional healing is literally the use of culture-specific skills to relieve pain from individuals or, in the case of spiritual and emotional healing, families and communities. Consumers may prefer traditional healing methods due to the perceived effectiveness of traditional medicine or because of cultural values and preferences. Either way, there is a market for indigenous healing, both physical and spiritual.

Capability as Gain Creator. Traditional arts are valued for their intrinsic beauty. Consumers value good beadwork, drumming, etc. because these crafts take decades for artists to master. Mainstream (non-Native) artists are also valued for the same reason. However, indigenous artists can protect their market space by using cultural authenticity as a barrier to imitation by non-Native American artists.

Summary. Everything about an entrepreneurial idea is merely a theory until tested. Validation is the process of generating evidence and data that either confirm or

---

[7] It is interesting to note that, in addition to using culture as an externally oriented marketing tool, American Indian business leaders also perceive culture as a benefit in the leadership and management of tribal businesses (Stewart, Daniel et al. "Being Native American in Business: Culture, Identity, and Authentic Leadership in Modern American Indian Enterprises." *Leadership* 13.5 (2017): 549–70).

reject your hypotheses regarding both the product/service itself and the business model and strategy that will be used to create a sustainable business. Validate early and validate often to reduce risk.

IV STEP 3: PIVOT OR PROCEED

It is uncommon for an idea to remain fully intact after the validation process. Entrepreneurs may find out that the original value proposition is slightly wrong, or the intended customer base isn't as strong as originally thought, or perhaps the business model is not sustainable because costs or revenue streams are not what the entrepreneur was expecting. Once an entrepreneur has more data to work with, a decision must be made: proceed on the same path or change directions. A change in strategic or operational direction is called a "pivot."

Pivoting is an essential part of the entrepreneurial process and the whole notion of changing midstream exemplifies why an entrepreneur should focus on being "lean." Imagine the risks a company would incur if it were to undergo an entire process of product development, production, marketing, and then distribution . . . only to find out that product isn't profitable! The financial and reputational losses could be catastrophic to an entrepreneur. Being lean implies that an organization constantly tests its hypotheses, whether those ideas are about product features, manufacturing feasibility, sales channels, or anything else that affects the viability of the business model, and then uses the results of those tests to inform change.

It should also be noted that pivoting is a process that requires humility. Individuals may become so personally attached to an idea or business model that pride can interfere with the ability to admit that changes must be made. There may be political and reputational risks that are associated with change. When ideas change, those changes may not be in everyone's best interest. For example, as casino gaming started to grow and become a major contributor to tribal economies, tribes had to decide whether to self-manage casinos or to outsource major components of casino management. A few tribes in my region (Pacific Northwest) decided to hire external managers or management firms to run their growing casinos. This path created more than a bit of internal consternation from tribal members who felt that tribes did not trust their own tribal members to do the job, many of whom already had experience running smaller tribal casinos. The decision to use outside contractors was certainly a political risk for council members.

An equally painful choice beside pivot or proceed would be to not proceed at all. If the validation process reveals that an idea is simply not feasible, then the idea should be laid to rest. Unfortunately, most entrepreneurs cannot see clearly enough to make this choice on their own. It helps to have some decision-making process or routine that will allow a bad idea to be terminated. For example, tribal council could create a review team that recommends go/no-go decisions on new tribal ventures.

In summary, each idea should be carefully vetted and tested before large amounts of resources are committed. Pivoting is the process of using data and evidence to change your idea as it develops, hopefully increasing the odds of the product or service doing well in the market.

V STEP 4: REPEAT

Once the choice to proceed or pivot has been made, the process becomes iterative. In other words, the entrepreneur must constantly reassess and revalidate whether it is still on the correct path with the idea, the product/service, and the business model. One reason to repeat the cycle often is that your customers evolve over time and, as their needs and preferences change, your product or service must also change. Another major driver of change is competition. If your product has competitors, you can rest assured that those competitors will be trying to create a better product than yours. If they do, you must react accordingly or risk failure.

VI FINAL THOUGHTS

Congratulations on completing the short, short course in entrepreneurship! If you've made it this far, I hope you have a greater understanding of the entrepreneurial process. Many of the students I work with comment that the process is much more iterative than they had imagined, resembling a quasi-scientific experiment that is played out in real time using real data. It is my belief that this is a process that can help increase the success rate of new entrepreneurial ideas emerging from Native American communities.

In the end, tribal entrepreneurship is simply entrepreneurship in a unique context. The fundamental principles of business do not change dramatically for tribal entrepreneurs compared to nontribal entrepreneurs. Entrepreneurship has always been, and will continue to be, extremely risky. It turns out that most new and novel ideas are bad (or at least "not good") and most new ventures are at a high risk for failure. However, tribal entrepreneurs can mitigate some risk associated with

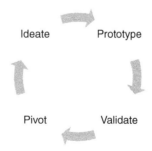

FIGURE 8.4: The entrepreneurial process

entrepreneurship through understanding the entrepreneurship process. Tribes should actively promote and cultivate a culture of entrepreneurship in which all tribal organizations and tribal entrepreneurs are encouraged to learn and engage in the process of ideation, prototyping, validation, and pivoting.

Doing so may be essential for the future of our people. Native America is primed for a revolutionary explosion in free market economic activity. However, for tribes and tribal members to become more entrepreneurial, tribal members must be educated in business and entrepreneurship, allowing entrepreneurship to become a key driver in economic development. Understanding the process of entrepreneurship and business creation will allow tribes and tribal members to set forth on a path of true economic independence. Hence, entrepreneurship should become part of the language we use when we discuss tribal sovereignty and self-determination. Control your own revenues, control your own destiny. That is true sovereignty.

9

Supply Chain Management and Native American Entrepreneurs

Stephanie L. Black and Deanna M. Kennedy

I INTRODUCTION

Although Indigenous peoples were once effective traders, barterers, and business-people across many areas of the world,[1] the introduction of new dominant cultures – and with them new laws and policies – changed the economic landscape, limiting traditional modes of commerce. In the United States, Article II, Section 8 of the U.S. Constitution granted Congress the authority to regulate both interstate commerce and commerce with "Indian tribes." This inhibited many opportunities for Native Americans to pursue entrepreneurial activities by minimizing autonomy or the autonomy of sovereign nations to develop their own economies. These past limitations started to relax with the Indian Self-Determination and Education Assistance Act in 1975 and the American Indian Gaming Act of 1988. These governmental changes have provided the grounding for Native Americans in the United States to regain some of their legal sovereignty and self-govern.[2] As such, across the past forty years there have been several Native American tribes able to develop a strong legal, political, and economic presence. This has created the opportunity and motivation for Native entrepreneurship and the establishment of new business ventures by and for Native peoples.[3] Nevertheless, Native American-owned businesses still represent the smallest number of minority businesses in comparison to other minority groups.

To effect change and help more Native American entrepreneurs prepare and manage successful business ventures, we aim to provide clarity and guidance on a major function of the business; that of supply chain management. While recent literature provides information about practices and principles of a Native American

---

[1] Gladstone, J. S., "Embracing Cultural Tradition," in *American Indian Business*, ed. Kennedy, D. M. et al. (Seattle: University of Washington Press, 2017), 16–26.

[2] Chaudhuri, J., "American Indian Policy," in *American Indian Policy in the Twentieth Century*, ed. Deloria, Jr., V. (Norman: University of Oklahoma Press, 1985), 15–34.; Jorgensen, M., *Rebuilding Native Nations: Strategies for Governance and Development* (Tucson: University of Arizona Press, 2007).

[3] Stewart, D., Gladstone, J., Verbos, A., & Katragadda, M., "Native American Cultural Capital and Business Strategy: The Culture-of-Origin Effect," *American Indian Culture and Research Journal*, 38, no. 4 (2014): 127–38.

business,[4] the function of supply chain management for Native business owners has yet to be discussed in depth. The supply chain of a product entails all of the providers and customers of direct or indirect components from raw materials to the delivery of a good or service to an end user. Simply put, the upstream of a supply chain considers who will be your supplier of parts or products, who are the suppliers of your supplier, and so on up the supply chain until you reach the providers of raw materials. The downstream of a supply chain considers who you sell your products or services to, and who your customers sell to, and so on until you reach the end user.

Although the decisions about who to buy from and who to sell to seem straightforward, they may not be as trivial as first perceived. Indeed, the operations of an organization that move the input of parts or products through to the customer is typically the highest cost center of an organization. This is because it is costly to buy goods, conduct any transformational processes that add value to the goods, hold inventory, and deliver goods to customers or the services that consume those goods. While it might seem that there are obvious decisions that can reduce costs (e.g., buy in bulk to obtain quantity discounts), these come with trade-offs such as creating more inventory that can require greater monitoring, insurance, and human resources. As well, supplier choices can be subject to customer opinion. For example, in the 1990s Nike fell under public scrutiny for the use of child labor and poor working conditions in their contracting manufacturing facilities.[5] Originally, Nike did not consider that they were responsible for their contractors, but consumers perceived that they were and Nike's failure to take action resulted in consumers boycotting their products at the Barcelona Olympics as well as colleges pulling their products due to student protests. Finally, Phil Knight, CEO of Nike, decided the negative consumer reactions were impairing the brand image. In 1998, Phil Knight stated, "The Nike product has become synonymous with slave wages, forced overtime, and arbitrary abuse," … "I truly believe the American consumer doesn't want to buy products made under abusive conditions."[6] Nike has become a proponent of change by increasing contract worker pay and supply chain monitoring, adopting Occupational Safety and Health Administration (OSHA) clean air standards, and establishing the first VP of Corporate Responsibility and a Corporate Responsibility Committee.

To understand the supply chain decisions for a Native business entrepreneur we use this chapter to clarify the entities of a supply chain, the different types of activities required by a business in the supply chain, the alignment of operational priorities across the supply chain, and the management of internal organizational and external supplier and customer relationships. We then expand our perspective to consider the influencing factors on supply chain entities and the impacts created.

[4] Kennedy, D. M., Harrington, C., Verbos, A. K., Stewart, D., Gladstone, J., & Clarkson, G. (eds.), *American Indian Business* (Seattle: University of Washington Press, 2017).
[5] Barnet, R. J. & Cavanaugh, J., "Just Undo It: Exploited Workers," *New York Times*, February 13, 1994.
[6] Nisen, M. "How Nike Solved Its Sweatshop Problem," *Business Insider*, May 9, 2013.

Specifically, we focus on those factors and impacts relevant for Native business entrepreneurs and the questions they create in making supply chain decisions.

II WHAT IS A SUPPLY CHAIN?

A supply chain refers to the entire network of entities (e.g., the individuals, organizations, resource activities, and technology) directly or indirectly involved in the creation and sale of a product or service. Figure 9.1 provides a diagram of the supply chain with various entities. The supply chain connects a supplier of raw materials to a manufacturer that uses those materials. In certain cases, the banks or venture capitalists must provide funding to pay the supplier for the release of raw materials. The manufacturer produces the product using the raw materials received. When the rate of production exceeds the rate of consumption by the next entity in the chain, the manufacturer may choose to send products to a warehouse or distribution center for storage. Then, when the retailer is ready to receive goods, they are shipped from the warehouse to the retailer. The customer, as the end user in the supply chain, then buys the product from the retailer.

As the figure shows, a supply chain is a complex network of business entities involved in the upstream and downstream flows of products and/or services that includes finances as well as information.[7] The management of a supply chain requires all entities to be present in the systematic and strategic coordination of flows within and across the organizations with the goals of reducing costs, improving customer relations, and gaining a competitive advantage for each organization in the supply chain.[8] The main flows of the supply chain, represented in the figure by arrows, are the product flow, the information flow, and the financial flow. While the product flow moves left to right, the financial flow or payments for goods and services moves right to left. The information flow occurs in both directions so that supply and demand can be effectively discussed and forecasted by entities.

One way to consider the importance of product, information, and financial flows to any given entity of the supply chain is to consider different primary and support activities. These activities determine how the company will work internally to take in inputs and produce outputs for customers. Organizational scholar Michael Porter[9] suggests that primary activities are directly related to the creation and delivery of

---

[7]   *See* Beamon, B. M., "Supply Chain Design and Analysis: Models and Methods," *International Journal of Production Economics*, 55 no. 3 (1998): 281–94.; Lambert, D., "The Eight Essential Supply Chain Management Processes," *Supply Chain Management Review*, 8 no. 6 (2004): 18–26; Mentzer, J. T. et al., "Defining Supply Chain Management," *Journal of Business Logistics*, 22 no. 2 (2001): 1–25.

[8]   *See* Cooper, M. C. & Ellram, L. M., "Characteristics of Supply Chain Management and the Implications for Purchasing and Logistics Strategy," *International Journal of Logistics Management*, 4 no. 2 (1993): 13–24.; Cooper, M. C., Lambert, D. M., & Pagh, J. D., "Supply Chain Management: More than a New Name for Logistics," *International Journal of Logistics Management*, 8 no. 1 (1997): 1–14.

[9]   Porter, M. E., *The Value Chain and Competitive Advantage. Understanding Business Processes* (London: Routledge, 2001).

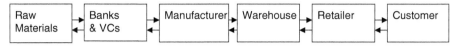

FIGURE 9.1: Supply chain example

a good or service. These primary activities are comprised of five main areas including inbound logistics, operations, outbound logistics, marketing and sales, and service, which are linked to support activities to improve their effectiveness or efficiency. The support activities are comprised of four main areas that include procurement, technology development (including R&D), human resource management, and infrastructure (systems for planning, finance, quality, information management, etc.).

Depending on the size of the organization and the quantity of a product produced, the primary and support activities will take on different levels of importance and resource requirements. For example, a start-up accounting office serving individuals may be created where the entrepreneur alone conducts the marketing and sales to drum up business, the operations of the accounting service, the procurement of office materials, the inbound logistics of receiving office supplies, and the outbound logistics of sending or delivering out completed forms. However, if the entrepreneur decides to start an accounting company that services a variety of clients, both individuals and organizations, then the entrepreneur may engage in additional primary and support activities. Indeed, primary activities will need to be expanded to ensure that the company has the required operations, logistics, marketing, and sales for each service. As well, the entrepreneur will have to hire and manage people with the expertise to address different service needs and build an infrastructure to support those employees and services.

While the primary and support activities are internal decisions, they should be informed by the activities of upstream and downstream partners in the supply chain. Indeed, because each entity in the supply chain of a product or service is connected through the product, information, and financial flows, the decisions made upstream and downstream will, for better or worse, impact the characteristics of the products and services that are offered. As well, how supplier inputs are transformed into company outputs determines what can be sold to downstream partners and customers. In particular, as an entrepreneur sets up a company, they must decide what their operational priority is and therefore what success for the company will look like. Four high-level operational priorities include cost, quality, on-time delivery, and flexibility.[10] When an entrepreneur prioritizes operational cost, a business decision-maker may focus on providing low-cost outputs by obtaining low-price parts and services from suppliers and minimizing the operational processes needed

[10]   Krajewski, L. J., Malhotra, M. K., & Ritzman, L. P., *Operations Management: Processes and Supply Chains*, 11th edition (New York: Pearson, 2016).

to turn the inputs to outputs. An entrepreneur hoping to achieve a high-quality product may intentionally source inputs that have an assurance of high quality so that the output offered from the company may in turn be of high quality. For an entrepreneur to achieve an on-time delivery priority, suppliers need to have goods available for quick delivery. When an entrepreneur desires the firm to be flexible, suppliers need to be able to change the characteristics or quantity of their goods and services in order to reflect new requirements.

In the past, entrepreneurs held that activities regarding the input materials, parts, and products purchased by their company and transformed into products and services sold to customers were unaffected by the decisions made by suppliers. Yet, successful businesses have shown that working with suppliers and customers to manage the production and delivery of goods and services to customers can create a more desired offering to the market. For example, Apple is a high-tech company that has been ranked among the best companies in supply chain management in the world. Apple has developed policies that enable it to be a leader in procurement of materials, manufacturing, and logistics. This company has outperformed many of its competitors by excelling in many areas including sourcing of global materials, working with suppliers to develop rigorous standards, managing inventory to maximize turnover and minimize waste, and developing responsible business practices. An example of how they manage one of their products can be seen in their iPhones. Apple works with different suppliers and has material shipped to their assembly plants. Currently the majority of Apple iPhones are assembled by Foxconn in China.[11] Once assembled these products are then shipped to consumers (via UPS/Fedex) if they are ordered from Apple's online store. They also use other distribution channels to sell their products (e.g., retail stores, other distributors), and these products are often shipped from their Elk Grove, California warehouse facility. When products such as older iPhones are deemed obsolete, customers may send the products back and they are recycled through dedicated recycling facilities. As part of their commitment to social responsibility, Apple has developed initiatives to reduce their waste, transportation costs, and carbon and water footprint.

Beyond alignment of decisions around operational priorities, there are other management strategies needed to ensure that the supply chain partners upstream and downstream work together to create a product that the customer is willing to buy. Based on the work of Lambert,[12] a successful supply chain management requires the management of eight key components as shown below. These

[11] SupplyChain 247, "Is Apple's Supply Chain Really the No. 1? A Case Study," www.supplychain247.com/article/is_apples_supply_chain_really_the_no._1_a_case_study (September 28, 2018).

[12] Lambert, D., "The Eight Essential Supply Chain Management Processes," *Supply Chain Management Review*, 8 no. 6 (2004): 18–26.

components are purposeful in directing the efforts of managers in attending to downstream customers (components 1–3), local operations (components 4–5), and upstream suppliers that produce goods and services for the company (components 6–8). Each of the eight supply chain management components encompasses strategic as well as operational elements, yet the implications of decisions for each component impact the entire supply chain. As such, it is in the interest of every entity in a supply chain to help each other improve management of each component in order to increase the profitability of the entire supply chain.

1. Customer relationship management – This is the process of managing, developing, and maintaining customers.
2. Customer service management – This is the process of managing face-to-face interactions with customers. It deals with aspects of real-time information on shipping, product availability, and providing customer service.
3. Demand management style – This involves managing customer requirements with supply chain capabilities.
4. Order fulfillment – This encompasses all activities for meeting customer requirements and creating a seamless system from the supplier to the firm and then on to the other customer segment.
5. Manufacturing flow management – This involves managing all activities necessary to obtain, implement, and manage manufacturing flexibility in the supply chain and move products through the plants.
6. Supplier relationship management – This provides the structure for managing the relationships with the supplier.
7. Product development and commercialization – This provides the structure for working with customers and suppliers to develop and commercialize new products.
8. Returns management – This is the process by which activities associated with returns, reverse logistics, "gatekeeping," and return avoidance are managed within the firm and across key members of the supply chain.

As we have described above, the supply chain is a network of entities with the goal of producing goods or services that the customer wants to buy. Within each entity an entrepreneur must manage primary and support activities that ensure the company can transform inputs into outputs. Further, an entrepreneur may set operational priorities that distinguish the goods and services offered. Yet, in order to meet these operational priorities, the entrepreneur should find suppliers with goods and services that align with these priorities. Finally, we presented eight supply chain management components that may affect the relationships between material providers, banks and venture capitalists, manufacturers, warehouses, retailers, and customers. At any link in the supply chain, an entity will have suppliers and customers and must successfully manage them and work with them in order to be profitable and successful in selling products and services.

III NATIVE AMERICAN BUSINESS AND THE SUPPLY CHAIN

Each business entity must manage the internal operations that transform inputs into outputs, while aligning with suppliers that can help meet operational priorities. While the simple framework suggests a straightforward approach in finding entities to fill each role, the job of identifying *the right* entity for a particular product or service is actually quite difficult. That is, there are a number of influencing factors that may affect the way an entrepreneur selects a company as a supplier. Moreover, for a Native American business entrepreneur, there may be specific influencing factors due to federal and tribal input that affect the selection of suppliers for a business. Although each tribe is distinct, traditionally tribal leaders make decisions that balance physical, economic, social, emotional, and spiritual implications.[13] Without considering these influential factors in business decisions, Native entrepreneurs may create a cognitive dissonance between their business strategy and Native identity. Indeed, scholars suggest that the lack of cultural salience and attention to community value may deter Native Americans from certain career paths and educational programs.[14] To relieve the potential dissonance, we connect the factors that may weigh on the supply decisions of a Native entrepreneur by adapting a recent supply chain framework as discussed below.

As a framework, we utilize the supply chain with influencing factors and impact from Newton, Agrawal, and Wollenberg.[15] In their model, the influencing factors of the supply chain include state, market, and civil society requirements. These factors may intervene with or direct decisions by producers of raw materials, manufacturers that process and package, warehouses and retailers that move goods closer to the consumer, and finally the customer that consumes the good or service. These entities, in turn, impact the economy, the environment, and society through the way they conduct their business.

We adapt the framework by Newton et al. to include additional aspects of the supply chain relevant to the Native American business entrepreneur. Figure 9.2 presents the adapted model, where shaded boxes represent additional influencing factors and more complex impacts. Below we will discuss the additional factors and impacts and suggest two supply chain considerations for the Native business entrepreneur.

---

[13] Stewart et al., "Native American Cultural Capital and Business Strategy."

[14] Verbos, A. K., Kennedy, D. M., Gladstone, J., & Birmingham, C., "Native American Cultural Influences on Career Self-Schemas and MBA Aspirations," *Equality, Diversity & Inclusion: An International Journal*, 34 no. 3 (2015): 201–13.

[15] Newton, P., Agrawal, A., & Wollenberg, L., "Enhancing the Sustainability of Commodity Supply Chains in Tropical Forest and Agricultural Landscapes," *Global Environmental Change*, 23 no. 6 (2013): 1761–72.

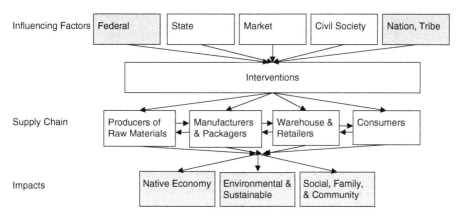

FIGURE 9.2: Supply chain adapted from Newton et al. (2013) for Native business context

A Federal Influencing Factor

Beyond state regulations, market demands, and societal guidelines for business practices, it is important to understand the federal implications for conducting a Native American business enterprise. Only a limited amount of non-Indian businesses and nongovernmental entities have sought to engage in business dealings with tribes due to the unique sovereign and jurisdictional characteristics attendant to business transactions in Indian Country. An important consideration in terms of who will take on a Native business as a producer, manufacturer, packager, or warehouse are the tax implications. "Generally, both federal and state taxes apply to tribes, tribal enterprises, and tribal members outside of a tribe's reservation. Within Indian country, on the other hand, the initial and frequently dispositive question in Indian tax cases is who bears the legal incidence of the tax. When the legal incidence falls on tribes, tribal members, or tribally owned corporations, states are categorically barred from implementing the tax."[16]

An area that complicates the use of tribal land and resources is the fact that the U.S. government has traditionally held trust over tribal lands for the benefit of tribal members, and because it is held in trust, tribal governments exercise sovereign authority within their boundaries and are generally not subject to state laws. The trust status places limitations on the use of these lands, and development may require federal approval. Tribal land usage is also complicated by its legal status. Indian land is either owned wholly by the tribal government or through a combination of tribal entities and individual tribal landowners that receive land allotments. The land ownership issue poses challenges for developers in order for development to occur. Indeed, new firms tend to face increased barriers in accessing

---

[16] Dreveskracht, R., "Doing Business in Indian Country: A Primer," www.americanbar.org/publica tions/blt/2016/01/05_dreveskracht.html (September 27, 2018).

their individual capital because of the limited individual property rights created by the way in which the reservation is organized. The reservation structure creates a collective ownership system that creates legal barriers and increases organizational and transactional costs for businesses.[17] Nevertheless, when resources and land are developed, successful projects enable multiple benefits as they provide employment opportunities for tribal members and improvements in health, education, and social services for tribal members, dividends that enure to all tribal members.

The stipulations around the use of tribal land resources may affect decisions of a business to provide a good or service. Specifically, tribal entities incorporate through Section 17 of the Indian Reorganization Act of 1934 (IRA) whereby the tribe creates a separate legal entity to divide its governmental and business activities. For example, "The Section 17 corporation has a federal charter and articles of incorporation, as well as bylaws that identify its purpose, much like a state-chartered corporation. The main differences between these entities and state-chartered corporations are that (1) the IRA places certain limitations on incorporated tribes, and the secretary of the interior issues the federal charter; (2) some corporate transactions, such as the sale or lease of tribal land or assignment of tribal income, require the approval of the secretary; and (3) the tribe retains sovereign immunity."[18]

Taken together there a number of rules and regulations that affect what and how goods can be offered, and this may affect how a business entity fits into a supply chain. In these regards, Native business entrepreneur considerations of federal influencing factors include:

1. How will the federal laws affect the taxation of the goods and service of my business?
2. What risks or opportunities does my business create for sourcing of goods and services?

B Nation and Tribe Influencing Factors

Although American tribes are sometimes referred to as "nations," for alignment in our framing we have chosen to use the term "tribe." A tribal government is defined as any Indian tribe, band, nation, or organized group or community that is recognized as eligible by the United States because of their special status as Indians. States usually do not interfere with tribal governance, but Congress may adopt laws that influence Native American governance. Each tribe has its own laws and government, and it has rights of self-government under the U.S. Constitution. Some tribes have adopted constitutions similar to that of the U.S. Constitution that allow for separation of powers. An example of this can be seen in the Yavapai-Apache Nation,

---

[17] Galbraith, C. S., Rodriguez, C. L., & Stiles, C. H., "American Indian Collectivism," *PERC*, 24 no. 2 (June 1, 2006).
[18] Dreveskracht, "Doing Business in Indian Country."

which has three branches of government: the judicial, legislative, and executive. Other tribes are unique and may be governed by a Tribal Council and Tribal Chair;[19] Indian corporations may also be organized under tribal or state law. "If the entity was formed under tribal law, formation likely occurred pursuant to its own corporate code – just as state entities incorporate via a state's corporate code. Under federal common law, tribal corporations enjoy sovereign immunity from suit. However, it is unclear whether a tribal corporation's sovereign immunity is waived through state incorporation. While courts are trending towards a rule that state incorporation waives sovereign immunity, there is no consensus at this point."[20]

Presently, there are 567 federally recognized tribes in the United States.[21] Tribes are influenced by U.S. federal laws and regulations even though each may have its own constitution, policies, culture, and customs. One distinguishing factor deals with sovereign immunity. "Tribal sovereign immunity protects tribal officials and employees acting in their official capacity and within the scope of their employment, as well as shielding tribes from suits for damages and requests for injunctive relief (whether in tribal, state, or federal court). Tribes have been held specifically immune from subpoena enforcement to compel production of tribal witnesses or documents. In addition, the doctrine of sovereign immunity usually extends to suits arising from a tribe's 'off-reservation' or commercial activities, including the activities of an off-reservation tribal casino."[22] With regard to business endeavors, federal courts generally do not distinguish between "governmental" and "commercial" activities. Thus, tribal entitles retain immunity whether those contracts involve governmental or commercial activities and whether they were made on or off a reservation.

Numerous courts have held that tribal sovereign immunity extends to tribal casinos, businesses, schools, and corporations. However, when conducting business with Natives, these organizations may require tribal enterprises to include sovereign immunity and tribal court jurisdiction waivers in contracts, which would mean that tribes sacrifice sovereign rights in order to conduct business. As such, Native business entrepreneurs' considerations of nation or tribe influencing factors should include:

1. How will the tribal laws affect the relationships with my suppliers and customers?
2. What risks or opportunities does sovereign immunity create for sourcing of goods and services?

---

19 U.S. Legal, "Tribal Governments," https://system.uslegal.com/tribal-governments/ (September 28, 2018).
20 Dreveskracht, "Doing Business in Indian Country."
21 National Conference of State Legislatures, "State Recognition of American Indian Tribes," www.ncsl.org /research/state-tribal-institute/state-recognition-of-american-indian-tribes.aspx (September 29, 2018).
22 Dreveskracht, "Doing Business in Indian Country."

C Native Economy Impact

Many Native nations are culturally influenced by a concern for the welfare of the community. Also, stewardship of resources and sustainability are woven into the fabric of many Native American-run businesses. In comparison to other minority businesses, Native American businesses tend to employ more people,[23] which may be attributed to their sense of community and the importance many tribes place on helping other members of the tribe. The Harvard Project on American Indian Economic Development recommends that tribes develop independent business boards to create a less political, more stable and certain "business" environment.[24] Native American tribes may optimally want to encourage more economic development by also adopting legal structures such as LLCs to imitate Western laws, limit legal liability, and be more attractive in creating outside capital. Native business entrepreneurs' considerations of the economic and sovereignty impact should include:

1. How will my suppliers and customers contribute to the economic development impact of my tribe?
2. What risks or opportunities do economic issues create for sourcing of goods and services?

D Environmental and Sustainable Impact

A group's worldview is reflected in their cultural values, which shape the values of future generations.[25] According to Hain-Jamal,[26] Native Americans' worldview embodies the notion of sustainability, with a few key values that are eco-friendly. Native American ecology contends that one is responsible to live harmoniously with one's surroundings, make as small an imprint as possible and take only what is needed to survive.[27] Native Americans display a respect for other life forms, seek to maintain a balanced system, and strive to coexist with other life forms with an inherent belief that we are all interconnected. For example, the Iroquois like other tribes believe in the concept of the Seventh Generation Principle, which is the foundation of their decision-making process. The decisions they make today will influence their children and seven generations going forward. The Great Law of the Iroquois Confederacy embodies this notion in the statement "*Look and listen for the welfare of the whole people and have always in view not only the past and present but*

---

[23] Bressler, M. S., Campbell, K., & Elliott, B., "A Study of Native American Small Business Ownership: Opportunities for Entrepreneurship," *Research in Business and Economics Journal*, 10 (2014): 1–13.

[24] Jorgensen, M., *Rebuilding Native Nations*.

[25] Oysermann, D., "Culture as Situated Cognition: Cultural Mindsets, Cultural Fluency, and Meaning Making," *European Review of Social Psychology*, 22 (2011): 164–214.

[26] Hain-Jamall, D. A. S., "Native American & Euro-American cultures: A Comparative Look at the Intersection Between Language & Worldview," *Multicultural Education*, 21 no. 1 (2013): 13–19.

[27] Cajete, G., *Native Science: Natural Laws of Interdependence* (Sante Fe: Clear Light Books, 2000).

also the coming generations, even those whose faces are yet beneath the surface of the ground – the unborn of the future Nation."[28]

Native American people display extensive knowledge of their environment. They inherently are a people of ecology and possess a closeness to their land or "mother earth," and a respect for all living things. This is part of their cultural identity and as such they have struggled with the development and preservation of their natural resources. Economic initiatives that do not incorporate environmental responsibility and sustainability within their business models are in direct conflict with Native American values. Therefore, ecosystem management concepts that combine Native values with modern science show promise among Native American fisheries within the United States, while exploitation of natural minerals and oil projects that are not environmentally friendly have been met with resistance among some tribal members. An example of this is seen in the National Indigenous Environmental Network, which was formed to combat environmental issues such as mining and oil projects. "Throughout Turtle Island and Mother Earth, Indigenous people are resisting transnational corporations and governments that are attempting to take from them all that is sacred."[29] Native business entrepreneurs' considerations of the environmental and sustainable impact should include:

1. How will my suppliers and customers contribute to the environmental and sustainable impact of my tribe?
2. What risks or opportunities do environmental and sustainable issues create for sourcing of goods and services?

E Social, Family, and Community Impacts

Native Americans tend to be collectivistic and as such community needs are primary, and economic development is centered around meeting the needs of the community.[30] Community values need to be linked with organizational practices and incorporated within the supply chain management to include tribal beliefs and priorities, as well as resources. An example of someone incorporating community values is Louie Gong, founder of Eighth Generation and a member of the Nooksack tribal community.[31] His company incorporates the intertribal value of "Seven Generations" within his business practices. He indicates that he embeds respect for the previous generations in his work and acknowledges that his success is a result of a collective effort. He encourages artists from various Native American tribes to

[28] Giants of the Earth Heritage Center, "The Great Law of the Iroquois Confederacy," https://spring grovemnheritagecenter.org/mission/their-eyes-were-my-eyes/iroquois-wisdom/ (September 28, 2018).
[29] Krech, S. III, *Natural Resource Issues in Indian Country. Sawyer Seminar, Modern Times, Rural Places* (Cambridge, MA: Massachusetts Institute of Technology, 2001), 15.
[30] Ratten, V., & Dana, L. P. "Gendered Perspective of Indigenous Entrepreneurship," *Small Enterprise Research*, 24 no. 1 (2017): 62–72.
[31] Eighth Generation, "Bio," https://eighthgeneration.com/pages/bio (September 28, 2018).

participate in the Inspired Natives Projects and sell handmade art. Eighth Generation also became the first Native-owned business to offer beautiful wool blankets. At Louie Gong's Pike Place Market store, phone cases, wool blankets, jewelry, and other items are all designed by Native American artists. As this example demonstrates, Native business owners may connect their cultural and tribal value into the operational priorities and therefore, the products that are sold to customers. The goal is to promote Native American artists and entrepreneurs.

The attention to community and the social and family connections by Native businesses may also change how a business owner measures success. Indeed, tribal businesses may not necessarily focus on profitability as the only goal; rather, tribes may seek to increase tribal employment opportunities, health care for the community members, social benefits, and other community-oriented initiatives. The efforts by tribal businesses to create economic opportunities are motivated by the need to improve the outlook of American Indians, who remain among the poorest minorities in the United States.[32] For example, the Cherokee Nation of Oklahoma owns the Cherokee Nation Businesses, a portfolio of thirty-five business ventures that strive to hire tribally owned and staffed suppliers of goods and services and service Native and non-Native customers. The benefit created includes investment in support services for Cherokee citizens and reinvestment in Cherokee businesses in terms of training and job creation. As this example suggests, Native businesses will need to consider what outcomes are desired and align supply chain entities to ensure the outcomes are obtained. In sum, Native business entrepreneurs' considerations of the social, family, and community impacts should include:

1. How will my suppliers and customers contribute to the social, family, and community impacts of my tribe?
2. What risks or opportunities do social, family, and community issues create for sourcing of goods and services?

IV PLANNING TO TAKE A SUPPLY CHAIN GLOBAL

With globalization and the emergence of new technologies, borders become less relevant and take on a global perspective. Global supply chain management is also referred to as the value chain and/or logistics network management, and consists of a network of suppliers, manufacturers, distribution centers, wholesalers, and retailers from around the globe. The value chain may also be comprised of a variety of specialized facilitating systems (e.g., transportation and information systems). Some of the reasons for firms taking on global suppliers are to achieve lower costs, diversify their offerings, access new markets, and improve operations by potentially learning better practices. Yet, the move to a global supply chain versus a local supply chain

---

[32] Cornell, S. & Kalt, J. P., "Sovereignty and Nation-Building: The Development Challenge in Indian Country Today," *American Indian Culture and Research Journal*, 22 no. 3 (1998): 187–214.

comes with some trade-offs. These may include large differences in distance and time, forecasting, exchange rates, infrastructure, variety of products, and legislation and foreign rules or laws.

Trends indicate that many companies are engaging in low-cost country sourcing, outsourcing, and customization, which has added to the complexity of supply chain management. The ability to manage the complexity of a global supply chain well leads to achieving better supply chain performance.[33] This includes the ability to take into consideration global factors such as a nation's economic and import and export policies (e.g., tariffs, customs regulations, trade agreements) as well as the logistics infrastructure influencing the growth of the firm and industry.

With globalization and technology many companies have also become more interlinked in their relations with their networks of suppliers, plants, distributors, retailers, and customers. Supply chain enterprise systems, which manage information, communication, and management technologies that support chain functions have developed as a central element in supply chain management strategy. Moreover, the supply chain management in organizations is increasingly becoming more concerned with creating a responsible innovation process that is based "on transparency, an interactive process by which societal actors and innovators become mutually responsive to each other with a view on the (ethical) acceptability, sustainability and societal desirability of the innovation process and its marketable products."[34]

Taking into consideration the opportunities that a global supply chain can provide, Native business entrepreneurs should ask:

1. Is it more affordable to manufacture locally or more cost effective to outsource the manufacturing of goods and services?
2. Where should the firm locate warehouses so that they can have a quicker response time for customers?
3. Is the product or service they provide in line with the core values of the tribe or does the firm need to develop a value chain that embraces core Native American values as well as the communal needs of the tribe?

V CONCLUSION

Native American entrepreneurs face additional challenges in developing their businesses. Much like multinational corporations, Native American enterprises need to take into consideration many factors such as geographic concerns, political

---

[33] Koudal, P. & Engel, D. A., "Globalization and Emerging Markets: The Challenge of Continuous Global Network Optimization," *Building Supply Chain Excellence in Emerging Economies,* 98 (2007): 37–66.

[34] Von Schomberg, R. (2011). Towards Responsible Research and Innovation in the Information and Communication Technologies and Security Technologies Fields, https://papers.ssrn.com/sol3/papers.cfm?abstract_id=2436399.

influences, legal policies, and economic forces, as well as cultural aspects of the supply chain. Moreover, some tribes may face more obstacles due to the resource constraints of their reservations and/or tribal land and autonomy from the U.S. government. In order for them to enjoy more economic development, collaboration with external partners and supply chain management are key factors.

10

Mapping the Sustainable Development Goals onto Indian Nations

Carla F. Fredericks

The Sustainable Development Goals (SDGs) are a collection of seventeen goals set by the United Nations in 2015, which form the backbone of the organization's 2030 Agenda for Sustainable Development, adopted by General Assembly on September 25, 2015 ("The 2015 Resolution").[1] The 2030 Agenda and the SDGs were designed to succeed the United Nations' Millennium Development Goals, eight goals for international development adopted in 2000 and that expired in 2015. The comprehensive aim of the 2030 Agenda and the SDGs is to "end poverty, protect the planet and ensure prosperity for all."[2] The United Nations recognizes sustainable development as "development that meets the needs of the present without compromising the ability of future generations to meet their own needs," dependent on "harmonizing three core elements: economic growth, social inclusion and environmental protection."[3] The United Nations describes each Goal as follows:[4] 1: no poverty; 2: zero hunger; 3: good health and well-being; 4: quality education; 5: gender equality; 6: clean water and sanitation; 7: affordable and clean energy; 8: decent work and economic growth; 9: industry, innovation and infrastructure; 10: reduced inequalities; 11: sustainable communities and cities; 12: responsible consumption and production; 13: climate action; 14: life below water; 15: life on land; 16: peace, justice and strong institutions; and 17: partnerships for the goals.[5]

---

[1]   G.A. Res. 70/1 (September 25, 2015), www.un.org/en/development/desa/population/migration/general assembly/docs/globalcompact/A_RES_70_1_E.pdf.

[2]   *Sustainable Development Goals*, www.un.org/sustainabledevelopment/sustainable-development-goals / (last visited July 16, 2018).

[3]   *The Sustainable Development Agenda*, Frequently Asked Questions, www.un.org/sustainabledevelop ment/development-agenda/ (last visited July 16, 2018).

[4]   *Sustainable Development Goals*, www.un.org/sustainabledevelopment/sustainable-development-goals / (last visited July 16, 2018).

[5]   In furtherance of the SDGs, the 2015 resolution assigns specific performance targets to each goal, with a total of 169 targets spread across the seventeen goals. In 2017, the General Assembly passed another resolution appending a global "indicator" framework to the SDGs – these indicators announce the specific data to be collected in relation to each performance target. The goal – target – indicator framework is the current format of the SDGs. This chapter refers to "the SDGs" to collectively describe the 2015 resolution and the set of goals, targets, and indicators in effect since 2017.

The SDGs, like many United Nations programs, were conceived to exist for the benefit of developing countries, not high-income or developed countries like the United States. However, the living conditions on many, if not most Indian reservations in the United States more closely resemble those of developing nations in the global South. According to the most recent United States Census, Indian reservations have a poverty rate for families of 36 percent, more than four times the national average.[6] Further, the status of tribes as sovereign entities affords an appropriate analogy to developing countries, and for that reason, mapping the SDGs onto Indian Country in the United States is a compelling proposition for both tribes themselves and outside actors. The SDGs may be implemented as a development compass externally by the public and private institutions that interact with tribes, to serve as a guide for partnerships with tribes, and internally by tribes themselves.

Native Americans require particular attention from the United States in implementing the SDGs, as they have explicit human rights protections beyond those articulated in the core internally recognized human rights instruments.[7] The United Nations Declaration on the Rights of Indigenous Peoples and International Labour Organisation Convention 169 (concerning Indigenous and tribal peoples) contain provisions pertaining to business activities on or near Indigenous land.[8] Most notably, the concept of free, prior, and informed consent is articulated multiple times. For example, Article 32 of the United Nations Declaration on the Rights of Indigenous Peoples states that "states shall consult and cooperate in good faith with the Indigenous peoples concerned through their own representative institutions in order to obtain their free and informed consent prior to the approval of any project affecting their lands or territories and other resources, particularly in connection with the development, utilization or exploitation of mineral, water or other resources."[9]

Pragmatically speaking, particular focus on tribes is crucial for attainment of the SDGs by the United States. For Goal 1: no poverty, Native American families are four times as likely to live in poverty than non-Native families nationwide.[10] Native Americans in the United States also disproportionately experience social, economic, and health problems, and lack adequate access to social protection systems and economic resources.

For the goal of "zero hunger" (Goal 2), Native Americans face disproportionately high levels of malnourishment. Further, threats to traditional subsistence foods and activities such as cultivation, hunting and gathering, and fishing and pastoralism are exacerbating this problem. As to "good health and well-being" (Goal 3), Native

---

[6]   National Center for Education Statistics, Statistical Trends in the Education of American Indians and Alaska Natives (Washington, DC: US Department of Education, 2008).

[7]   U.N. Declaration on the Rights of Indigenous Peoples, G.A. Res. 61/295, U.N. Doc. A/RES/61/295 (October 2, 2008).

[8]   *Id.*

[9]   *Id.*

[10] U.S. Census Bureau, *Poverty Thresholds* (archived from the original on December 21, 2011).

Americans' life expectancy is five and a half years less than non-Native counterparts, and inadequate access to health services and information leads to disproportionately high levels of preventable and curable diseases.[11] Also, disproportionately high suicide rates plague Native communities. "Quality education" (Goal 4) would require addressing the lack of access to quality education and training in reservation and urban Indian communities. "Gender equality" (Goal 5) would require serious efforts to address problems in the United States of exploitation and violence against Native American women and girls. "Clean water and sanitation" (Goal 6) has been a long-term problem in tribal communities, where contamination of water sources due to natural resource development has been a widespread issue for reservations.

"Affordable and clean energy" (Goal 7) presents significant issues for Native Americans in the United States. Not only do Indian communities wrestle with inadequate access to affordable and clean energy, but have for generations borne negative consequences of fossil fuel development via land alienation, resource contamination, and forced displacement. In the context of large-scale renewable energy development, several case studies of the issues arising in the United States related to Goal 7 follow in the latter part of this chapter.

Of course, "decent work and economic growth" (Goal 8) has long been an issue for Native Americans. Globally, this continues to play out for Indigenous peoples in a similar fashion, where modern trends of globalization, noninclusive economic growth, and environmental conservation threaten traditional livelihoods dependent on access to lands and territories. Further, continuing barriers to participation in modern market economies render Native Americans and Indigenous peoples highly vulnerable to the negative impacts, without realizing the benefits, of economic growth and development.

The lack of high-quality, reliable, sustainable, and resilient infrastructure in Native communities implicates Goal 9, "industry, innovation and infrastructure." The lack of opportunity manifests in the challenges Native Americans face stemming from increasing migration to urban centers, which relates to the goal of "sustainable cities and communities" (Goal 11). Native Americans for generations have experienced inequality, lack of opportunity, discriminatory laws, exclusion in public policies, and nonrecognition of their rights. Further, the exclusion of Indian people from national governance processes, fundamentally stemming from a lack of consultation and participatory mechanisms in decision-making, renders achieving "reduced inequalities" (Goal 10) of critical importance in the United States.

"Responsible production and consumption" (Goal 12) is an important target for Native Americans in the United States because unsustainable production and consumption processes have for centuries driven Native Americans from traditional lands and territories and excluded them from management of their own lands, territories, and resources. From the destruction of the buffalo in the 1800s to the

---

[11] *Indian Health Service Fact Sheet*, April 2018, www.ihs.gov/newsroom/factsheets/disparities/.

Dakota Access Pipeline in 2018, it is clear that Native American people in the United States pay a high price for unsustainable practices of the larger consuming majority. Similarly, Native Americans are among the first to face the direct consequences of climate change, implicating Goal 13, "climate action." From the Alaska Native village of Kivalina to the Biloxi-Chitimacha-Choctaw Tribes in Louisiana, Native Americans are under direct and persistent threat from the consequences of climate change and are fighting for their very subsistence and lifeways.[12]

Goal 14, "life below water," requires particular consideration in the United States, as Native Americans continue to face overexploitation of water resources that threatens their subsistence and livelihoods, and that for centuries has also resulted in ongoing encroachment on their fishing and water rights and resource management. Similarly, Native Americans are closely tied with the situation addressed in Goal 15, "life on land." Chief Edward Moody of the Nuxalk Nation recently articulated this connection as follows: "We must protect the forests for our children, grandchildren and children yet to be born. We must protect the forests for those who can't speak for themselves such as the birds, animals, fish and trees."

Native American history is riddled with the suffering of grave injustices and, unfortunately, Native Americans continue to face severe and ongoing violence and serious violations of their human rights.[13] The lack of effective preventative and remedial processes that ensure inclusive, participatory, and representative decision-making at all levels must be addressed in the United States for the SDGs to be achieved. Similarly, the United States may implement Goal 16, "peace, justice and strong institutions," by supporting the crucial role Native Americans can play as partners in the efforts to achieve the SDGs themselves. Given the complex jurisdictional frameworks that exist throughout Indian Country, it is critical to put in place strong and effective national processes for dialogue, consultation, and participation with Native Americans to include them and harness the potential they have to address the serious problems that exist in the development context. Finally, Goal 17, "partnerships for the goals," envisions a new process for engagement with peoples throughout the world, which recognizes the importance of inclusion and equality for addressing the global challenges of sustainable development and the betterment of humanity.[14]

[12] David Usborne, *Meet America's First Climate Change Refugees, Whose Island Is Disappearing Under Rising Seas*, THE INDEPENDENT, March 31, 2018, www.independent.co.uk/news/world/americas/time-almost-up-island-louisiana-sinking-into-the-sea-american-indians-coastal-erosion-isle-de-jean-a8280401 .html; *see also* Native American Rights Fund, *NARF & Alaskan Native Village Sues 24 Oil and Energy Companies for Destruction Caused by Global Warming*, February 29, 2008, www.narf.org/narf-alaskan-native-village-sues-24-oil-and-energy-companies-for-destruction-caused-by-global-warming/.

[13] *See* Report of the Special Rapporteur on the rights of Indigenous peoples on her mission to the United States of America, Human Rights Council, thirty-sixth session, United Nations General Assembly, A/HRC/36/46/Add.1.

[14] International Labor Organization, *Sustainable Development Goals: Indigenous Peoples in Focus* (July 26, 2016), www.ilo.org/wcmsp5/groups/public/–ed_emp/–ifp_skills/documents/publication/wcms_503715.pdf.

The SDGs explicitly refer to Indigenous peoples in several places; there are also certain targets and indicators that do not refer directly to Indigenous peoples, but that the United Nations Department of Economic and Social Affairs has identified as particularly relevant to Indigenous peoples.[15] Particularly, the 2015 resolution recognizes that the vulnerable must be empowered, including Indigenous peoples. The 2015 resolution further commits to "providing inclusive and equitable quality education at all levels – early childhood, primary, secondary, tertiary, technical and vocational training. All people, irrespective of sex, age, race or ethnicity, and persons with disabilities, migrants, indigenous peoples, children and youth, especially those in vulnerable situations, should have access to life-long learning opportunities that help them to acquire the knowledge and skills needed to exploit opportunities and to participate fully in society. We will strive to provide children and youth with a nurturing environment for the full realization of their rights and capabilities, helping our countries to reap the demographic dividend, including through safe schools and cohesive communities and families."

Finally, the 2015 resolution commits to inclusion, stating: "'We the peoples' are the celebrated opening words of the Charter of the United Nations. It is 'we the peoples' who are embarking today on the road to 2030. Our journey will involve Governments as well as parliaments, the United Nations system and other international institutions, local authorities, indigenous peoples, civil society, business and the private sector, the scientific and academic community – and all people. Millions have already engaged with, and will own, this Agenda. It is an Agenda of the people, by the people and for the people – and this, we believe, will ensure its success."

The SDGs have been criticized for overlooking Indigenous peoples, principally for 1) inadequate recognition of IPs in the goals and targets themselves,[16] 2) the indicators' failure to disaggregate IP-specific figures from country-level data, and 3) for failure to recognize the potential contributions of IPs as active participants in attaining the Goals, as opposed to mere recipients.[17] In the United States, it is a missed opportunity for full implementation of the SDGs if tribal nations are not considered partners in achieving the SDGs domestically, first disaggregating data to capture poverty, employment, and education challenges in Indian communities, then incorporating the situation into United States SDG reporting, as well as considering how implementation of the principles of the United Nations

[15] United Nations Department of Economic and Social Affairs, *Indigenous Peoples and the 2030 Agenda*, www.un.org/development/desa/indigenouspeoples/focus-areas/post-2015-agenda/the-sustainable-development-goals-sdgs-and-indigenous.html (last visited July 16, 2018); United Nations Department of Economic and Social Affairs, *Infographic: Indigenous Peoples & the 2030 Agenda*, www.un.org/esa/socdev/unpfii/documents/2016/Docs-updates/Indigenous-Peoples-and-the-2030-Agenda-with-indicators.pdf.

[16] U.N. Permanent Forum on Indigenous Issues, *Indigenous Peoples and the 2030 Agenda*, www.un.org/esa/socdev/unpfii/documents/2016/Docs-updates/backgrounderSDG.pdf.

[17] U.N. Major Group for Indigenous Peoples, *2016 High Level Political Forum Paper*, https://sustainabledevelopment.un.org/index.php?page=view&type=30022&nr=282&menu=3170.

Declaration on the Rights of Indigenous Peoples can be effected by pursuing the SDGs.

Of course, the SDG framework envisions a new future for development for all peoples that is grounded in sustainability for all, inclusive of sustainability for the natural environment. For that reason in particular, renewable energy on tribal lands provides an interesting lens through which to examine the ways the United States, tribes, and partners are already participating in achieving the SDGs domestically, and shows the necessity of SDG implementation within a framework that protects human rights, particularly the rights expressed in the United Nations Declaration on the Rights of Indigenous Peoples.

Renewable energy is the key to implementing Goals 7 and 13: sustainable, modern energy for all and urgent action to combat climate change. Indian Country comprises 2 percent of U.S. land but accounts for 5 percent of U.S. renewable energy potential.[18] The raw *potential* for renewable energy resources in the United States is staggering – on the Navajo Nation alone, the potential for solar photovoltaic (PV) generation is nearly twenty-four times what the entire state of Arizona generated from all power sources in 2017.[19] However, renewable energy development in Indian Country is still in its infancy.[20]

For renewable projects to be consonant with the SDGs, tribal involvement in the procedural aspects of developing the projects in a manner consistent with tribes' cultures and traditions – consultation and mitigation of impacts to cultural resources – must be a cornerstone of such development.[21] The Navajo Nation has confirmed this sentiment in its commitment to a current renewable project: "[T]he recently announced second phase of the Kayenta Solar project, which will be constructed by the Navajo Tribal Utility Authority ... will put over 50 MW of electricity into our local grid and reduce our reliance on outside sources of energy. With each one of these endeavors we are working with companies engaged in the next generation of technological advances that will assist us as a Nation to transition

---

[18]   United States Dep't of Energy, Office of Indian Energy, DOE/IE-0012, *Developing Clean Energy Projects on Tribal Lands*, at 3 (2012), www.nrel.gov/docs/fy13osti/57048.pdf.

[19]   Navajo PV solar potential = 2.5 billion mwh annual, United States Dep't of Energy, Office of Indian Energy, DOE/IE-0012, *Developing Clean Energy Projects on Tribal Lands*, at 3 (2012) www.nrel.gov/docs/fy13osti/57048.pdf; Arizona generation 2017 = 105 million mwh, data from *Electricity Data Browser*, United States Energy Information Administration, www.eia.gov/electricity/data/browser/#/topic/0?agg=2,0,1&fuel=g&geo=00000000001&sec=g&freq=A&rtype=s&maptype=0&rse=0&pin=&ltype=pin&ctype=map&end=2017&start=2001.

[20]   United States Gov't Accountability Office, GAO-15-502, *Poor Management by BIA Has Hindered Energy Development on Indian Lands*, at 2 (2015), www.gao.gov/assets/680/670701.pdf; Nicholas Ravotti, *Access to Energy in Indian Country: The Difficulties of Self-Determination in Renewable Energy Development*, 41 AMER. IND. L. REV. 279 (2017), https://digitalcommons.law.ou.edu/cgi/viewcontent.cgi?article=1078&context=ailr; Michael Maruca, *Working Draft, From Exploitation to Equity: Building Native-Owned Renewable Energy Generation in Indian Country* (March 31, 2018), https://papers.ssrn.com/sol3/papers.cfm?abstract_id=3153556.

[21]   Ryan D. Dreveskracht, *Alternative Energy in American Indian Country: Catering to Both Sides of the Coin*, 33 ENERGY L.J. 431 (2012).

our use of natural resources to more economically viable and environmentally friendly markets while maintaining and growing our jobs and revenues."[22] In January 2018, the Navajo Nation further articulated its self-determined perspective as follows:

> With the signing of a landmark agreement between the Navajo Tribal Utility Authority (NTUA) and Salt River Project, a solar plant on the Navajo Nation will soon be expanded to provide more renewable energy to the Nation. The agreement also paves the way for future renewable energy projects. The NTUA and its wholly-owned subsidiary NTUA Generation, Inc., will expand the Kayenta Solar generation facility, labeling it Kayenta II. The announcement was made Friday on the same day NTUA and the Phoenix-based Salt River Project (SRP) signed a long-term solar confirmation for the sale of firmed energy and the Environmental Attributes from Kayenta II along with a Memorandum of Understanding (MOU) for future energy development on the Navajo Nation. The MOU identifies that SRP will provide technical support in developing interconnection facilities for large scale renewable development within the Navajo Nation, as well as provide procurement and financing expertise related to the development and ownership of such projects. The agreement targets the development of at least 500 MW of renewable energy projects over the next 5–10 years within the Navajo Nation.[23]

The Hopi Tribe has also committed to renewable energy in its 2016 Comprehensive Economic Development Plan, and the City of Flagstaff and the Hopi Tribe have agreed to partner on a renewable energy project.[24]

The Oceti-Sakowin Power Project, to be located on tribal lands throughout the Dakotas, is on track to be the largest clean energy project ever established on tribal land. The ultimate goal of the project is to produce a series of wind projects with a cumulative installed capacity of two gigawatts.[25] The first project comprises two facilities in areas of South Dakota with wind resource that rank among the best onshore in North America. The 450 MW Ta'Teh Topah facility will be located on the Cheyenne River Reservation and the 120 MW Pass Creek facility on the Pine Ridge Reservation.[26] Estimates are that each wind farm will have a 50 percent net

---

[22] *The Benefits of the Navajo Generating Station to Local Economies: Hearing Before the Subcomm. on Energy and Mineral Resources of the H. Comm. on Natural Resources, 115th Cong.* (2018) (statement of LoRenzo Bates, Speaker, 23rd Navajo Nation Council), https://docs.house.gov/meetings/II/II06/20180412/108127/HHRG-115-II06-Wstate-BatesL-20180412-U1.pdf.

[23] Press Release, Salt River Project, *Kayenta Solar Farm to Expand; Commitment Between NTUA and SRP to Develop Renewable Energy Projects on Navajo Nation* (January 26, 2018), www.ntua.com/assets/kayenta-solar-farm-to-expand-(1-25-18)-(002).pdf.

[24] Hopi Tribe, *Hopi Tribe Comprehensive Economic Development Strategy 2016*, at 58 (2016), www.hopi-nsn.gov/wp-content/uploads/2016/09/Hopi-Comprehensive-Economic-Development-Strategy-Final-Draft-2016.pdf; Emery Cowan, *City of Flagstaff and Hopi Tribe Partner on Renewable Energy Project*, AZDailySun.com, March 17, 2018, https://azdailysun.com/news/local/city-of-flagstaff-and-hopi-tribe-partner-on-renewable-energy/article_303b0c8b-38ba-515a-af97-b26a027a85b3.html.

[25] Oceti Sakowin Power Authority, *The Oceti Sakowin Power Project*, http://ospower.org/the-project/.

[26] Richard Kessler, Apex and Sioux to Develop Largest U.S. Tribal Wind Projects, RechargeNews.com, March 2, 2018, www.rechargenews.com/wind/1445692/apex-and-sioux-to-develop-largest-us-tribal-

capacity factor and together generate 2.5 million/MWh of electricity annually.[27] To shepherd the project, the six of the tribes of the Great Sioux Nation joined together to form the Oceti-Sakowin Power Authority, an independent, nonprofit governmental entity.[28] Self-determination is central to the project, and the partners have stated, "[while] the OSPA is based on the successful public power models that exist in other jurisdictions throughout the U.S., it has been adapted to the unique status of the Tribes as sovereign nations, and is modeled after governing bodies that have already been placed in operation by several of the participating Tribes."[29] The project partner also acknowledged that "for years, the South Dakota tribes 'have been trying to do clean-energy projects, but we all run into the same problems, such as investors wanting to come in and own the project, and to just lease the land from the tribes. The tribes want to control their own energy resources.'"[30]

The project envisions a model that rejects a passive role for the tribes whereby outside investors lease tribal land, erect turbines, take advantage of federal tax breaks, pay the tribe royalties, and receive the lion's share of the benefits, only to eventually leave the tribe with old turbines and no power purchase agreement in place.[31] Instead, the OSPA board selected a partner on the project and formed a joint venture to develop wind energy on tribal lands and split the profits, whereby Apex, the outside investor, agreed to give the power authority a "51 percent majority ownership."[32] The project also contains a workforce development component that requires Apex to train residents to work on turbine construction, operations, maintenance, and financial aspects of the industry, to further the goal of tribal members eventually running the wind farms.[33]

These types of ventures require the partnerships to raise their own capital, but conversely afford the possibility of retaining more tribal control and profits.

The Quechuan Tribe's engagement with the Imperial Valley Solar Project provides a key United States example of how clean energy project proponents cannot, simply by virtue of alignment with the SDGs, disregard the rights of Indigenous peoples who have an interest in lands upon which projects will be located.

wind-projects, reprinted at www.apexcleanenergy.com/article/apex-clean-energy-recognized-best-largest-pipeline-wind-projects-u-s-2/.

[27] *Id.*

[28] Oceti Sakowin Power Authority, *About Us*, http://ospower.org/about-us/ (last visited July 16, 2018).

[29] *Id.*

[30] Karen Uhlenhuth, *Amid Dakota Access Protests, Tribes Continue to Pursue Clean Energy*, EnergyNewsNetwork.com, December 1, 2016, https://energynews.us/2016/12/01/midwest/amid-dakota-access-protests-tribes-continue-to-pursue-clean-energy-standing-rock/.

[31] Stephanie Woodard, *It's Clear Sailing for a Giant Sioux Wind Power Enterprise*, IndianCountryToday.com, May 20, 2017, https://newsmaven.io/indiancountrytoday/archive/it-s-clear-sailing-for-a-giant-sioux-wind-power-enterprise-kBTlpjpOloaJ6wtQiXBoqA/.

[32] Frank Jossi, *Can Sioux Tribes Pull Off Largest Ever Clean Energy Project on Tribal Land?*, EnergyNewsNetwork.com, May 9, 2018, https://energynews.us/2018/05/09/midwest/can-sioux-tribes-pull-off-largest-ever-clean-energy-project-on-tribal-land/.

[33] *Id.*

In 2010, the Bureau of Land Management approved a 709-MW solar project to be located on roughly 6,000 acres of public land in California's Imperial Valley, lands estimated to contain 459 cultural resources of significance to the Quechan Tribe of the Fort Yuma Indian Reservation ("Quechan").[34] The Quechan opposed the project on the grounds that the tribe was not adequately consulted, and it was able to obtain an order enjoining the project. If built, the project would have been one of the largest solar facilities in the nation. Instead, because of the Bureau of Land Management's failure, the Imperial project lost most of its backing.[35] The Imperial project seems to have disappeared. In 2011, Tessera Solar, the Imperial project's original developer and owner at the time of the lawsuit, sold the project to AES Solar.[36] AES soon thereafter wrote California regulators detailing its intent to move forward with the project, but a week later withdrew the letter with no further details.[37]

As these tribal government ventures demonstrate, tribal nations have a unique opportunity to be thought of as partners in achieving the SDGs domestically. The potential for Indigenous participation increases further when the tribal private sector is taken into account. Many Native entrepreneurs working in Indian Country already recognize a double bottom line in their businesses – that is, the need to make a profit and the need to operate within the bounds of sustainability as defined by the SDGs. As Stephanie Gutierrrez, an Oglala Lakota woman explains, "[C]ommunity wealth building begins with loyalty to geographic place … Even though we were nomadic people, we have always had our sacred sites and a land base that was deeply spiritual to us. It provided for us and therefore, we honor and care for all living things."[38] This SDG-relevant orientation is evident in larger-scale businesses, such as the efforts of Aki Development LLC, a green economy-focused corporation owned by Native residents of the Leech Lake Reservation,[39] and in smaller entrepreneurial ventures, such as the fifty-dollar chiller invented by eighth-grade Navajo students at the STAR school, a charter school on the Navajo reservation.[40]

[34] Ryan Dreveskracht, *Alternative Energy in American Indian Country: Catering to Both Sides of the Coin*, 33 Energy L.J. 431, 433–34 (2012).

[35] *Id.* at 433.

[36] Press Release, AES Solar, *AES Solar Buys 709 MW Imperial Valley Solar Project*, February 21, 2011, www.aescalifornia.com/files/pdf/11-02-solar.pdf.

[37] *Solar Thermal Plants Scrap Steam for Photovoltaic*, CNET.com, July 1, 2011, www.cnet.com/news/solar-thermal-plants-scrap-steam-for-photovoltaic/; Ucilla Wang, *The Mystery of the Imperial Valley Solar Project*, Gigaom.com, June 3, 2011, https://gigaom.com/2011/06/03/the-mystery-of-the-imperial-valley-solar-project/.

[38] Stephanie Gutierrez, An Indigenous Approach to Community Wealth Building: A Lakota Translation 27 (November 2018), https://democracycollaborative.org/community-wealth-building-a-lakota-translation.

[39] Lee Egerstrom, *Indian Country Moves Closer to the Sun; Takes Saga Solar with It*, The Circle: Native American News and Arts, December 11, 2016, http://thecirclenews.org/environment/indian-country-moves-closer-to-the-sun-takes-saga-solar-with-it/.

[40] Katherine Locke, *STAR School Creates Solutions for Staying Cool in Off-Grid Housing*, Navajo-Hopi Observer, February 13, 2018, www.nhonews.com/news/2018/feb/13/star-school-creates-solutions-staying-cool-grid-ho/.

Acknowledged areas in which SDG implementation has shortcomings provide insight into possible initial frameworks for the successful implementation of SDGs in Indian Country. The SDGs have been criticized for overlooking Indigenous peoples, principally for 1) inadequate recognition of Indigenous peoples in the goals and targets themselves,[41] 2) the indicators' failure to disaggregate Indigenous peoples-specific figures from country-level data, and 3) the failure to recognize the potential contributions of Indigenous peoples as active participants in attaining the Goals, as opposed to mere recipients.[42] Each of these oversights hold particularly true for Indian Country in the United States, the most clear-cut being the failure to disaggregate figures relating to Indigenous peoples from country-level data – the United States National Statistics for the SDGs aggregate the data at the country level, which masks the destitute conditions defining many Indian communities. The first critical step for the United States would be to compile appropriate statistics specific to Indian Country – even looking to using and expanding upon data on poverty, employment, and education from the United States Census, which would be specifically incorporated into the country's SDG reporting.

Finally, countries throughout the world have committed to full implementation of the SDGs in the global context. Tribes in the United States have the potential to play an essential role in achieving the SDGs domestically and aiding in the implementation of the aims of the United Nations Declaration on the Rights of Indigenous Peoples. The recognition and protection of human rights for Native Americans alongside realization of the SDGs would allow for fundamental and internationally accepted mechanisms for the United States to carry out its stated commitments and responsibilities to Indigenous communities domestically.[43] The inclusion of tribal communities as a focus for the United States in mapping the SDGs therefore requires thoughtful consideration as a possible mechanism to achieve human rights and suitable development.

---

[41]   United Nations Permanent Forum on Indigenous Issues, *Indigenous Peoples and the 2030 Agenda*, www.un.org/esa/socdev/unpfii/documents/2016/Docs-updates/backgrounderSDG.pdf.

[42]   U.N. Major Group for Indigenous Peoples, *2016 High Level Political Forum Paper*, https://sustaina bledevelopment.un.org/index.php?page=view&type=30022&nr=282&menu=3170.

[43]   Carla F. Fredericks, *Operationalizing FPIC*, 80 Albany L. Rev. 469 (2016).

PART IV

From Learning to Doing: Examples of Entrepreneurship in Indian Country

11

Indigenous Arts Ecology – A New Investment Model for Indian Country

Lori Lea Pourier

Art and culture are integral to every aspect of ancestral and modern life in Indigenous societies. In tribal communities, art and culture are deep and inseverable roots that reflect humans' relationships with and interdependence on land, water, plants, animals, and one another. For centuries, art and culture have been inherent to the functional and spiritual practices of surviving, flourishing, and bringing meaning to life. Yet for generations, ceremonies, language, and cultural practices deeply rooted in ancestral knowledge and ways of being were prohibited by law, stripping Native peoples of their rights to carry on the traditions and lifeways that always had sustained them. Destructive federal policies, Indian boarding schools, racism, and entrenched inequities fractured the connection between Native peoples and our cultures. It wasn't until 1978, when the U.S. Congress enacted the Indian Religious Freedom Act, that Native Americans, Alaska Natives, and Native Hawaiians reclaimed the right to practice our cultures and spirituality freely and independently. The myriad challenges that have affected Native communities for generations – and continue today – are in many ways a consequence of this fracturing and our disconnections from land and place, cultural identity, and the traditional art forms passed on from one generation to the next.

First Peoples Fund (FPF) is guided by the belief that restoring the practice of cultures rooted in ancient traditions is what is most vital to healthy tribal communities and thriving economies that lift up Indigenous lifeways. Restoring this link is a critical first step in generating sustainable Native economic development. Our work is enlivened by the conviction that Native culture bearers and emerging artists embrace social entrepreneurship but their potential has not been fully realized. In many Native communities, an understanding of the critical role that culture bearers and artists can play in building vibrant tribal economies has yet to take hold, and many emerging artists residing on Indian reservations today live on less than $10,000 per year.[1]

It is this set of complex federal policies and human relationships to which FPF has dedicated its resources and programs. FPF is a carefully designed program model

---

[1] First Peoples Fund, "Establishing a Creative Economy: Art as an Economic Engine in Native Communities," First Peoples Fund, Rapid City, SD, July 2013.

that takes Native culture bearers and artists at any stage in their entrepreneurial development and connects them with the business training, cultural grounding, and social networks that will expand their opportunities and horizons as cultural practitioners, artists, entrepreneurs, and ultimately skilled and knowledgeable culture bearers. Since 1999, FPF has provided $4.5 million in grants to 381 individual Native artists and their families across Indian Country and has certified over 50 Native artists and business coaches who in turn have trained 1,800 more emerging artist-entrepreneurs. From our extensive data and narrative about the impact of our work with artists and their families on their entrepreneurial growth, financial independence, and community involvement, we know that small investments (project grants ranging from $5,000 to $10,000) coupled with tailored technical assistance, mentoring, and small business loans help increase artists' annual incomes by 20 percent, on average, after just one year in our fellowship program. The data also demonstrate that when artists are well supported and achieve financial security for themselves and their families, they turn their gifts and energy toward their communities, and pass on their skills and knowledge. This approach is what restores and strengthens the very cultural fabric of a community.

This chapter describes the work of the First Peoples Fund and how reflection and research have made our efforts more effective. It presents additional evidence on the importance of culture bearers' role in driving an artist-led entrepreneurial and community development strategy. It concludes with a description of the Indigenous Arts Ecology framework, a model uncovered by our work and that now guides all our efforts to improve the cultural and economic lives of artists, their families, and their communities.

I ENVISIONING ECONOMY-WIDE IMPACT

In 1995, independent philanthropist Jennifer Easton founded First Peoples Fund and began providing support to Native artists and culture bearers in tribal communities. Focused on rural, reservation-based artists, First Peoples Fund invests in the quilters, bead-workers, basket weavers, quill-workers, traditional and contemporary musicians, dancers, storytellers, and next generation artists who, when fully supported, have the potential to become viable economic engines and social change-makers.

FPF's initial work revolved around three grant programs. The Jennifer Easton Community Spirit Awards are national fellowships that honor and provide resources to culture bearers based on their exceptional abilities to pass on cultural knowledge and sustain community spirit. Artist in Business Leadership Fellowships recognize tribal artists for the critical role they play in strengthening their communities' economies. They provide artists with working capital grants, mentoring, training, networking, and access to new markets. Cultural Capital Fellowship Project Grants are awarded to members of the FPF network of artists to support the design and implementation of community projects that strengthen and revitalize tradition-based practices. Projects that commemorate a tribe's history, protect and preserve ancestral practices, support the collective creation of tradition-based art, or that encourage younger generations to develop as artists and culture bearers all have been funded through this grant program.

These three initiatives have been impactful. They have motivated artists to think bigger, to be entrepreneurial, and to have greater confidence in their own abilities. Without question, the grants changed recipients' lives. Lauren Good Day (Arikara, Hidatsa, Blackfeet, and Plains Cree), who was both an Artist in Business Leadership Fellow and a Cultural Capital Fellow, offered this testimony about the awards:

> My grandmother taught me what she had learned from her grandmother. She gave me her songs, the rules about how to make things and the prayers that go along with them. These are things I hold really dear to me, they were handed down from my ancestors. First Peoples Fund helped me connect the past to the future. They let me see that artwork is something you can do as a career, something you can do to support your family. First Peoples Fund helped me make my dreams a reality.[2]

Today, the Jennifer Easton Community Spirit, Artists in Business Leadership, and Cultural Capital grants remain at the core of FPF's efforts – but they are only a part of our activities. After a dozen years of consistent and sustained grantmaking, First Peoples Fund's board and staff came to realize that to make real and lasting change, we must go beyond simply providing support at the individual level. We realized that we also needed to invest in the systems that support artists and their families. Our attention was drawn to community-based organizations with the potential to serve Native artists, imagining that if FPF could help grow the capacity of these organizations and help them understand how to better serve artists, artists' incomes would improve, sustainably benefiting their families and communities. The board and staff were especially interested in the development of community-specific programming that could give culture bearers and artists access to the resources they needed to develop and grow as entrepreneurs.

II GATHERING THE EVIDENCE FOR A NATIVE ARTS ECONOMY

As a result, First Peoples Fund began partnering with Native community development financial institutions (CDFIs). Native CDFIs are specialized community-based organizations that work in underserved markets and communities and provide a wide range of financial products and services including financial education, asset-building programs, mortgage finance, and loans to start or expand small businesses. The last eighteen years have seen a surge in the number of Native CDFIs operating in rural and urban communities, growing from 12 in 2004 to 73 in 2017.[3] Early in this

---

[2] First Peoples Fund, "Investing in the Indigenous Arts Ecology," First Peoples Fund, Rapid City, SD, 2018, p. 11.

[3] CDFI Fund Native Initiatives, "Fostering Economic Self-Determination for Your Native Community," U.S. Department of the Treasury, Washington, DC, December 2017.

growth period, First Peoples Fund partnered with the Oweesta Collaborative to offer small grants, training, technical assistance, and support for arts-focused program development to a cohort of Native CDFIs based in rural reservation communities. Our goal was to encourage these Native CDFIs to provide services tailored to the entrepreneurial and business development needs of artists and culture bearers.

Stories from the field told us that using a wider lens to view FPF's work and guide our grantmaking was the right approach. As expressed by Tawney Brunsch, executive director of Lakota Funds, a Native CDFI that was an early (and now long-time) partner in FPF work,

> Working with First Peoples Fund has been so inspiring. We have worked together to establish relationships with artists who are now growing their businesses with help from loans and matched savings accounts. Our work with artists continues to grow . . . All of this means artists are better able to do their work, sell their products and at the same time manage their funds and build credit.[4]

But we also realized that quantitative data would help FPF tell a more complete story, help us better mark progress, and provide additional persuasive evidence for our partners and funders. What were the household economic status and entrepreneurial needs of Native artists in the Great Plains region? In 2011, in partnership with Artspace, Colorado State University, Leveraging Investments in Creativity (LINC), and the Northwest Area Foundation, FPF embarked on the American Indian Creative Economy Markets Study Project to examine these questions.

The study primarily sampled households on the Pine Ridge Reservation and Cheyenne River Reservation and in the state of South Dakota: of the 143 study participants, 67 percent lived on the Pine Ridge Reservation, 7 percent lived on the Cheyenne River Reservation, and 3 percent lived elsewhere in the state. Among the remaining participants, 13 percent hailed from either Montana, Oregon, or Washington, and 10 percent were from still other places in the United States. Emerging artists constituted 71 percent of the sample (102 individuals).

First Peoples Fund published the study report, *Establishing a Creative Economy, Art as an Economic Engine in Native Communities*, in 2013. The findings unequivocally established that art can be a significant economic development lever in Native communities. In Lakota communities, for example, the study found that artists comprise a third or more of the population. Further, it found that more than half (51 percent) of the reservation-based households sampled relied on a home-based business to support themselves, and that 79 percent of those home-based businesses consisted of traditional art forms. The 2015 report *Voices—Our Survey, Our Voice, Our Way*, which was based on a representative sample of

---

[4]   First Peoples Fund, "Investing in the Indigenous Arts Ecology," First Peoples Fund, Rapid City, SD, 2018, p. 25.

households in the Cheyenne River Sioux tribal community, provided independent confirmation of these statistics.[5]

The *Establishing a Creative Economy* report also shed light on the key resources that Native artists need in order to grow as entrepreneurs and cultural leaders – credit and capital, new markets, knowledge and training, informal networks, creative space, and supplies. In each instance, these resources were nonexistent or sorely undersupplied in the studied reservation communities.

On the one hand, these data backed up FPF's understanding that artists constitute a large – and perhaps the largest – subset of entrepreneurs in Native communities. The data also affirmed our belief that complementing FPF's grant and award programs with activities that strengthened artist-serving community-based organizations could amplify our impact. On the other hand, revealing the truly acute lack of capacity and infrastructure in tribal communities to provide artists with access to critical resources suggested that an even broader approach might be necessary. A desire to spur the transformative effect that artist-led entrepreneurship and business development could have in tribal communities set First Peoples Fund on a path to deepen our work with Native CDFIs. Our goal shifted from helping Native CDFIs create and/or adapt programs to better serve artists-as-businesspeople to building Native CDFIs' capacity to develop local arts *economies* that support artists' creative and entrepreneurial development.

III INVESTING IN THE ARTS ECONOMY

In 2013, with funding from the Northwest Area Foundation and the Surdna Foundation, First Peoples Fund piloted the Native Arts Economy Building grant program to leverage the potential of Native CDFIs to support artists. From 2013 to 2016, FPF made seventeen $20,000 seed grants, with accompanying technical assistance, to Native CDFIs and similar artist-serving organizations across Indian Country. The funding and technical assistance were focused both on increasing the organizations' appreciation for artists as economic drivers and on strengthening their capacity to provide artists with access to capital, markets, networks, trainings, and the other resources they need to create and sell their work.

By growing their understanding of the value of artists as economic drivers and of providing products and services tailored to meet the needs of artist-entrepreneurs, the Native CDFIs achieved a deeper reach into their local artist communities. With support from First Peoples Fund, each partner organization undertook an asset-mapping exercise to determine how best to complement existing services and artist-support systems. Each Native CDFI then developed programs, projects, and financial projects tailored to the needs of its community. These variously included

---

[5] See Eileen Briggs and Kathleen Pickering, "Cheyenne River Tribal Ventures Voices Project, Our Survey, Our Voice, Our Way, Executive Summary Report," Cheyenne River Sioux Tribal Ventures, Eagle Butte, SD, 2015.

professional development focused on pricing and marketing artwork; business planning trainings; unsecured micro loans to assist artists in purchasing supplies and building inventory; informal artists' cooperatives; space for artists to gather and create work; matched individual savings accounts, in which the match was tied to arts business training and the accumulated capital could be leveraged for business expansion; access to local and regional art markets; and online artists' directories.

Continuing our deliberate and proactive effort to mark progress and to refine our unique-to-tribal-communities model for building creative economies, FPF undertook an impact evaluation of the pilot Native Arts Economy Building grant program. The rich assortment of quantitative and qualitative data produced through this effort shows that Native artists are good business for Native CDFIs. On average, at the end of the pilot grant period (2013–16), participating Native CDFIs increased the proportion of artists in their client pools from 12 percent to 26 percent.[6] In other words, the typical Native CDFI participating in the FPF Native Arts Economy Building grant program more than doubled the number of artists it served.

The impact evaluation also showed that Native artists, especially those in rural reservation communities, see Native CDFIs as an important resource for their entrepreneurship efforts. In particular, surveys of more than seventy artists from the grantees' communities show that a majority (51 percent) of artists view their Native CDFIs as a critical source of support to create and sell their work. This finding is especially significant considering that a decade ago most artists entering First Peoples Fund's programs did not know what a Native CDFI was or if one existed in their community.

IV THE INDIGENOUS ARTS ECOLOGY FRAMEWORK

Certainly, these results are promising regarding the potential for significant impact through small investments at the nexus of Native artists and Native CDFIs. But as First Peoples Fund evaluated the data that emerged from the Native Arts Economy Building grant program in the context of the larger trajectory of our programs, we found our conception of FPF's creative economy-building work shifting once again. In analyzing the data, we immediately noticed better outcomes for artists and partners with whom we have long-term relationships. We also saw better results in communities where the partnering organizations and their leaders placed value on their communities' cultural assets and culture bearers, and where we perceived these organizations and their leaders to be committed to upholding the traditional values of generosity, integrity, wisdom, and fortitude. The Indigenous Arts Ecology – a more holistic framework for the field in which First Peoples Fund works – began to emerge.

---

[6] First Peoples Fund, "Investing in the Indigenous Arts Ecology," First Peoples Fund, Rapid City, SD, 2018.

The Indigenous Arts Ecology framework is more than a relationship-based model. It is propelled by the Indigenous value of making relatives, where we invest in long-term relationships with a sense of interconnectedness and inter-responsibility. Within the Indigenous Arts Ecology, art and culture are valued well beyond their worth as commodities. The Indigenous Arts Ecology taps into the innovative and generous spirit that always has guided the intertribal ecosystems and trade routes that existed long before Indian reservations. Culture bearers form the central hub of the Indigenous Arts Ecology, and it encompasses the Native artist's leadership journey from an internal focus to gradually turning outward to build partnerships with others in their communities; it is a place-based model that, over time, rejuvenates individual artists' focus on a collective way of life in which they are working as culture bearers for the benefit of their own communities and other communities. Culture bearers are the carriers of ancestral knowledge who connect Native communities to their cultural assets and their collective identity, enabling them to envision a future in which they are strong and whole. The Indigenous Arts Ecology also includes modern institutions like tribal colleges and governments, Native CDFIs, youth services organizations, and local businesses. First Peoples Fund's guiding principle, Collective Spirit® – that which manifests self-awareness and a responsibility to sustain the cultural fabric of a community – circulates throughout. Alfred "Bud" Lane III, vice president of the Siletz Tribal Council, president of the Northwest Basketweavers Association, FPF Community Spirit Award honoree, and FPF board member explains the framework this way:

> All Native models exist because of culture bearers, including Native business models. They are the nucleus of culture that all of our art, modern and traditional, flows from, and none would exist without the traditional ways and belief systems. Identity, knowledge, teachings, traditions – that stream that exists with the individual people – they all emanate from the beliefs and practices held and passed on by our culture bearers.[7]

In 2017, based on data and learning from our pilot study, First Peoples Fund revamped the Native Arts Economy Building grant program and relaunched it as the Indigenous Arts Ecology grant program. We extended the grant period to up to three years, deepened the technical assistance, added opportunities for convenings and peer-to-peer learning, and developed an online resource library. We have long recognized the exceptional potential of small investments in Native artists and their families not only to create meaningful gains in income and improved business practices but also to induce the regeneration of cultural practices and intergenerational mentoring. Based on our learning and data, we firmly believe that this holistic ecosystems approach, in which FPF continues and further strengthens our partnerships with Native CDFIs and other community-based organizations, has the

---

[7] First Peoples Fund, "Investing in the Indigenous Arts Ecology," First Peoples Fund, Rapid City, SD, 2018, p. 25.

potential to exponentially multiply the impact of artist-led entrepreneurship and business development in Native communities.

V THRIVING INDIGENOUS ARTS ECOSYSTEMS

The Pine Ridge Reservation provides an example of what is possible when artists, their families, Native CDFIs, and other community-based organizations are supported to strengthen the local Indigenous arts ecosystem. First Peoples Fund has directly supported nearly seventy-five artists and culture bearers with grants and technical assistance on Pine Ridge through our programs, and annually invests in substantial fees and honoraria for local artists. These artists have expanded their networks, markets, and businesses and measurably improved their individual and family incomes. Emerging and established artists on Pine Ridge are able to build and grow their arts businesses with financial products, business trainings, new markets, and other services developed specifically for them by the Native CDFI Lakota Funds. After a two-year, $40,000 total investment in the pilot phase of First Peoples Fund's regrant program, 20 percent of Lakota Funds' clients were artists, up from 7.5 percent at the outset of the program. Lakota Funds has continued to participate in the Indigenous Arts Ecology grant program and has developed an annual art market and exhibit, expanded its artists' directory, added new training programs, and designed financial products specifically for artists. The latter include an Art Builder Microloan program ($500 unsecured loan) and an Art Equity Grant (up to $2,500 on top of a secured loan).

To date, the Rolling Rez Arts bus may be the best example of an arts ecosystem project serving the Pine Ridge reservation. Collaboratively developed by Lakota Funds, First Peoples Fund, and the Minneapolis-based nonprofit Artspace Projects, designed with input from the local Lakota art community, and launched in 2016, Rolling Rez Arts is a state-of-the-art mobile arts space, business training center, and bank that delivers art, business, retail, and financial services that were previously inaccessible to many of the artists and culture bearers who live and work on the Pine Ridge Reservation. For example:

- The Lakota Federal Credit Union, established in 2012 as the reservation's first FDIC-insured financial institution, uses the bus twice each month to offer mobile banking services. In part due to this partnership, the credit union is chipping away at the large number of unbanked reservation residents. In 2018, approximately 10 percent of the reservation's population were members of Lakota Federal Credit Union.
- The bus's arts teaching program employs twenty Native artists as part-time teachers, bringing art and cultural classes and workshops, such as beadwork, film, and ledger drawing, to far-flung reservation communities. By 2018, these

programs had engaged more than 800 culture bearers and artists living in all districts of the 3,500-square-mile reservation.

- Through a partnership with The Red Cloud Heritage Center, which monthly uses the bus to purchase more than $3,000 in artwork from local artists for its gift shop, Rolling Rez Arts is able to bring income and wholesale opportunities to artists across the vast reservation by providing a transport option for individuals with art to sell.

Piggybacking on the success of Rolling Rez Arts, FPF, Artspace, and Lakota Funds are working to bring a fixed art space to the community as well. In September 2018, construction began on the Oglala Lakota Artspace, a first-ever art studio and artist community space on the Pine Ridge reservation. Not only its internal design but also its geographic location – in the town of Kyle near the headquarters of the Pine Ridge Area Chamber of Commerce, Lakota Prairie Hotel, and Oglala Lakota College – reflect the possibility for synergy that an ecosystems approach takes into account. While its success has yet to be proven, its grounding in the Indigenous Arts Ecology Framework strengthens its chances. As former Oglala Sioux Tribe President Troy Scott Weston puts it,

> This [Oglala Lakota Artspace on the Pine Ridge Reservation] is what we as tribal leaders push for. This is what will build our economy. This is about sustainability for our tribe, our ways, our culture, and our nation. Art and culture are the base of who we are going to be and who we always were.[8]

There also is promising growth in the other Indigenous arts ecosystems where First Peoples Fund has invested deeply, including the Red Lake (MN), Colville (WA), Cheyenne River (SD), and Blackfeet (MT) reservations. This growth and the analysis contained in *Investing in the Indigenous Arts Ecology*, our impact evaluation report, validate First Peoples Fund's long-held understanding of how to approach the process of igniting Indigenous arts economies – by placing artists and culture bearers at the center and keeping the focus on building lasting relationships. When relationships between community organizations and artists are woven more tightly together, the entire local arts ecosystem is strengthened, allowing the Indigenous Arts Ecology to thrive and improving the economic and cultural lives of artists, their families, and communities.

---

[8] Remarks at the ground breaking for Oglala Lakota Arts Space, Kyle, SD, September 28, 2018.

12

Native American Food Sovereignty and Youth Entrepreneurship

Raymond Foxworth, Krystal Langholz, and Vena A-dae Romero-Briones

Food is foundational to society. In Native nations in the United States, food is more than physical nourishment, it is interwoven into social, cultural, and community bonds that sustain Native beliefs, practices, and traditions. In short, food is central to lifeways. Colonization of North America has disrupted, altered, and in some cases destroyed the traditional food practices and lifeways that have sustained Native communities since time immemorial.

In recent years, more and more Native communities are taking active and deliberate steps to reclaim local food systems. Recognizing that healthy Native citizens are the cornerstone of a healthy community and nation, the work to reclaim Native food systems has been aimed at increasing direct control over food production, consumption, distribution, regulation, thought leadership, and more. Many have conceptualized this work to reclaim local food systems as food sovereignty.

Although food sovereignty and youth entrepreneurship are not widely studied or documented, both are being practiced across Indian Country as mechanisms to grow local economies and empower youth. In this chapter, we discuss food sovereignty and its intersection with youth entrepreneurship in Native communities. We define food sovereignty, discuss the history of food system colonization, and show how three Native communities have invested in local agriculture as a way to push back on colonization and to grow entrepreneurial values and skills among Native youth.

I WHAT IS FOOD SOVEREIGNTY?

The emergence of the term food sovereignty has been traced to the 1996 World Food Summit where La Via Campesina, an international peasant movement, used the term to express the rights of peoples to define their own food systems, including agriculture, livestock, and fishery systems. La Via Campesina called for more responsive free-trade policies to meet demands of rural and marginalized farming communities.

Throughout Indian Country, Native communities have adopted the term food sovereignty to describe a myriad of local efforts to transform and reclaim local food systems. In some Native communities, food sovereignty has been used to describe efforts to combat hunger and increase access to healthy and traditional foods. In other Native communities, the term food sovereignty has been used to describe Native-led movements that enhance community health, create food policies, or target food as a mechanism for entrepreneurship and economic development. In other words, definitions of food sovereignty may look different across Native nations and are dependent on local land, geography, economies, and belief systems.

II THE COLONIZATION OF NATIVE FOOD SYSTEMS

Prior to the arrival of European colonizers, Native nations of the Americas had their own systems of food generation, relying on Indigenous knowledge for harvesting, planting, processing techniques, and consumption behaviors. In fact, the Americas were one of the birthplaces of modern agriculture as Indigenous peoples developed a sophisticated agricultural system based on corn (Dunbar-Ortiz, 2014; Stinchcomb, Messner, Driese, Nordt, & Stewart, 2011). In addition, early agriculturalists cultivated beans, squash, pumpkins, and varieties of potatoes. Significantly, food systems formed the economic backbone of numerous settlements and civilizations, as these staples were a common means of commercial and cultural exchange along the precolonial trade routes and road systems that extended from South to North America (Hardoy, 1968; Hyslop, 1984; Trombold et al., 1991).

The struggle for Native people and nations to maintain this healthy existence of land, water, food, and community is rooted in battles against colonization dating back to first contact with European colonizers. Initially the arrival of Europeans to the Americas transformed Indigenous food systems through the incorporation of Native people into the European mercantile economy. One example is the fur trade; another is the repressive labor practices initiated by European colonizers, especially the Spanish and British (Cornell, 1988; Gifford-Gonzalez & Sunseri, 2007; Usner, 1992).

The ongoing exploitation of Indian labor and the encroachment onto Native lands intensified conflicts between Native nations and European colonizers. As a result, Europeans targeted and destroyed Native food systems in an effort to force Native people into compliance with various colonial agendas. For example, during the Revolutionary War, George Washington torched hundreds of thousands of bushels of Iroquois corn to deliberately starve Iroquois men, women, and children into submission. In the Southwest, Spanish missionaries controlled agricultural harvest yields as a way to force Pueblo people to comply with the dictates of the Catholic Church (Liebmann, 2012). Events like these emphasize that altering and destroying Native food systems was a significant part of Native colonization (Bailey et al., 2017; Calloway, 1995; Diné Policy Institute, 2014; Hardeman, Murphy, Karbeah, & Kozhimannil, 2018; Iverson, 2002; Pearsall, 2015).

After the formation of the United States, control of land and its associated resources was the central issue structuring interactions and conflicts between Indian nations and the new American republic. U.S. federal Indian policy continued to disrupt, and in some cases destroy, Native food systems – either through policy creation to remove Indians from territories known for their rich agricultural lands and other natural resources or through deliberate attempts to starve Indians into submission.

Indian removal policies during the early years of the new American republic took agricultural land away from Cherokee and other Native nations in the southeastern United States. While historical data suggest that the majority of Cherokee households were producing diversified, surplus agricultural yields, Jacksonian-era rhetoric held that Native nation land was idle. These arguments cleared the way for the Indian Removal Act (1830), population removal via the Trail of Tears, and land theft through the transfer of valuable Native land to white farmers (Wishart, 1995).

Similarly, during the late nineteenth century, food was weaponized in the assimilating and Christianizing efforts of U.S. federal policy. Policies like the General Allotment Act (1887) forced Indian people to abandon communal lifeways and ownership in favor of individual property ownership, Western agriculture, and other modes of "civilized" life. When individuals refused to "engage in civilized pursuits or employments," Indian agents withheld their food rations, deeming these individuals vagrants in need of punishment (Cornell, 1988; 57). Westward expansion necessitated new railway systems that took nearly two hundred million acres of Indian land for tracks that crosscut Native farms, hunting grounds, cultural sites, and homelands (Strickland, 1985; White, 2011).

Not only did land tenure systems drastically change during this time period, but the U.S. army also significantly altered cultural landscapes closely connected to food. In the Great Plains for example, Buffalo mercenaries slaughtered tens of millions of buffalo – the source of subsistence and trade for many Native nations, especially the Očhéthi Šakówiŋ. By the 1880s, the buffalo had been slaughtered to near extinction, only a few hundred buffalo remained, and hunger became a devastating way of life for once buffalo-dependent populations (Feir, Gillezeau, & Jones, 2018). During this same period, the military forcefully removed tribal children to boarding schools, which in turn created a dependence on new food diets. These eventually were transferred to communities as children grew up and returned home.

In the twentieth century, federal policies transitioned to reorganizing American Indian governments. The Indian Reorganization Act (1934) stopped explicit allotment polices aimed at breaking up tribal lands and "civilizing" Native Americans. But other policies sought to disrupt the relationship of Native nations to the land by relocating Native people off the reservation in favor of urbanization. For some Native communities, this policy disrupted the generational transference of traditional agricultural practices and has manifested in the loss of farmers in Native communities.

Today, accessing healthy foods is a challenge for many Native Americans, particularly in rural reservation communities. Native households experience food insecurity at greater rates than most Americans. Recent data indicate that 23 percent of Native households (nearly one in four) are food insecure compared to 15 percent of all U.S. households. Almost all Native American reservations are located in what the USDA identifies as "food deserts" (Gordon and Oddo, 2012). Some reservation communities experience even greater rates of food insecurity. For example, research in Oglala Lakota County, South Dakota, entirely encompassed by the Pine Ridge Indian Reservation, has found that in households with kindergarten-age children, 40 percent experienced food insecurity (Bauer et al., 2012). Similarly, research on the Navajo reservation has noted that 75 percent of individuals are food insecure (Pardilla, Prasad, Suratkar, & Gittelsohn, 2014).

Recognizing that the loss of self-sufficient food systems is a contributing factor to myriad issues Native communities face today, many Native communities are working to reclaim control of local food systems. Local food-system control is foundational to reversing years of colonization aimed at the disintegration of cultural and traditional belief systems and the dismantling of Native social and economic systems. If Native communities can control local food systems, food can become a driver for cultural revitalization, improved community health, and economic development.

III   NATIVE YOUTH AND ENTREPRENEURSHIP

Today, there are more businesses and entrepreneurs than ever before in Native communities (McManus, 2016; Minority Business Development Agency, ND; U.S. Small Business Administration, ND). Though a bright spot, many Native communities still struggle to create conditions that facilitate a vibrant private sector where entrepreneurs can thrive. Some Native nations have focused on local governance and on the creation of policy responses to make Native communities more desirable for local business development. Other efforts, including those by nonprofits such as community development financial institutions (CDFIs), have focused on creating mechanisms for business finance and service delivery to local entrepreneurs.

There are strong justifications for this latter response. In 2001, a study by the U.S. Department of the Treasury CDFI Fund documented that financial services in Native communities were virtually absent and that inflexible rules and regulations of mainstream lenders were barriers to Native American local business development (CDFI Fund, 2001). Beyond access to capital, the study cited the need for programs and services (including financial education, business plan development, and credit repair) to help prepare entrepreneurs for financing products. Research also has noted that would-be Native entrepreneurs have a high degree of mistrust for service providers and financial institutions, feelings that are rooted in negative interactions with service programs and in generations of historical trauma (Dewees & Sarkozy-

Banoczy, 2008; First Nations Development Institute, 2007; Jorgensen, 2016; Native CDFI Network, 2017).

One specific strategy that many Native nonprofits and Native CDFIs are pursuing in response to these needs is the development of youth-focused entrepreneurship programs. Focusing on youth entrepreneurs provides a mechanism to build and grow human capital within Native communities – and ultimately build Native economies. At a minimum, youth entrepreneurship programs build leadership and problem-solving skills that can serve youth over a lifetime. Though research on youth entrepreneurs is limited and has been conducted largely in the context of developing countries, evidence suggests that building entrepreneurial skills in youth increases self-esteem and that entrepreneurship training allows youth to see active pathways to formal economic participation and economic security (Dolan & Rajak, 2016; Ojeifo, 2013; Rasheed & Rasheed, 2003; Walstad & Kourilsky, 1998).

Below we highlight three Native community initiatives that have focused on food sovereignty as it intersects with local economies and youth empowerment and development. The programs highlight the adaptability of this combined approach and show various ways to incorporate entrepreneurial skill development. For example, for the Crow Creek Fresh Food Initiative, entrepreneurial and financial skills development was an intentional and important part of the partnerships formed to make the program successful. On the other hand, for the Cochiti Youth Experience, skill-building primarily focused on the cultural and social connections to food and on empowering youth with cultural teachings around food – expansion of the local food economy was a secondary outcome, which occurred as youth engaged in farmers markets and other empowering economic activities. Regardless of such differences, all three highlighted programs are grounded in the understanding that as the youth population of Native communities continues to grow, this population cohort will become an even more important piece of the puzzle in creating economically, culturally, socially, and physically thriving Native communities. The programs also demonstrate the close connection between the food sovereignty and Native youth entrepreneurship movements.

A *The Crow Creek Fresh Food Initiative*

The Crow Creek Fresh Food Initiative was started in 2009 on the Crow Creek Reservation, located in central South Dakota. Led by the local Native CDFI, this innovative program was supported financially over the years by many partners, including First Nations Development Institute (First Nations). The initiative focused its efforts on youth in response to local community demographics. With approximately half of the population of the reservation under eighteen, a large land mass that was leased to white ranchers, and high levels of unemployment, community members saw the initiative as a chance to invest in the future of the local economy through fostering a culture of food systems-based entrepreneurship among the youth.

Using a multipronged approach, a large community garden was the cornerstone of the initiative. This garden was located next to the Crow Creek Elementary School, where classrooms planted and tended their own raised beds. The same children, ranging from six to twelve years old, tended these beds during the summer months through a partnership with the Boys and Girls Club. Individuals seeking a community atmosphere or lacking their own land for growing also kept plots in the community garden. A third portion of the garden was tended by four to six teen workers hired and employed each summer by the Native CDFI. These teen workers ran the community garden program, selling their produce at local community farmers markets that they organized. The initiative averaged six farmers markets per summer, events that welcomed participation not only from the community gardeners but also from other local food vendors. Food that was not sold in the farmers markets was given to the Golden Age Nutrition Center to be used for elders' meals.

Boys and Girls Club members and teen workers who tended the garden were automatically enrolled in the youth and teen Summer Savers Program. They then participated in culturally and age-relevant financial education classes, as well as in experiential learning activities focused on individual savings, budgeting, and more. While no money was exchanged for children under legal working age, Boys and Girls Club members earned stipends toward their "savings accounts," which they carefully monitored throughout the course of the summer. By the end of the summer, these younger children would have enough money in their accounts to make a major asset purchase, such as a bike or laptop for school. Teens who worked in the garden saved in a matched savings account held by the partner CDFI that could be used for college or for food entrepreneurship. In 2013, over fifty youth participated in the two programs.

Teen gardeners regularly chose to use their matched savings to start their own food-related businesses. Receiving support from the Native CDFI to develop a business plan, the most successful of these businesses was "Fresh Grown Goodies." This small business was owned by two young women – cousins – who learned food preservation from another partner in the initiative, the Healthy Heart Program of Indian Health Services (IHS). In an effort to teach community members how to cook with all the fresh produce from the garden, the IHS taught classes on the preparation of traditional foods, food preservation, and other related subjects. Using their learning from the IHS classes, Fresh Grown Goodies sold canned produce, and the owners used their profits to support their college funds.

Small agricultural businesses, such as beekeeping, were also formed as the community grew more interested in food entrepreneurship. For these burgeoning entrepreneurs, the Native CDFI provided culturally relevant entrepreneurship education through a twelve-session course designed to help aspiring entrepreneurs build a business plan. Individuals who completed the class were eligible to receive small business loans to make their dreams a reality. When asked to describe the program, members of the initiative would laugh and say, "it's an entrepreneurship, youth, food, community, health, workforce, financial education, and matched savings program" – a response that acknowledges the value of an intersectional approach to local food sovereignty, youth empowerment, and local economic development.

B *Cochiti Youth Experience, Inc.*

Cochiti Youth Experience, Inc. (CYE) is a Native-led nonprofit organization located on the Cochiti Indian Reservation in Cochiti Pueblo, New Mexico. Originally established in the late 1990s as a U.S. Department of Agriculture (USDA) Cooperative Extension 4-H program serving the youth of Cochiti Pueblo, CYE reincorporated in 2008 to focus on the revitalization of pueblo traditional agriculture, to reengage youth in farming, and to encourage healthy lifestyle choices. Youth engagement was a community-identified goal, and CYE provided a useful organizational structure for bringing Native youth and elders together to apply traditional agricultural knowledge and continue to grow healthy Cochiti people.

Cochiti Pueblo is located in northern New Mexico, twenty-two miles south of the capital of Santa Fe and fifty-four miles north of Albuquerque. While Cochiti people have resided near the riverbanks and in the canyons of this area for thousands of years, the present village has been occupied for only 800 years. It is home to approximately 800 Cochiti tribal members.

In the late 1970s, the Army Corp of Engineers chose the portion of the Rio Grande River that flows through Cochiti Pueblo as the site for a dam that would aid downstream flood and sediment control. Despite the pueblo's resistance to the dam, the Army Corps of Engineers began construction in 1965. Completed in 1975, the dam's reservoir flooded one half of the pueblo's primary and pristine agriculture fields. Several years later, water from the poorly constructed reservoir floor began to seep into the pueblo's remaining fields, making them unfarmable as well. From 1980 to approximately 1998, Cochiti had no arable lands. Consequently, an entire generation of Cochiti youth did not have the privilege of learning the traditional agricultural practices that had sustained the community for centuries.

Through wisdom, contemplation, and reflection, Cochiti leadership decided to file suit against the U.S. Army Corps of Engineers for faulty dam construction and for the restoration of Cochiti agricultural lands. After long years of negotiation and legal posturing, the United States government settled with Cochiti Pueblo, and it eventually developed new technology to create a drainage system under the fields so that Cochiti lands could be farmable again.

CYE's efforts began with a few cooking classes but grew every year, creating opportunities for youth to establish food networks, such as farm-to-table programs and programs that provided food to tribal elders and the local school district. As the Pueblo's agricultural lands became viable again, CYE established its Farmers Mentorship Program, which paired youth farmers ranging in age from five to early teens with adult mentors in order to perpetuate the transmission of traditional agricultural knowledge. Because the community's agricultural lands had been unusable for so long, many systems of knowledge transmission had been disrupted, so getting young people into the fields and creating opportunities for the pueblo's few remaining traditional farmers to share their expertise were the very first steps in rejuvenating community agriculture. By continuing this work, CYE helped to reinvigorate the role of family, community, and intergenerational relationships in teaching and learning agricultural skills that are deeply tied to Cochiti culture and values and is supporting a self-determined future for the Pueblo.

Beyond learning the cultural practices of Cochiti agriculture, youth and mentors had the opportunity to become entrepreneurs by creating a local farmers market for the community. Over one summer, CYE also registered in the USDA Double-Up Food Bucks program, an initiative that doubles the value of Supplementary Nutrition Assistance Program (SNAP) dollars spent on fresh and healthy foods at local markets. Although program bureaucracy makes local implementation extremely laborious, CYE's investment paid off. Its participation in the Double Up Food Bucks program increased the value of goods sold at local farmers markets and incentivized the purchase of healthy foods from local farmers.

As these outcomes show, CYE programming created numerous benefits for many young citizens of Cochiti Pueblo. Fundamentally, success was achieved because youth were once again introduced to agriculture through mentorship with local Cochiti adult farmers. Significantly, the process of learning Cochiti agricultural practices included cultural learning that will sustain youth for a lifetime. Youth also were exposed to employment opportunities, educated about the local food economy, and encouraged to practice entrepreneurship by creating local farmers markets and thinking of other ways to get their produce to market.

Even so, using farming to generate economic activity was not accepted by the entire community. This is understandable, because for Cochiti people, agriculture and food are part of a complex spiritual and social system that centers on caring for the individual, family, and community. Nonetheless, the program helped start conversations and raise consciousness about the local economy, especially as it relates to food.

C California Indian Museum and Cultural Center

The California Indian Museum and Cultural Center (CIMCC) was established in 1996 within the Presidio of San Francisco, California. The purpose of CIMCC is to culturally enrich and benefit the people of California and the general public. The goals of the CIMCC are to educate the public about California Indian history and cultures, to showcase California Indian cultures, to enhance and facilitate these cultures and traditions through educational and cultural activities, and to preserve and protect California Indian cultural and intellectual properties. CIMCC also creates relationships with nontribal and tribal partners including the Native communities in Lake Sonoma and Mendocino counties.

The CIMCC created the Tribal Youth Ambassadors (TYA) program to empower young people and grow their leadership and as a means to address food sovereignty through the execution of various youth-led projects. California has one of the most tumultuous Native histories in the United States, and CIMCC has been active in creating programs that allow Native youth to explore their own histories, to create venues and mediums to tell their stories, and to develop other responses to their learning.

In 2016, the TYA conducted a food sovereignty assessment. As part of this assessment, youth interviewed elders to collect data on the history of their local food system. These data pointed to the significance of acorns, which contain complex carbohydrates, fiber, and other properties that help regulate glucose and prevent diabetes. Prior to the disruption of local food systems, acorns were central to the diets of Indian people in California. Because of this important food staple, historically diabetes was not a common disease among California's Native peoples.

With new knowledge acquired through their food sovereignty assessment, the TYA decided to create a youth-led social enterprise to produce and market an acorn energy bar. The TYA noted that they wanted to produce and sell the acorn bar to address the diabetes epidemic, revitalize California Indian acorn traditions, and protect and cultivate oak trees. Today, California Indians are hindered from incorporating acorns into their diets on a daily basis because of issues related to colonization and contemporary circumstances. The acorn energy bar addresses the need to incorporate acorns back into their daily diet, while addressing the challenges Native communities face in a fast-paced society. Generally, the goal of these Native youth is to adapt traditional tribal dietary traditions to modern lifestyles (California Indian Museum and Cultural Center, 2017).

In 2017, the CIMCC Tribal Youth Ambassadors presented acorn bar prototypes to a national audience at the Food Sovereignty Summit held in Oneida, Wisconsin. Since then, the TYA have been conducting consumer testing by providing samples at local community events, a process that also helps reestablish local tribal communities' connections with this traditional food source. The long-term goals of the acorn bar project are to secure and advance California Indians' reciprocal relationship with acorns by increasing their consumption of acorns; to advance local tribal traditions associated with acorn caretaking, gathering, and processing; and to advance tribal stewardship of acorn food system landscapes.

Overall, the acorn project emerged as a youth-led effort to gain more knowledge about the local food system through a food sovereignty assessment. Collecting data allowed tribal youth to harvest traditional knowledge that they could use to reintroduce traditional foods into local Native people's diets and combat health issues. Once again, this is a Native youth-led project that shows how a dual focus on Indigenous food sovereignty and youth entrepreneurship creates the potential for significant local social and economic change.

IV CONCLUSION

While each of the programs highlighted in this chapter is uniquely adapted to the cultural values and economic context of its communities of origin, there are several common themes. Each approached food holistically – understanding its spiritual, cultural, health, and economic value. This approach led to multidimensional programs that worked to address local barriers to true food sovereignty. The programs also relied on youth to be leaders of local food sovereignty initiatives, which built self-confidence while also teaching practical entrepreneurial skills. While the long-term economic impact on the private sector of this type of youth engagement is still unknown, short-term impacts include a more hopeful and skilled youth workforce, increased access to healthy foods and, in some cases, local business development.

Ultimately, these programs – and their results – demonstrate the close connection between the food sovereignty and Native youth entrepreneurship movements. There is significant crossover in values. There are similar demands on youth to increase knowledge, hone skills, dream big, and be creative. And there is a shared focus on the generational thinking necessary to build strong, healthy, and vibrant communities.

REFERENCES

Bailey, Z. D., Krieger, N., Agénor, M., Graves, J., Linos, N., and Bassett, M. T. (2017). "Structural Racism and Health Inequities in the USA: Evidence and Interventions." *The Lancet*, 389 (10077), 1453–63.

Bauer, K. W., Widome, R., Himes, J. H., Smyth, M., Rock, B. H., Hannan, P. J., and Story, M. (2012). "High Food Insecurity and Its Correlates Among Families Living on a Rural American Indian Reservation." *American Journal of Public Health*, 102(7), 1346–52.

Briones, V. A. (Forthcoming) "Fighting for the Taste Buds of Our Children." *Journal of Agriculture, Food Systems, and Community Development*.

Brown, T. L. (2013). *Pueblo Indians and Spanish Colonial Authority in Eighteenth-Century New Mexico*. Tucson: University of Arizona Press.

California Indian Museum & Cultural Center. (2017). "Cuh:uyaw: Increasing Tribal Family Access to Healthy and Traditional Food Resources Food Sovereignty and Security Assessment Findings." Santa Rosa, CA: California Indian Museum and Cultural Center. Retrieved from: https://cimcc.org/wp-content/uploads/2017/10/CIMCC-Food-Sovereignty-Assessment-Report.pdf.

Calloway, C. G. (1995). *The American Revolution in Indian Country: Crisis and Diversity in Native American Communities*. Cambridge: Cambridge University Press.

Community Development Financial Institutions Fund. (2001). *The Report of the Native American Lending Study*. Washington, DC: U.S. Department of the Treasury.

Cornell, S. (1988). *The Return of the Native*. New York: Oxford University Press.

Denetdale, J. (2007). *Reclaiming Diné History: Legacies of Navajo Chief Manuelito and Juani*. Tucson: University of Arizona Press.

Dewees, S., and Sarkozy-Banoczy, S. (2008). *Investing in Native Community Change: Understanding the Role of Community Development Financial Institutions*. Longmont, CO: First Nations Oweesta Corporation.

Diné Policy Institute. (2014). *Diné Food Sovereignty: A Report on the Navajo Nation Food System and the Case to Rebuild a Self-Sufficient Food System for the Diné People*. Tsalie, AZ: Diné Policy Institute.

Dolan, C., and Rajak, D. (2016). "Remaking Africa's Informal Economies: Youth, Entrepreneurship and the Promise of Inclusion at the Bottom of the Pyramid." *The Journal of Development Studies*, 52(4), 514–29.

Feir, D., Gillezeau, R., and Jones, M. E. (2019). *The Slaughter of the Bison and Reversal of Fortunes on the Great Plains* (No. 1–2019). Minneapolis: Federal Reserve Bank of Minneapolis.

First Nations Development Institute. (2007). *Integrated Asset-Building Strategies for Reservation-Based Communities: A 27-Year Retrospective of First Nations Development Institute*. Longmont, CO: First Nations Development Institute.

Gifford-Gonzalez, D., and Sunseri, K. U. (2007). "Foodways on the Frontier: Animal Use and Identity in Early Colonial New Mexico." In Twiss, K. (ed.), *The Archaeology of Food and Identity*, Carbondale: Center for Archaeological Investigations, Southern Illinois University, 260–87.

Gordon, A., and Oddo, V. (2012). Addressing Child Hunger and Obesity in Indian Country: Report to Congress (No. 69cb021705cf40e798d8ca9922a3d013). Mathematica Policy Research.

Hardeman, R. R., Murphy, K. A., Karbeah, J., and Kozhimannil, K. B. (2018). "Naming Institutionalized Racism in the Public Health Literature: A Systematic Literature Review." *Public Health Reports*, 133(3), 240–49.

Hardoy, J. E. (1968). *Urban Planning in Pre-Columbian America*. New York: Braziller.

Hyslop, J. (1984). *The Inka Road System*. Orlando, FL: Academic Press.

Iverson, P. (2002). *Diné: A History of the Navajos*. Albuquerque: University of New Mexico Press.

Jorgensen, M. (2016). *Access to Capital and Credit in Native Communities*. Tucson: Native Nations Institute, The University of Arizona.

Liebmann, M. (2012). *Revolt: An Archaeological History of Pueblo Resistance and Revitalization in 17th Century New Mexico*. Tucson: University of Arizona Press.

McManus, M. (2016). Minority Business Ownership: Data from the 2012 Survey of Business Owners, U.S. Small Business Administration Office of Advocacy Issue Brief Number 12.

Minority Business Development Agency. (No Date) Fact Sheet: American Indian and Alaska Native-Owned Firms. U.S. Department of Commerce. Retrieved from: www.sba.gov/sites/default/files/SBO_Facts_AIANOB.pdf.

Native CDFI Network. (2017). *Revisiting Native American Entrepreneurship in South Dakota's Nine Reservations*. Rapid City, SD: Native CDFI Network.

Ojeifo, S. A. (2013). "Entrepreneurship Education in Nigeria: A Panacea for Youth Unemployment." *Journal of Education and Practice*, 4(6), 61–67.

Pardilla, M., Prasad, D., Suratkar, S., and Gittelsohn, J. (2014). "High Levels of Household Food Insecurity on the Navajo Nation." *Public Health Nutrition*, 17(1), 58–65.

Pearsall, Sarah M. S. (2015). "Madam Sacho: How One Iroquois Woman Survived the American Revolution." *Humanities*, 36(3).

Rasheed, H. S., and Rasheed, B. Y. (2003). "Developing Entrepreneurial Characteristics in Minority Youth: The Effects of Education and Enterprise Experience." In Stiles, C. H., and Galbraith, C. S., eds., *Ethnic Entrepreneurship: Structure and Process*, 261–77. Bingley, UK: Emerald Group Publishing Limited.

Reséndez, A. (2016). *The Other Slavery: The Uncovered Story of Indian Enslavement in America*. New York: Houghton Mifflin Harcourt.

Stinchcomb, G. E., Messner, T. C., Driese, S. G., Nordt, L. C., and Stewart, R. M. (2011). "Pre-colonial (AD 1100–1600) Sedimentation Related to Prehistoric Maize Agriculture and Climate Change in Eastern North America." *Geology*, 39(4), 363–66.

Strickland, R. (1985). "Genocide-at-Law: An Historic and Contemporary View of the Native American Experience." *U. Kan. L. Rev.*, 34, 713.

Trombold, C. D., Audouze, F., Renfrew, C., Schlanger, N., Sherratt, A., Taylor, T., and Ashmore, W. (1991). *Ancient Road Networks and Settlement Hierarchies in the New World*. Cambridge: Cambridge University Press.

Usner, D. H. (1992). *Indians, Settlers, & Slaves in a Frontier Exchange Economy: The Lower Mississippi Valley Before 1783*. Chapel Hill: University of North Carolina Press.

U.S. Small Business Administration. (No Date) American Indian- and Alaska Native-Owned Businesses in the United States. Retrieved from: www.sba.gov/sites/default/files/SBO_Facts_AIANOB.pdf.

Walstad, W. B., and Kourilsky, M. L. (1998). "Entrepreneurial Attitudes and Knowledge of Black Youth." *Entrepreneurship Theory and Practice*, 23(2), 5–18.

White, R. (2011). *Railroaded: The Transcontinentals and the Making of Modern America*. New York: W. W. Norton & Company.

Wishart, D. M. (1995). "Evidence of Surplus Production in the Cherokee Nation Prior to Removal." *The Journal of Economic History*, 55(1), 120–38.

Index

CPSIA information can be obtained
at www.ICGtesting.com
Printed in the USA
LVHW052031260722
724434LV00004B/264

9 781108 703758